DYNAMIC ORGANISATIONS

Dynamic Organisations

The challenge of change

David Jackson

Foreword by John Humble

First published 1997 by
MACMILLAN PRESS LTD
Houndmills, Basingstoke, Hampshire RG21 6XS
and London
Companies and representatives
throughout the world

ISBN 0–333–66645–3

A catalogue record for this book is available
from the British Library.

10   9   8   7   6   5   4   3   2   1
06   05   04   03   02   01   00   99   98   97

Copy-edited and typeset by Povey–Edmondson
Tavistock and Rochdale, England

Printed and bound in Great Britain by
Antony Rowe Ltd
Chippenham, Wiltshire

This book is written for the brave people who know there is a better way to run their organisations . . . and are doing something about it.

It is dedicated to my family, who are my greatest source of pleasure.

Contents

List of Tables and Figures   ix

Foreword by John Humble   xi

Preface   xiii

Acknowledgements   xx

Part I   The Dynamic Organisation
1   A New Scheme of Things   3
2   Getting Close to Customers   22
3   A New Approach to Change   54
4   Leadership in the Post-Industrial Era   87
5   People Do It All   112
6   Building a Well-Oiled Machine   127
7   Dynamic Organisations: The Greater Context   151
8   Change: Seven Sins, Seven Virtues   158

Part II   Dynamic Organisations in Action
    Introduction to Part II   169
9   Avis Europe   171
10 The Birmingham Midshires Building Society   185
11 Cigna UK   197
12 Disneyland Paris   207
13 KLM   215
14 The National and Provincial Building Society   222
15 RAC Motoring Services Ltd   230

Appendix I   The Voice of the Customer Handbook   237

Appendix II   Dynamic Organisation Audit   243

Notes   249

References   257

Index   261

List of Tables and Figures

TABLES

1.1	The rate of economic change	4
7.1	Regular use of IT by social group	157
10.1	Measure of employee satisfaction	193
10.2	Interpreting First Choice	194
10.3	Comparison of retail financial service providers	195
13.1	Decathlon scores, 1993	218
13.2	KLM service decathlon weighting	219

FIGURES

1.1	The 'S' curve shift	6
1.2	Growth in banking product revenues at non-bank institutions	8
1.3	Key capabilities	11
1.4	External pressures on the dynamic organisation	17
2.1	Context-based segmentation	30
2.2	The dimensions of quality	33
2.3	ABB's staircase of advantage	34
2.4	The butterfly model	36
2.5	The house of quality	38
2.6	The enhanced listening cycle	40
2.7	Information not included in customer records	50
2.8	Contact management system	52
3.1	Culture and the environment	66
3.2	The cultural onion	66
3.3	Dimensions of organisational culture	68
3.4	Delivering change	73
3.5	Opportunity, work and teams	77
3.6	Linking direction through measurement	83
3.7	Mitsubishi Heavy Industries – Pentagon Campaign	83

4.1	Developing middle managers	108
5.1	The vicious circle of low pay	115
6.1	The ideas hierarchy – ideas generated each day	128
6.2	The relationship between results and IT spend	135
9.1	Avis organisational processes	177
10.1	Continuous performance improvement cycle	188
11.1	Cigna UK facilitator skills model	200
11.2	Maturing teams	205
12.1	Disneyland Paris 'raison d'être'	210
13.1	Service performance and repurchase intention	216
13.2	Percentage of passengers experiencing problems	217
13.3	Satisfaction ratings by nationality of traveller	217
14.1	The basic process cycle	223
14.2	Cascading processes	223
14.3	N&P's reward system	228
15.1	RAC's quality management system	235
A1.1	Voice of the Customer and continuous improvement	238
A1.2	The House of Quality	239

Foreword

Perhaps the best way to test David Jackson's thesis that exponential change is transforming literally every aspect of a manager's life is to reflect on one's own personal experiences. When I started work forty years or so ago, we took for granted a long hierarchical structure, with its strict line of command, precisely defined jobs and tight control from above. The big idea at the time was selling: persuading customers to buy the products and services we had created. Information systems were primitive and computers unknown. In manufacturing a high proportion of jobs were unskilled or semiskilled. There was a high expectation that an employee who consistently performed to standard had job security. Playing one supplier off against another was seen as an effective way of purchasing at the lowest prices.

Today the big idea is that our greatest asset is satisfied customers. Satisfaction does not arise out of selling them what we have produced, but understanding what customers really want. These needs are objective – measured performance and quality – and subjective – courtesy, listening and relationships. Only by satisfying these needs better than our competitors can companies survive. Managing knowledge workers has become an imperative as it becomes clear that success lies in managing intellectual capital rather than physical resources. As the separate revolutions in computers, communications and content interact, information is now an incredibly powerful force that permeates every part of the organisation. Partnerships with fewer suppliers is the only way to manage quality and to have effective just-in-time systems. Individual managers increasingly face the harsh truth that job security means constantly widening and deepening their skills and knowledge. Employability rather than employment for life in one job is the name of the game. New social issues such as concern for the environment and equality of opportunity are high on the agenda.

Buffeted by the turbulence of change, we have to hang on to some basic truths:

- Saying that our job is to satisfy customers is correct, but simplistic. Which customers do we really want? How do we keep these customers? How do we measure satisfaction? Responding to expressed needs is essential but beyond that we have to innovate in order to deliver the goods and services that customers want, but did not ask for.

- We have to take a holistic view of managing organisations. A change in one part of the system always has an impact on other parts. Downsizing, for example, has been an unenviable but necessary task in organisations that had become inefficient and overstaffed. However, some organisations have taken out costs crudely, and in so doing have damaged customer service. Creating profitable growth, not just chasing efficiencies, has to be the goal.
- Competition is global. We have to benchmark ourselves against the best of our international competitors. For European organisations competing against businesses in the dynamic Pacific Rim, adding value is the only strategy. More investment in truly innovative products and services and getting them to market faster is essential.
- In a knowledge-based world, empowering staff and providing opportunities and stimulus for learning and growth are no longer options. Since behaviour is governed by beliefs, people need the stability and guidance of clear corporate values during times of rapid change.

David Jackson has a rare gift for identifying the few critical issues that managers face in the late 1990s. Drawing on original research and front-line experience in many organisations, David considers the practical implications of each major issue and forces us to think about where we stand. As one might expect from a Yorkshireman, his conclusions are outspoken and provocative.

This book should be read by every manager who wants to win in the new millennium.

JOHN HUMBLE
Author and international consultant

Preface

W. Edwards Deming told us that the system is to blame for 90 per cent of quality problems, not the people. I did not truly understand this until 1987. I was working for Management Centre Europe (MCE) as a programme director, responsible for developing a range of executive training programmes. MCE is a leader in this field in Europe and attracts senior managers from blue chip organisations.[1]

Following the publication of Lord Cockfield's white paper on the formation of the European single market, '1992' was a big issue for European managers. MCE developed a range of functionally based programmes to help managers think through and address the significant change involved, based on customer research. The functional focus of the programmes exactly matched the structure of the programmes group, which mirrored the functional structure of major companies in the 1960s and 1970s.

Talking with colleagues, it became clear that none of us were looking at the big picture – what 1992 meant for organisations as a whole. We were not addressing a prime part of our customer base – the chief executive officer or general manager. It also became clear that this was a great opportunity, but one which none of us could tackle alone. We had to combine our knowledge and contacts to put together a first-class event. Two of us agreed to work together to put a proposal to our bosses. We sketched out a two-day conference programme, calculated a budget and identified some of the key speakers we wanted. We presented our proposal.

Management was enthusiastic about the idea, liked the programme, tweaked the budget and gave us the green light. There was just one question: which programme director's budget was this going on? We explained that this was a joint effort and that we would share the effort, costs and revenues. You could almost hear the spanner jamming the works. The controller had no way of splitting the costs involved. The head of programmes had no one point of contact. Our respective bosses both wanted all of the revenues to boost the turnover of their divisions. I was nominated to run the programme – on my own, despite the fact that my colleague, Jenny, had a better track record of running conferences like that.

The conference ran and was a success. Not a huge success, but it was profitable and earned good reviews from the participants. Jenny felt bitter. I felt embarrassed and annoyed. It was *our* idea; it was *our* effort; it was *our* creativity. I seriously doubt that I would ever have got the conference off the ground had I been working on my own. What could have been great was merely good. What could have been fun became routine. The system ground us down.

On reflection, the experience was a truly valuable one. I learned about what makes the difference between good organisations that survive and great organisations that truly thrive. I learned the difference between managers, who apply a process, and leaders, who enable results.

What happened to me in 1987 was a function of decades of Western thinking and teaching. We learn more in our first two years than we do in the rest of our lives. In those early days we have no formal teachers and no set curriculum. Much of our learning is collaborative – we interact with other children and adults. It is also experiential, we learn by doing. Then of course we end our informal learning and begin 'a proper education'. The more we progress in our education, the more we specialise. In the land of formal education we learn about the world in discrete elements. Of course, as our knowledge expands we have to specialise; we cannot know everything about everything. Unfortunately this truism has caused us to lose sight of the fact that everything is connected to everything else. There is only one world. We must be able to place our specialist knowledge in the context of the greater picture. In our quest to improve our specialist knowledge, we have lost sight of the need and ability to understand the big picture.

This influence has carried over into our thinking about organisation. The industrial revolution heralded the growth of the organisation – a place where work was organised. Or perhaps more specifically, a place where workers were organised.

Modern organisation theory can be traced back to Frederick Winslow Taylor and his infamous quest for '*a fair day's pay for a fair day's work*'. Taylor taught us that not only should management determine what work should be done but also how it should be done.

This breakthrough spurned others to turn their minds to the organisation of labour. Whereas Taylor focused on the organisation of work, Henri Fayol, originator of the organisation chart, focused on the operation of the organisation. Fayol (another engineer) expounded his credo of organisation in his principles of management, addressing planning, organising, unity of command, coordination, control and management theory. These same elements can still be found in the curricula of many business management training programmes today.

These were of course perfectly natural, indeed innovative responses to the problems of the time. Taylor lived in an era when education for the masses was, by today's standards, pitiful. Only the upper and middle classes had the opportunity to obtain a decent education. Those with money viewed those without as a resource, a disposable source of labour to fund their own wealth. It is interesting to note that many organisations still use the term 'Human Resource Management', a vestige of the exploitative school of management.

In the 1920s and 1930s new views started to enter management thinking. These views took a psychological view of work with far greater emphasis on people.

At General Electric's Hawthorne plant in 1924, Elton Mayo's experiments with working conditions showed that if working conditions changed, for better or worse, productivity improved. The simple act of making people the focus of attention was the salient activity. Abraham Maslow came to similar conclusions when he presented his 'hierarchy of needs', arguing that once basic needs were met, people looked to relationships and fulfilment for motivation.

Likewise Herzberg told us of the important difference between the hygiene and motivation factors, an understanding of which is essential for improving personal performance in organisations.

Despite this research and thinking, few organisations have taken the messages to heart. When seeking to introduce change, most organisations still turn to rewards – and monetary rewards at that – with little thought for recognition and the higher motivational forces identified by Maslow and Herzberg.

The scientific school of management reinforced specialisation, which became embedded in organisational structures. Driven by the notion of scientific management and specialisation, we created the functional organisation. Specialist departments dealing with specialist issues became the order of the day – and still are in most organisations. The theory was fine. Working towards a common goal, individual functions would implement specific elements of the strategy. In practice, however, the understanding of the goal was not common, and politics and power got in the way of the common good.

Functions, being specialisms, needed to ensure their specialisms were properly implemented and thus sought greater and greater control over the practice of their specialism across the organisation. Power was accumulated at the centre, the habitat of the superspecialists. Line managers, those running the part of the business responsible for generating revenues and profit, found themselves with less control over their costs.

As the functional organisation grew, coordination became a greater issue. To deal with the problems of the disconnected functional organisation we designed strategic planning processes. Of course, in the realm of the specialist functional organisation, strategic planning became another specialist function. Indeed it was the jewel in the crown of the specialist functional organisation. The process, introduced to solve the problems facing organisations, became a major part of the problems. Specialist strategic planners studied the market through countless figures. The results of the company were dissected, reconstituted and extrapolated. Business plans of wondrous complexity were developed, handed down to the line to implement – and failed. So further analysis, extrapolation and planning was called for but the results were the same.

The building blocks for our organisations have become ever more specialised, and until very recently measurement has remained singularly focused on financial factors. This again reflects the thinking that has dominated recent history, finding its peak in the 1980s. The belief, held by some aspects of both business and government, that everything can be valued in economic terms *alone* has done much damage. This is not to decry the good things done during that period. But government is about more than just money. Interestingly, just as business was advocating a broader basket of measures, the government was focusing on financial results to the exclusion of almost everything else. This has served to reinforce the financial aspects of life and business when a broader, more holistic view that incorporates finance is needed.

Short termism, a disease often associated with the West, is a purely financial disease. Returns have to be generated in shorter periods of time. Success is measured in six-monthly cycles, with huge anticipation among financial analysts. Failure to deliver – which is defined as meeting the analysts' expectations – is met with analysis of what went wrong and what needs to be done. Interestingly, this analysis is done from outside the organisation and is focused on the activities relating to financial measures.

Recent thinking about organisations is forcing people to consider the interconnectedness of organisations. Whilst this might be new to organisational thinking, it certainly is not new in itself.

It has been difficult over the past thirty years not to notice the relative success of Japanese companies compared with their Western competitors.

Many point to the Marshall Plan and the significant investment it generated. But the UK received more aid under the Marshall Plan than either Germany or Japan. There is no doubt that Japan and Germany invested their aid wisely. But this alone cannot explain the relative success of these economies.

In 1988 I led a study tour of 35 senior European managers to examine how the Japanese managed their manufacturing companies. We had heard much about the techniques of Japanese management: just-in-time, preventative maintenance and zero defects. In preparation we had read about lifetime employment, the *keiretsu* (highly organised networks of companies), and quality circles. Our two weeks included visits to leading companies and workshops with leading academics and officials. We all had our own ideas about why the Japanese were so successful – the unquestioning loyalty and work ethic of the Japanese worker, the guiding hand of the Ministry of Trade and Industry (MITI) and of course the techniques. The techniques were much in evidence. Toyota explained the *kanban* system (a card-based method of inventory management), Komatsu demonstrated the rapid setting-up of machine tools. The technology was rudimentary – paper-based processing and home made jigs and tools – but it worked.

During our visit we came to realise that there was much more to Japanese manufacturing excellence than mere techniques. We constantly observed a level of communication none of us had experienced in Western companies. We experienced a great respect for people: one of the main driving forces behind automation at Toyota is the removal of drudgery from work.

Of course experienced Japan watchers will know that beneath the large companies, where lifetime employment has been the norm, is a myriad of small, underprivileged suppliers. Here employment is only as secure as the current order and working conditions are as bad as you will find anywhere. But this does not detract from the quality of management we found in the larger organisations.

As a summary of the tour I produced the following *Ishikawa* (fishbone) diagram of Japanese manufacturing excellence (on the following page).

My conclusion was that the Japanese had designed – or more accurately, evolved – an holistic system of organisation to suit their culture and heritage. Copying their ideas would not work, as many have found to their cost. One Japanese lecturer pointed the way when he advised us to 'study and understand the Japanese way, then use that understanding to build a system which works for your culture'. This does not fit easily with the quick fix mentality of many Western managers. I

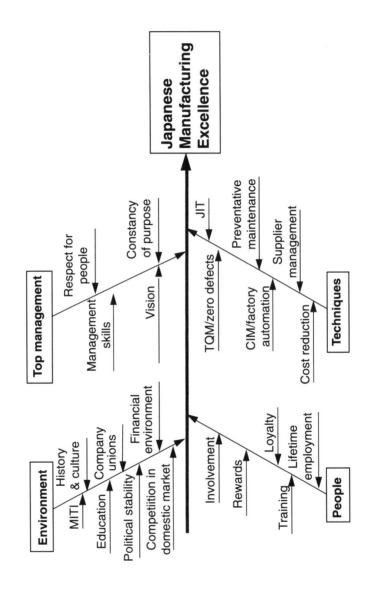

had heard the same message of study and adapt a few years earlier on one of my several visits to the plant (then under construction) of Nissan Motor Manufacturing in Washington, Tyne and Wear. Newly appointed managers were sent to Japan for several months to study how Nissan plants in Japan operated. They were however instructed not to copy what the Japense plants were doing but rather to design a system to suit the British way of life and work.[2] Peter Wickens, Nissan's personnel director recognises this in the acknowledgements in his book, *The Ascendant Organisation* (1995), saying:

Of Toshiaki Tsuchiya, Nissan's first Managing Director, all I can say is that I owe him a great deal. He had the wisdom to appoint people who had independent minds but an empathy with the Japanese way. He then created the environment in which these people could build a company which hopefully pulls together the best of the Orient and the Occident, and rejects that which is not transferable.

This is a lesson that many multinational organisations have yet to learn.

In this book I will to outline my views about leading and managing an organisation. It is based on experience, and much research. As Peter Wickens said, I hope you will find a number of ideas that are transferable to your own situation. But if you do learn something from the book, remember there is an important difference between using learning to adapt and innovate, and simply copying.

DAVID JACKSON

Acknowledgements

I have been working in organisations for 20 years and advising managers for more than 10 years. What has surprised me is the number of fads and fashions that have arisen – and fallen – in those few short years. Much like the clothing industry, the length of time a fashion remains current has shortened. Fortunately, within this plethora of ideas, concepts and guru speak there are a number of common themes; seemingly eternal truths. They are what successful organisations have always done. They are the basics of life in organisations – people, change, customers and leadership.

This book is an attempt to synthesise my ideas and prejudices about how organisations should be run and to provide guidance to people who want to change organisations for the better. In writing this book I am mindful of the many people who have shaped my thinking. I have been truly fortunate to have met and had the opportunity to exchange views with some remarkable minds. To paraphrase a Chinese proverb, it is easy to look tall when you stand on the shoulders of a giant. I have known many giants.

John Humble – a guru by any measure – has been a great source of inspiration. Our work together in the area of service excellence provided the basis of much in this book. I never cease to be amazed by his ability to come up with ideas and insights. I am grateful beyond measure for his permission to use material we have developed together. Peter Moyes and Colin Van Orton, colleagues from my days at Digital, also deserve sincere thanks. Peter, a fellow Yorkshireman, would bring me back to reality with a bump when my mind wandered off in some of my more esoteric periods of thought. Peter's constant drive for elegant simplicity and incisive clarity are a lesson for all managers and especially for many of the consultants who have pedalled recycled hype. If Peter bullied my thinking, Colin Van Orton nurtured it. His relaxed, comforting manner and constant support was backed up by questioning that cut to the quick. Charles Savage, author of *Fifth Generation Management* (1990), deserves credit, together with John Humble, for expanding my thinking. His work on the issues of succeeding in the knowledge era have been truly valuable to me.

I am an avid student of organisational life and have been fortunate to meet some of the great management thinkers of my time. Top of the list must be Peter Drucker, who seems to have thought of almost everything before anybody else. I always look for a quotation from Drucker to illustrate my points. I met Peter Senge and Bill O'Brien at a seminar in London in 1992. They gave me a language for many of the ideas I had been struggling with. Of the most recent developments, the concept of the learning organisation is one of the most important. I recommend you all to read Margaret Wheatley's book *Leadership and the New Sciences* (1992). When I read it, my head was popping with thoughts and insights. The books by Robert Pirsig – *Zen and the Art of Motorcycle Maintenance* (1974) and *Lila: An Enquiry into Morals* (1991) – were hard work for me. Not because they are difficult to read but because of the sheer number of ideas they triggered in my own mind. I wish I had such a talent for thinking.

Special thanks go to people who have given me their support and friendship throughout the long period of thinking and development that was the gestation of this book. Russell Syson, Emeritus Professor of International Purchasing at The Derbyshire Business School, is the one who started me off in the thinking business, a process others have continued. Sultan Kermally and Jackie Merckx, with whom I worked at The Management Centre Europe, made an overseas move not just tolerable, but enjoyable. I value their continuing friendship. Indeed my belief in the talent of people and the ability of management to repress it (although never fully) was founded in my conversations with wonderful colleagues at MCE, not only Sultan and Jackie, but also Eduardo Medeiro, Paul de Wouters, Jenny Webb-Bastin, and Karen O'Donnell. Lesley Colyer of Avis, Doug Cowieson of Cigna, Paul Chapman of National and Provincial Building Society have been valuable sounding boards and exemplars of the type of people we have all too few of. There are many others, too many to list, who have been important in contributing to my thinking.

The staff at Macmillan, notably Stephen Rutt, Nicola Young, and Keith Povey have shepherded this work through its final stages. Their efforts are deeply appreciated. Thanks also to Peter Wickens, a fellow Macmillan author who reviewed the first draft and made many points that resulted in subsequent changes.

Finally and most importantly, thanks to my wonderful family. Having them around me means I can truly claim to be a lucky person. My Mum and Dad nurtured my early life but it is my wife, Janet, and our children, Christopher, Andrew and Claire, who provide a constant reminder of what life is really all about.

Work of this type does not finish. Writing the book has been a mixture of pleasure and pain. It will be nice to get back to decorating . . . for a short while at least. But the world of organisations is a living laboratory. I would love to hear about your experiences, your prejudices, your war stories and your ideas. If you have any comments – good or bad – please let me know.

Thank you.

DAVID JACKSON

12 Bramdown Heights
Basingstoke
RG22 4UB

David@davjac.demon.co.uk

Every effort has been made to contact all copyright-holders, but if any have been inadvertently omitted the publishers will be pleased to make the necessary arrangements at the ealiest opportunity.

Part I
The Dynamic Organisation

1 A New Scheme of Things

We have it in our power to begin the world over again.
(Thomas Paine 1737–1809)

Whilst we are the products of our heritage, we do not have to be victims of it; there have already been enough of those. Everyone in organisations talks of the constant change, but one poster sums up many people's attitude. It reads '*We welcome change provided it does not affect us.*' Well, now there is no hiding place. Many people talk of a new paradigm of business, of new realities and a new era. Much is changing, but not all that much is really new. This chapter will briefly examine some of the key changes and provide a thumbnail sketch of how organisations have to change to meet the challenges facing us as we approach the millennium. The rest of the book expands this sketch, describing how organisations will have to respond to meet these challenges. As I gathered examples and constructed my thoughts, I was struck by how little of what we think of as new, is actually new. Most things being promoted as modern solutions have their origins in the ideas and practices of yesteryear. It is what many would describe as common sense. But as Lord Sieff of Marks and Spencer fame was reputed to have said, 'The problem with common sense is that it's not very common.'

There is so much talk about change being the new imperative that we could be excused for thinking it is a new phenomenon; something modern business executives have just discovered. Every article and book seems to begin or end with an exaltation for us to recognise that, today, change is the only certainty. Well that saying originates from Heraclitus in ancient Greece. Hardly new then. But it was true then and it is true now. We are also told that the rate of change is increasing. This is easily explained by the mechanism of compound interest

In their desire to paint a black picture, many commentators ignore one important fact. The point at which change begins is also changing. The advent of the computer as a ubiquitous tool in the workplace is a change most of us have experienced directly. But for our children it is a given. They start from a new base, as does each new generation. Of course admitting we are getting older is hard for us all.

3

There is some evidence that change comes in waves, and that as the new millennium approaches we are in a period where that wave is at or approaching its peak. People wiser than I believe we are in the transition from the industrial era to the knowledge era. Shifts like this produce periods of excessive discontinuity – change to you and me. The wave theory of change is well recognised in several disciplines, including economics, which studies long cycles (the Kondratieff wave) as well as the short cycles so beloved of politicians and the City.

The important trends impacting on organisations, and people generally, are the following.

FASTER, FASTER, FASTER

John Heywood, former vice chairman of Hambros Bank, once said that today's *status quo* is the current rate of change. The wind of change has become a hurricane of change – and a hurricane that never lets up. We all face this phenomenon. Product life cycles have shrunk. Newly designed personal computers come onto the market every 9–12 months. Speed of operations and response has become a key part of competitive productivity. Fred Smith, the chief executive officer of Federal Express, tells us bluntly: 'Organisations must adopt fast cycle methodologies or succumb to those that do.'

Economic change is also speeding up. The following table shows the time taken to double real income per capita.

Table 1.1   The rate of economic change

Country	Time Period	Time Taken (years)
UK	1780–1838	58
US	1840–1887	47
Japan	1885–1919	34
Turkey	1957–1977	20
China	1977–1987	10

COMPLEXITY

We are living in an increasingly complex world. Let me give you a few examples.

Ten years ago, the average supermarket stocked 5000 lines, of which 3000 were food items. Today the average supermarket stocks 19 000 lines, 10 000 of which are food. The ease with which we can and do travel has broadened our horizons – gastronomically as well geographically. And the supermarkets have latched onto this in their search for a bigger slice of our cash, giving us far more choice than ever before.

'Specialisation has bred feelings of isolation, futility and confusion in individuals. It has resulted in individuals leaving responsibility, thinking and social action to others.'
(Richard Buckminster Fuller)[1]

The Gartner Group, a research company, estimates that a typical multinational organisation holds over three trillion bytes of information, not all of it electronically. Yet when you ring one of them they never seem to have the answer to your question. And it is going to get worse. The report predicts an order of magnitude growth in the amount of information an organisation will need to hold. This is very easy to understand. If our organisations are going to be truly customer focused, we will need much more information about customers' habits, preferences, foibles and changes. Stafford Beer (1972) calculated that even a small organisation with only 300 inputs and outputs had 3×10^{92} possible permutations of activities within it. Far too many to comprehend. But that is exactly what we try to do.

But for all this complexity, you could argue that fundamentally little has changed. We are born, we live and finally we die. There are still rich and poor. We continue to love and hate. Throughout the turbulent changes, much has remained the same. Human nature has changed little, and shows no signs of doing so. I venture to suggest that the world is not really vastly different. The big difference is our increased understanding and our desire to understand more. The more we learn, the more we realise how little we know. This learning points to new ways, as it has always done. What is needed, and what I believe is happening, is that an increasing number of people in organisations are saying 'stop, it doesn't have to be like this'. To date we have tried to manage our complex organisations through the decomposition of command and control mechanisms; and in so doing we have dampened their souls. We need fresh ideas. I will deal with this in Chapter 3.

UNCERTAINTY

There is much conjecture about the degree of change we are facing. I favour the view that proposes a move into a new era – the knowledge era. This is a change of similar proportions to the shift from the agricultural to the industrial era. A shift of this type disturbs the natural order that we have come to accept. It is a well-known phenomenon. Any system is born, lives and eventually dies. But as one system begins to die, another evolves to replace it, with an overlap between them (Figure 1.1)

In the period of the overlap we are leaving the past, but have not yet reached the future. We are constantly oscillating between the two. This so-called period of discontinuity causes uncertainty and frustration but it can also provide opportunities. Unfortunately too many organisations feel themselves victims of the uncertainty and frustration. Entrepreneurs and leaders focus on the opportunities.

> 'Opportunities are usually disguised as hard work, so most people don't recognise them.'   (Ann Landers)

Uncertainty is a natural part of our lives. We have, however, built our organisations on the premise that the future will be more or less a continuation of the past. This is an acceptable premise when we are climbing up the straight slope of the S curve. But as soon as we meet a

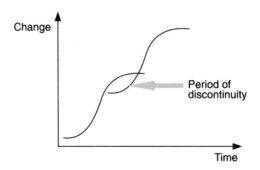

Figure 1.1   The 'S' surve shift

period of change the structures, beliefs and techniques that helped manage that growth become the very things that prevent us from making the next, necessary changes. And as change speeds up, the problem is exacerbated. It is this problem that many organisations face now. They have been successful, but the very things that brought them that success, now hold them back. The future cannot be predicted; anyone who has worked in inventory control knows the pitfalls of attempting that. The former president of Sony, Akio Morita, had it exactly right (and displayed a deep meaning of the role of leaders) when he said 'The only way to predict the future is to create it.' It is the work of leaders to change these mechanisms. Managers only seek to improve them, and in so doing create a more effective process to manage decline.

There are parallels between golf and the situation faced by many organisations. Every hole is always a new challenge; even what seems to be the same situation is different. As with golf, we can practice, and thereby get better. Some people might have more natural talent, others might have more ambition, but we can all master the basics and get around – if we put our minds to it. One of the best descriptions of change came from an outstanding golfer, Jack Nicklaus. Describing his game, he said 'Golf is 40 per cent set-up, 10 per cent swing and 50 per cent vision'.

One parallel does not however hold true. Golfing equipment and techniques have moved on significantly in the past 100 years. Unfortunately the approach to change used by many organisations has not.

GLOBAL COMPETITION

New competitors are entering traditional markets. Who would have expected a pop record producer to fly you to Japan and offer you financial services and a vodka and coke on the way. Branson's Virgin empire can. These days banks are as concerned about software manufacturers taking market share from them as they are about other banks doing the same (Figure 1.2).

With the development of new information technologies the cost of entering new markets can be reduced. Global networks make it possible to reach new markets, particularly for information-based products and services, at minimal cost. India is now one of the world's leading suppliers of software development services, with most of its customer base in the US and Western Europe. This all adds up to more intense competition than ever before.

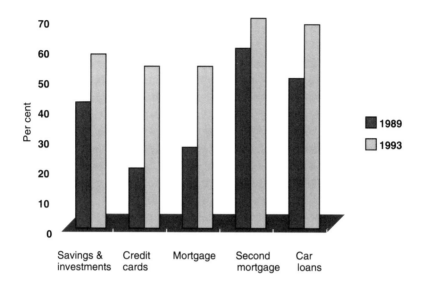

Figure 1.2   Growth in 'banking product' revenues at non-bank institutions

RISING EXPECTATIONS

One of the most fundamental changes facing organisations, and indeed society as a whole, is the impact of the demand for a better standard of living. This is not new. We have always wanted better for ourselves and our children than was available to our parents. Just compare a wedding present list of now and 20 or 30 years ago. Luxuries become essentials. This is never more true than with the information technologies, which have the potential to increase the gulf between the haves and the have nots. What has also changed is our increasing belief that certain things are ours as of right and the pressure we are all under to 'keep up with the Jones'. In the UK and the US this reached fever pitch in the 1980s with the advent of yuppies.

Rising expectations are not restricted to material possessions. The standards of health care, education and social welfare provided in most Western countries far exceed any expectations our grandparents had. The vast majority of people now working in organisations have attended full-time education to at least the age of sixteen. That certainly wasn't the situation at the turn of the century – the height of the industrial era – when it was not uncommon for children to be working from the age of eleven or twelve. At school and at home, being told what to do and how to do it was the norm. Working life was no different – just a second spell of being treated like a child. For some that is the still the reality of life in the organisations they work for.

Improved education has given people the confidence to ask why, to question the instructions handed down from on high. The workforce, many of whom are now the intellectual and educational peers of their bosses, are less willing to accept the 'I know best' attitude. People are also much better off today. Whilst the global recession of the late 1980s and early 1990s hit hard, and poverty still exists, few people living in the developed countries have to worry about survival. The combination of improved pay and the welfare state has put the physical needs of Maslow's hierarchy essentially behind us. Yet we still manage according to them. Reward and recognition are still manifested in pay. Motivation is still mainly encouraged in terms of carrot and stick – with an emphasis on stick. Improvement is upward. What of Maslow's others needs: self-steem and self-actualisation?

PEOPLE

People have always been an important resource in organisations. Now they are critical. The skills, knowledge and behaviours of people will become more important as the shift to knowledge work increases. Even in a manufacturing company the vast majority of people work away from the factory floor. They work in warehousing, distribution, sales, service, marketing, finance, training and management. And further up the supply chain, more people are employed in distribution and selling. Capturing the knowledge that is locked in people's head is a major challenge, as is building a culture and processes where one person's learning can be shared across the organisation. But most of all, we have to learn how to build organisations where people willingly give of their best.

CUSTOMER FOCUS

Whilst business is an age-old activity, the challenges never cease. As the golfing analogy above explained, you can meet the same situation many times, yet it is always different. No matter how hard we practise, we are never able to say we have totally mastered it. Customers have been around as long as business, but if you read the business press, you would think some organisations have just discovered them. Well there is perhaps more than a grain of truth in that for too many organisations.

In research carried out a couple of years ago,[2] companies around the world were asked about customer service. To a person, they all said that customers would become more important in the next five years, but half of them also said their organisations were not really doing anything about it yet. Chapter 2 addresses this important area.

> 'There is nothing more difficult to handle, more doubtful of success and more dangerous to carry through than initiating change in a state's constitution. The innovator makes enemies of all those who prospered under the old order and only lukewarm support is forthcoming from those who prosper under the new.'
>
> (Niccolo Machiavelli)

The reality of change is not new, nor is its management. The tools at our disposal might not have been around in the fifteenth century, but the nature of change has changed little. It is very much more about power, *realpolitik* and the teachings of Machiavelli. Ambitions, aspirations, fears and values dominate. Change is about people, and people are not logical; they are emotional and irrational. Black and white give way to a myriad shades of grey. Machiavelli taught us that people and power produce unlikely results, and despite hundreds of years at the school of hard knocks we still have not learned. There is an excellent text on the subject, *Management and Machiavelli* by Anthony Jay (1967), author of the excellent TV series *Yes Minister*, which should be on the reading list of every student and practitioner of management.

The problem is that we take a very rational view of change management. I have a favourite saying: 'I think sex is better than logic, but I can't prove it.' Think about it. It's true isn't it? We put so much faith in logic in our organisations. We seek a systematic answer to it all. Buyer behaviour is a classic case. A significant part of the buying decision is based on the feel-good factor – the commercial world's equivalent of the political phenomenon of the same name. It is very difficult but not impossible to describe, and the absence of it does not bode well for those in power, who until recent years have been the suppliers. It is often *not* based in fact, but it is nonetheless very real in the influence it has on voters' and, in my commercial equivalent, buyers' behaviour.

THE NEW SCHEME

What will the organisation of the future do? The dynamic organisation is one that is capable of quickly and continuously adapting to meet the changing needs of its environment. Figure 1.3 shows the areas an organisation has to excel at. It is not enough to be good at any one of them. An organisation succeeds because of the sum of what it does, not because it does one thing particularly well. It is these areas that this book will describe in great detail.

Understanding Customers

Organisations are not an end in themselves. They exist to serve: above all a business exists to serve its customers. Understanding them is therefore the obvious starting point.

Most new businesses start because their founders believe they can provide customers with something better, faster, cheaper or – occasionally – totally new. They have an implicit understanding of and a real feel for their customers. They have to, because if they don't, they don't eat. As they grow however, many lose sight of this basic premise. In 1989 research[3] showed the impact of size on an organisation's ability to focus on its customers. When asked 'Is bureaucracy eliminated if it gets in the way of good customer service?' about half said no, although the majority of those thought it should be. But in small organisations this figure was less than 25 per cent. Small organisations cannot afford complex policies and procedures that take time away from the customer. Neither can large organisations; but many have yet to realise it.

Figure 1.3   Key capabilities

The survey also asked whether customer satisfaction was measured; only half said they did this. These figures are several years old, but my experience is that still only a few organisations put any real effort into truly understanding their customers. Many are still using nothing more than the annual 'do you love us survey'.[4] They seek answers only to the questions they want to ask. These questions are based on their beliefs about what is important to the customer. That is just not good enough. Any organisation needs the answer to three questions: who are our customers, what do they want, and how are we performing in providing their needs? Sounds simple doesn't it. But given the rate at which customers change their minds and become blasé about what once delighted them, there has to be a constant cycle of questions, answers and actions. J. P. Morgan, the international banking group, puts it simply: 'Everything we do starts with knowing a client's business inside out. That's the key to anticipating their needs, solving their problems, to bringing them opportunities they might not find on their own.'

Many organisations fail to deliver outstanding service to their customers – what Bob Galvin of Motorola calls the 'Wow'[5] factor – because they overlook much of what satisfies the customer. Recent experience suggests that the soft factors – interest in the customer's business and problems, quality of relationships, responsiveness and friendliness – are increasingly important in a world where the quality of the basic product or service merely confers the right to exist in a market. But how do you systematically capture and act on soft information about customers? How do you ensure you are not taking a narrow view of customer satisfaction? Is customer satisfaction regularly and systematically measured, with clear links to action planning to improve shortcomings? I will address these issues in Chapter 2.

Operational Excellence

Customer understanding has to be turned into products/services and the processes that deliver them. The choice available to customers means that organisations have to deliver what customers want at a competitive price. The opportunity to charge a price premium for outstanding service still remains, but competition will continually squeeze that. Providing value and bringing about constant productivity improvements are the focus of dynamic organisations. Do not assume therefore that product quality and innovation are no longer important. They are crucial. They are the foundation upon which customer satisfaction is built. Alone, however, product excellence is not enough.

Manufacturing productivity has improved greatly in the last twenty years. This has not been matched by the productivity of white-collar workers. The recent focus on business process reengineering (BPR) has heightened the importance of cost-effective processes in a dynamic organisation. Unfortunately few BPR projects have delivered the desired results. Eric Cairns at Nottingham University calculates that it often takes the National Health Service 7.5 weeks of administration to deliver 1.5 hours of patient care. Hardly a model of operational excellence. Despite the massive investments in information technology, white-collar productivity has not significantly improved.

Synergy and efficiency of processes within the organisation is not enough. The idea that an organisation can work alone is clearly out of date. The 'boundaryless organisation' is coming closer with the approach of the twenty-first century. How could 'just in time' systems operate without close cooperation with major suppliers? Shared processes and systems are important but need the backdrop of shared purpose and a willingness to work together to solve problems.

As organisations outsource more of their non-core activities, the demand for partnership behaviour grows. Outsourcing requires organisations to operate within a closely integrated partnership, as though the service had remained 'in-house'. Here again organisations have much work to do. An adversarial approach to suppliers predominates. The type of supply chain partnership that Wal-Mart and Procter and Gamble have developed and the Inland Revenue's partnership with EDS for the supply of IT services are still the exception.

Have you weeded out the bureaucracy in your organisation that not only obstructs the effort to satisfy customers, but also gnaws away at people's time and motivation and adds significantly to costs? Done properly such an exercise can increase the useful information available to people whilst reducing the amount of data that typically engulfs people. Chapter 6 will examine these issues further.

Engaging People

Innovative, intelligent and committed people are the key asset of organisations. People working through and with organisations produce results. Dynamic organisations build both the culture and the processes to bring together teams of people with the right skills, knowledge and behaviours. They place intense emphasis on the development of people. They innovate with approaches to recognition, reward and forms of employment.

Staff will demand new career paths as the old ones disappear in flattened organisational structures. However full-time workers are only part of the picture. Many organisations use more part-time and contracted staff to help accommodate the shifts in the type and volume of business; a trend that is set to continue. Gaining the commitment of these important contributors is no less important than for full-time staff. Dynamic organisations have worked out how to attract the right people without offering the security of permanent employment. They know the importance of capturing the learning individuals gain and making it available for the good of the whole organisation; a process they have embedded into their culture.

Empowerment is not just the latest buzzword: it is a commitment to a common purpose and shared values. It demands authority to match accountability and a greater degree of self-discipline. It is founded on shared information and mutual trust. Above all it is the only way to deal with the increasing complexity we are all faced with. Only by tapping the skills, knowledge, wisdom and creativity of everybody in the organisation can we deal with this complexity. The critical role of people will be covered in Chapter 5.

Leadership, Vision and Values

At the heart of a dynamic organisation lies leadership. Anyone looking to this book for a quick fix will be disappointed, because unless their organisation has, or can acquire, the leadership skills needed, the changes described will not happen. This capability of the dynamic organisation is about creating an environment in which people want to give of their best. This requires a clarity of vision and values that few organisations possess today. A dynamic organisation has, and continually develops, a management team that has given full thought to what it wants to be and how it wants to work. It communicates intensively. The management team – collectively and individually – presents a compelling case for change. Leadership in dynamic organisations focuses on the purpose and values of the organisation, leaving to others the freedom and responsibility to determine how. By focusing on creating the right environment, leaders of dynamic organisations encourage others to take responsibility.

This lies at the heart of the complex interactions that make an organisation tick, or perhaps I should say buzz, for anyone who has worked in such an organisation will be aware of the positive energy it generates. Life here is a constant battle between self-confidence and self-doubt; a battle perpetuated by its leaders. They celebrate success and those who create it, whilst never letting the organisation sit on its laurels.

Dynamic organisations also work hard at building a cohesive management process, incorporating the development of values with the achievement of the hard goals of the organisation. They place less emphasis on creating structures, and more on the soft aspects of organisational design: values, power and relationships. Organisations can look incredibly neat and tidy when they are analysed in terms of structures, processes and information flows drawn on paper. Like a well-designed engine, all the pieces fit beautifully to precise tolerances, each piece moving in synergy with the others.

A good organisational structure helps people to work together, but a poor structure obstructs this. The shift has been to flatter, smaller organisations with more inter- and intraorganisational team working. The benefits of this are obvious: shorter lines of communication, reduced costs, greater flexibility and quicker response. Those at the corporate centre do only that which cannot be delegated.

But formal structure is only part of the picture. The organisation of the future will place greater emphasis on the design of the soft aspects of the organisation. Most companies have explicit statements of corporate values. Often these have been extensively communicated through pamphlets, videos and discussions. However research has revealed that only 6 per cent of managers say that their organisations' values make a difference to their daily work behaviour.[6] Have you considered the fit between your current values and those you will need to thrive in the brave new world?

There is another potential problem. Design faults in a car are easy to spot; there are rattles, loss of power and so on. Faults in organisational structure are not so obvious, for the simple reason that people are gifted at making bad structures work. They have had lots of practice. What is hard to measure is the lost time, frustration and lower productivity incurred when forcing poor structures to function. Too many managers enjoy the process of structural design, little boxes and lines, precise definitions of duties and responsibilities. The dynamic organisation calls for the 'under design' of organisation, leaving space for people to exercise their personal judgement and freedom of expression.

I am not advocating a soft touch. What is needed is balance between the soft and the hard. Robert Haas, chairman of Levi Strauss, says his toughest challenge is to mix the 'hard stuff of getting pants out of the door with the soft stuff of worker empowerment' (Howard, 1990). Jack Welch, chief executive officer of General Electric, represents a yardstick for leaders operating the new paradigm. But even he recognises the need to balance hard and soft. He was once known as Neutron Jack – when he left a plant the buildings remained but most of the people had gone. Both Welch and Haas are clear that success needs attention to both soft and hard. For many managers, that represents a significant change in skills and attitude. Not all will, or can, make the change.

These important areas of the dynamic organisation are addressed in Chapter 4.

> 'Life is a lot more like riding a bike than building a fortress. A rider needs alertness, flexibility, intelligence and skill. The fortress mentality is stupid in this world and we're more likely to be done in by our psychological and spiritual armour.'
>
> (Charles Milligan)

Watching the environment

In addition to the four core capabilities outlined above, dynamic organisations have to keep an eye on three things in the outside world. It is from the world outside that the organisation draws its energy in the form of information. Many of the problems organisations face can be traced back to their lack of external focus. They are so busy managing internal politics, game playing and looking good to their bosses that they fail to spot the weak signals of change that the environment presents to them. Even when they do spot them, managers mindsets are often so closed that they fail to question their beliefs about how the world works. They might see the signals, but they fail to take notice of them or, even worse, choose to ignore them. This path leads only to failure. A Harvard professor, Ted Levitt said, 'It is impossible to buck the market, so why bother?' Many a corporate disaster has its roots in management's attempts to do just that.

The three things an organisation has to watch out for are competition, the changing environment and innovation.

Competition

You may look with pride on improvements made in customer focus, empowering your people, the new products you have developed and your success in turning strategy into action. It may not be enough. Your

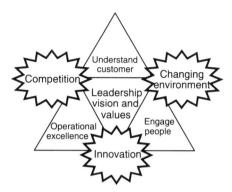

Figure 1.4 External pressures on the dynamic organisation

competitors may have secured more significant improvements, thus worsening your comparative position in the market place.

Literally every organisational activity must be made more productive. The goal must be to be a low-cost producer *and* deliverer of the highest added value for the customer. It is no longer an either/or decision. The constant fight to increase customer value and reduce costs is not a contradictory one, as some commentators believe. Rather it calls for a balancing of conflicting demands, an activity many organisations shy away from in their quest for simplistic solutions.

Benchmarking is an important tool – not just for the financial performance so beloved of the City of London, but in the quality and price of products and services, the effectiveness of delivery, the quality of relationships with customers, the workings of organisations and so on. Benchmarking is not a tool to identify the measurement hurdles so beloved of the cut, cut, cut school of management, but rather a learning path towards the greater understanding that fuels growth. The learning that benchmarking facilitates is not the same as copying. Copying leads to 'me too' products and organisations. By all means learn from the leaders, but do not just copy.

Watching the competition is particularly important when an industry is in turmoil. A recent report commissioned by the European Commission points out that the productivity of Japanese vehicle makers is around 30 per cent higher than that of their European rivals, which in the components sector Japanese productivity is 250 times higher. If you are in those industries every single part of your organisation must be competitive if you are to survive.

Changing Environment

A wide-angle view is needed of the changes in the outside world. It is in the world of society, politicians and regulators that things happen. They are important for two reasons.

Firstly, changes in these areas often impact on an organisation's ability to do business. Witness the fall in revenue of financial services companies after the introduction of disclosure. Regulation forced suppliers of certain life and pension products to show clients the charges and commissions involved in their policies and many customers decided against investing in such products when they saw how much was being raked off their payments in non-invested charges. The growing concern of the general public about the efficacy of the industry failed to cause industry players to rethink. I believe many simply did not see the signals. After all, they were not included in reporting systems, so how could such a trend be important. Many companies do keep track of demographic changes, but how many seek a meaningful understanding of shifts in the values of society?

> 'Knowing is not enough, we must apply. Willing is not enough, we must do.'   (Bruce Lee)

Secondly, changes in these areas can point to new opportunities. An organisation that is quick to spot external changes and strives to understand what they mean for their customers, has an opportunity to develop new products and services; sometimes before the customer has fully appreciated the nature of the problem. In my mind this is moving from merely listening to customers to understanding customers. It provides a mechanism to support a proactive strike.

One of the most important factors an organisation has to monitor is the shifting value sets of the customer groups they serve. In the battle for the hearts and minds of the UK voting public, the emphasis is increasingly focusing on matters of the heart. Organisations are recognising the importance of values and cultures in their organisations, and are making much greater effort to understand and deal with them. If they are so important in driving the behaviour of our voting intentions and our behaviour at work, why do most organisations pay scant regard to them (or just ignore them) when it comes to dealing with customers? When was the last time you spoke to your key customers about what makes them tick? Values lie at the heart of what we all are and do. They must be included in the picture an organisation builds of its environment.

The most fundamental social dilemma we face is implicit in Charles Handy's book *The Empty Raincoat* (1994), where he says that $\frac{1}{2} \times 2 \times 3$ is becoming the formula for those who want to remain competitive in an interconnected world: half as many people, being paid twice as much (because the organisation keeps the best), producing three times as much added value. A society operating with today's principles and beliefs about work will pay a high price in long-term unemployment, whilst those at work face increasing pressures and risk of burn-out before the traditional retirement age. Yet the alternative to such a formula may well be bankruptcy, with even worse social consequences. Employment and profits fund our social fabric. Finding the right balance is going to be a major challenge in the coming century, and one in which business must play an active part. This is too important to be left to the politicians. This will be debated further in Chapter 7.

If changes of this type are monitored by organisations, it is typically done at the senior level. Of course senior managers need to know this critical information. But how many share it with the product development staff, service managers and other middle and junior managers who are responsible for the real work of the organisation? It is through the decisions they make that the public face of the organisations is formed. Do they know what they are dealing with?

Dorothy Leonard-Barton coined the term 'core rigidities' to describe the infliction facing many organisations.[8] Their world-view is fixed, causing them to fail to see, or explain away, important changes in the environment. An organisation that cannot or does not read its environment can never be dynamic. Information from the outside world is the lifeblood of a dynamic organisation.

Innovation

The final aspect of the outside world that needs to be watched is innovation – innovation in products, processes, process technology and, perhaps most importantly, information technology (IT). Again, a wide-angle lens is required. Whilst an extremely sharp focus must be kept on product and process innovations within the industry, ignoring developments in other industries, indeed in other walks of life, could mean missing early opportunities. Andy Green, a former purchasing manager at Nissan, once explained to me how Nissan placed great emphasis on learning from other industries.

> 'If you're doing today what you did yesterday you'll be out of
> business tomorrow.'   (Dale Carnegie)

Information technology is the area where innovation has most shaped
our lives. The silicon chip is perhaps the greatest invention since the
wheel. To date, most computer power in organisations has been applied
to doing work better. In the last decade we have seen a shift in emphasis
of IT into the home. The growth of the Internet has amazed many, and
much of the recent growth has been in consumer sales. Consumers'
spending power will bring further, radical change to the organisations
serving the market.

The development of IT and the changing fashion of organisations
seems to have gone hand-in-hand. There are clear parallels between the
dominant form of computing and the types of organisation we have
adopted (a point I will explore further in Chapter 6). This of course
should come as a surprise to no one. Organisations spend much of their
time collecting and manipulating information, and computers are the
technology of information. The question organisations have to ask is
'what is the next key development IT is going to throw at us, and what
will that mean for our organisations?'

> 'There are no conditions of life to which a man cannot get
> accustomed, especially if he sees them accepted by others.'
>   (Leo Tolstoy)

That brings me neatly to the final area of innovation organisations
have to watch out for. New technologies and old management just won't
work. Our ideas about how organisations are managed are being questioned by many companies. Ricardo Semler of Semler Industries, Jack
Welch of GE, Bill O'Brien formerly of Hanover Insurance, Percy
Barnevik of ABB and Alun Cathcart of Avis Europe are among the
leaders of this movement. They have built very successful organisations
and attribute much of their success to the changes they have made in the
way their organisations work, rather than any brilliant new product
strategy or some daring acquisition. There is no shortage of material
seeking to understand and explain these changes, to which this book is a
further testament, but there is a lack of active debate and action in far too

many organisations. These changes are written off as fads, and some undoubtedly are. But to ignore the growing weight of evidence suggests to me a degree of arrogance that will cost people their jobs. Unfortunately, all too often it is the wrong people who bear the cost.

Having studied and advised on these issues for many years, to say nothing of the struggles I have been involved in when trying to change things in organisations, one thought has always come to the fore: the changes needed in organisations should not be difficult to understand. Customer focus, process improvement, people development, values and culture, leadership and the rest are all areas that have been extensively studied. The problem is twofold. The first, as Lenin commented, is that 'Everything is connected to everything else.' Organisations are not like puppets where pulling one string will move an arm and another a leg. Change something in an organisation, and the ripples often appear in an unexpected place. Cause and effect are disconnected by both time and space. It is what chaos theorists call the butterfly effect.[9] Simple cause and effect is not how organisations work. Only by understanding and managing organisations as complete systems can we hope to make change really work.

To instil this we need to change how we manage change. Instead of always demanding change master plans that embrace the whole organisation, we need to encourage and harness multiple experiments; what Bob Waterman, coauthor with Tom Peters of *In Search of Excellence*, calls 'informed opportunism'. The late Christopher Lorenz of the *Financial Times* reported that one of the findings from a major internal review made by the successful IT services company EDS was that, in order to occupy new competitive space, a company does not always have to take giant steps and put itself at risk; 'bet the farm' in EDS parlance. Instead it can move step by step with relatively small investments. As one EDS manager put it 'Ah! I see what this means; that we only need bet the pig.'

The second problem is that much of what has to be done to change organisations involves people, and we attempt to use logic and reason when people are illogical and irrational. Our moods guide our actions and responses. We cannot expect to manage change unless we understand and focus much more of our time and effort on people. So often they are the last consideration. Training, communication and consultation are all seen as add-ons to the real work of change.

If this book achieves anything, I pray it will be that people are placed fully at the top of our agendas.

2 Getting Close to Customers

You can automate the production of cars but you cannot automate the production of customers.

(Walter Reuther)

Many organisations find themselves between a rock and hard place. As markets mature and life cycles shrink, differentiation of the core products/services becomes increasingly difficult. Almost any innovation brings an immediate response from competitors, applying what Tom Peters called creative swiping.[1] There are signs that the customer is feeling shell shocked from the rate of innovation. We are not happy when, having bought the latest model, we find six months later that we are now behind the times: we feel cheated. On the other hand, customers are becoming more demanding, more vocal and more willing to exercise the choice they have. As consumers we are raising our sights. Organisations that once could feel secure in the knowledge that they were the best at serving the customer, now find themselves under pressure. Industry standards are no longer sufficient: we expect the same level of service from our bank that we get from our car hire company; we want large corporations to be as friendly as our local pub. We translate our experiences across industries with consummate ease, and wonder why suppliers find it so difficult to do the same. We are also learning to be more vocal, even the normally reserved English are now more likely to complain. I use the term 'vigilante customer' to describe people who know what they want and hang on until they get it.

The huge increase of interest in customer satisfaction we have witnessed in the last six years is welcome, but at the same time worrying. If

'To sustain competitive advantage requires a total commitment to your customers – to understanding what they want now and anticipating what they will want tomorrow – and to being there on cue, first choice, every time.' (Sir Michael Perry)

organisations are now focusing on the customer, what were they doing before? Some organisations, for example Marks and Spencer, have always placed the customer at the centre of their activities, but many are more recent converts. There are plenty of examples. Xerox Corporation started its quality drive when, on losing patent protection, some Japanese competitors, notably Canon, began to take huge tranches of its market share. British Airways was losing about £2 million pounds a day when Lord King and Sir Colin Marshall began to build 'the world's favourite airline'. Royal Automobile Club Motoring Services Ltd almost went bankrupt before embarking on an organisation-wide change, led by Arthur Large. Difficulties such as these tend to focus the mind.

> 'To know what a business is we have to start with its purpose. Its purpose must lie outside the business itself. In fact it must lie in society since business enterprise is an organ of society. There is only one valid definition of business purpose – to create a customer.' (Peter F. Drucker)

In all cases the turnaround was focused on the needs of the customer and certainly wasn't a quick fix. One common thread running through companies I have studied was their determination, often through great difficulties, to stick to their guns. Customers are unique in their role as a focus for change: they are dynamic – their needs change, often in response to what we provide for them. This provides a continuous stream of ideas, opportunities and threats, upon which innovation can be based.

But many organisations do not tap into this rich vein. They suffer from the CIA syndrome. We all know the CIA (the US Central Intelligence Agency) exists, but it is spoken of in hushed tones. Many of its activities are unseen – at least until after the event – and the outcome of its activities are often blamed on other factors. Well the CIA is alive and well in many organisations. It takes the form of *complacency, ignorance and arrogance* (I have borrowed and embellished this phrase from a former colleague who once used it in a presentation).

Complacency is commonplace. In the 1960s and 1970s the West could never imagine a Japanese luxury car – it was unthinkable. Some organisations are too easily pleased. Growth may be slowing, but it's still growth. There are always factors that can explain the slip in performance, and profits are still being generated, so things can't be that bad, or so they argue. Underperforming becomes a way of life, and a growing malaise sets into the organisation. It's business as usual. Jose Ignacio Lopez, an executive poached by Volkswagen from General Motors, said 'We must transform the Western ability to create intelligent excuses into positive creativity.' The game playing that takes place in these organisations saps energy that could otherwise be channelled into positive results.

Ignorance is perhaps less common, but just as destructive. Ignorant organisations just don't know what is happening. They often have a narrow focus, perhaps seeing themselves as a product supplier in a marketplace where customers are wanting solutions. Ignorant organisations make little or no effort to understand shifts in their industry and markets. They keep their heads down and plough on regardless. I was once told by the finance director of a multinational company I worked with that the company's problems had been minimised because 'the directors had been unable to really interfere with the running of the shops because they did not how it all worked'. An honest statement, but damning indictment.

Arrogance abounds in some organisations. Often these organisations were founded on an outstanding idea or product, from which they enjoyed huge success. But they have held onto this idea beyond its sell-by date. Every idea has its time, and equally its limits. But many organisations are so wedded to the ideas and products that brought them success in the past that they are blind to new markets and possibilities. *Fortune* magazine once described Ken Olsen, the founder of Digital Equipment Corporation, as the ultimate entrepreneur. Olsen built up Digital from nothing to a $13.5 billion company in 30 years, a remarkable achievement in anyone's book. He founded Digital on the idea of the minicomputer, arguing that the mainframe was remote from the people it served and promulgated large centralised bureaucracies. His vision of the mini-computer was to bring computing closer to the people. His ideas on computing changed the industry and spawned a new breed of computer. How strange then that, when commenting on the emerging market for personal computers, he should say 'I cannot see why anyone would want a computer on their desk.' In exactly the same way that the minicomputer fuelled huge growth of the IT industry in the late 1970s and early 1980s, the PC became the largest growth sector of the late 1980s, a trend that continued into the 1990s. Indeed there is every sign that as computing enters the home, as the song says 'we aint seen nothing yet'. It is very difficult for an organisation to admit that its great idea has run its course, nut not many individuals would dispute that most ideas have a limited life. Misplaced self-confidence is fuelled by a lack of willingness to listen to the market, to customers, indeed to anyone who does not support the creed.

'At some time in the life cycle of virtually any organisation, its ability to succeed in spite of itself runs out.'   (Richard O'Brien)

All three aspects of the CIA syndrome share a common feature: too little attention is paid to the outside world. It is the external world that provides the energy – in the form of information – that fuels an organisation's development. In 'Planning as learning' (1988) Arie de Geus, then working in corporate planning at Shell, researched organisations that had succeeded in business over the long term. He found that the average lifespan of a large industrial enterprise is less than 40 years, and that in most cases, the source of their problems and viable solutions are known within the organisation ahead of them impacting on performance. It is the shared mindset of the organisation that blinds them to the answer. As Arnold Toynbee said, 'Nothing fails like success.' [2]

Avoiding the CIA syndrome means developing a strong external perspective. In reality, however, most organisations make decisions on the basis of information that is both historic and essentially internally oriented. This internal perspective fuelled the cut, cut, cut management style of the 1980s and early 1990s. Of course monitoring customers is at the core of what is needed, and is discussed in detail later in this chapter. However knowing the customer is not enough. It is a paradox that whilst customers are the referees of business today, they do not always know what they want. The dynamic organisation keeps its eye on three particular elements of the outside world in addition to customers: competitors, innovation and socioeconomic trends. Let's look at these in turn.

COMPETITION

Most organisations have competitors, and those competitors have customers, so they must be doing something right. Does your organisation know what its competitors are doing right? Competition monitoring is not difficult. 'Shop at, eat at, fly with, have your hair cut by . . . your best competitor' says John Humble. Manufacturing companies use a technique known as reverse engineering: stripping down a competitor's product to see how it works and to gain an insight into the competitor's production methods. Without breaching intellectual property and copyright laws, and within the bounds of ethical behaviour, organisations should study their competitors' products, services and organisation more rigorously.

But today's competition is only half the picture. Many new developments of the past years have come from companies that are not recognised as players in a particular industry. The entry of Virgin and Marks and Spencer into financial services are just two high profile examples of how new entrants are threatening established market players.

SOCIOECONOMIC TRENDS

The outside world and how it is changing is of vital importance to the dynamic organisation for two reasons. The first is that changes impact on the ability of the organisation to operate. International and national politics, legislation and industral regulations directly limit what the organisation can do; witness the effect of regulation on insurance and pensions providers. But other, more subtle forces such as changing lifestyles and values have just as strong an impact on the organisation. More importantly, these same trends affect customers. They impinge on their ability to operate, and they create new opportunities for the customers. Spotting the changes early is therefore a vital activity, providing you with opportunities to consider and develop new products and services. Obvious trends are the changing demographics of the world – the increase in the average age of the population for example.

A more subtle and perhaps more important trend is the change in the values. The individualism of the 1980s is being challenged by an increasingly vocal group that is concerned about the state of our society. Collective responsibility is, perhaps, just beginning to peek out from behind the parapet again. A MORI poll conducted in the UK the day after·the 1995 November budget reported that over 60 per cent of people would have preferred the 1p reduction in the basic rate of income tax to have been spent on improving services. The oil company Shell was twice the butt of public disquiet in 1995: first over the disposal of the Brent Spar oil rig and then over their investment in Nigeria, a country with a poor human rights record. These values shifts are reflected in consumers' buying habits. Shell's revenues from petrol sales fell at the time of these two incidents.

Consumers, shareholders and employees are of course all drawn from the same pool. The vast majority of shares in UK plc are held by pension funds. The trade unions represent people upon whom the City relies for a significant part of its funding. Employees are customers, and viceversa. A dynamic organisation recognises these interconnections and seeks to balance the needs of all stakeholders, rather than focus on just one group. Taking an external view requires changes in the culture and processes of an organisation – particularly the former.

There are plenty of sources of pertinent information for those interested, including customers, whose views are always welcome. Academic-based forecasting groups such as the centres at Henley and the London Business School and pollsters such as MORI, NOP and Gallup regularly publish studies of social issues. Futurologists also make for interesting reading.

INNOVATION

As discussed in Chapter 1, the dynamic organisation also has to keep an eye on innovations in new products, services and process technologies, including information technology, and on new ideas about how to manage organisations.

> 'Research carried out into the workings of the candle will not reveal the existence of the light bulb.'   (Anon)

The quartz watch decimated the Swiss watch industry and for a time consigned it to the luxury watch market niche, even though the quartz watch was invented by Swiss watchmakers. The powers within the industry failed to grasp how this upstart technology was destined to play a major role in the precision engineering industry until the Japanese took a significant market share from them. IBM invented the reduced instruction set chip (RISC), an approach creating computer chips of greater power. However, IBM's mainframe mentality, reinforced over years by the huge success the mainframe had brought to the firm, led it to reject the idea and it was left to others to develop. RISC is now seen as the mainstream computer architecture, enabling the continuing growth in computer power.

> 'The world is moving so fast these days, that the man who says it can't be done, is often interrupted by the one doing it.'
>   (Data Logic)

In all industries, new process technologies spawn new winners. The traditional steel suppliers in the US have lost market share to Nucor, which introduced the minimill. Forsaking the conventional wisdom that steel mills had to be huge to gain the benefits of economies of scale, Nucor have developed and built minimills and is now the fastest growing company in the US steel market. Now US steelmakers are saying the minimill technology will not work on strip products. Nucor is quietly confident.

Innovation applies not just to technology. Much thought is being given (as I hope this book reflects) to the management of organisations. A working group of senior managers at computer manufacturer Hewlett Packard is considering the fundamental purpose of the organisation: the reason for it's existence. Charles Handy (1991) considered the same issue and concluded that the basic purpose of an organisation is to perpetuate itself, to guarantee its own survival in the context of the society within which it operates. Such questioning may seem academic, but it has a truly valuable role: it requires people to consider the basic principles upon which the organisation is built. This opens up new possibilities of management. Many winning organisations are innovators.

Many organisations have come to chastise themselves for being internally focused, and have set themselves the goal of becoming customer focused. Whilst this is an absolutely essential element of a dynamic organisation, the term customer focused should be replaced by externally focused. It is also the case that a strong external focus has to be matched with a propensity for action. The eyes that watch developments in the outside world are important, but they are only part of the body corporate. Without legs and arms to move and act, brains to think and a heart to feel, the eyes have little value.

UNDERSTANDING CUSTOMERS

Understanding customers is a simple concept but it is enormously difficult to do well. Each customer is an individual, and as such is a collection of experiences, moods, prejudices, aspirations and expectations. Unfortunately these characteristics change according to which side of the bed the customer gets out of, the phase of the moon or what a friend said an hour ago. Customers are people, and as such are unpredictable, irrational and emotional. Having said that, there is no choice other than actively to build both a more complete understanding of our customers and an organisation that can deal with their individual needs and aspirations.

Understanding customers is about constantly seeking the answers to three questions:

1. Who are our customers?
2. What are the needs and aspirations of these customers?
3. Are we meeting those needs and aspirations?

Many organisations seek answers to at least two of these questions through the annual 'do you love us' survey. In an environment where needs and choice are changing so quickly, can you really afford to wait a year to find out what your customers want, or how your competitors are outperforming you? The dynamic organisation is one where listening to customers is a continuous, not a discontinuous activity.

Let's take a more detailed look at these questions.

Who are our Customers?

Many businesses have failed by trying to be all things to all people. The corollary of this is that organisations choose which products and services to offer and which customers to serve. Whilst there is plenty of evidence of the former, there are fewer examples of the latter. Most organisations' customer bases are an accident of history, not a result of intellectual thought. Choosing customers is a complex decision that interacts with decisions about which products and services to offer. Often the two conflict, hence the frequency of the discussion about whether to be product focused or customer focused. But the act of choosing which customers to serve is not a one-way street. Customers also choose which suppliers to buy from.

The question of which customers to serve is more important to some organisations than others: packaged consumer goods manufacturers will be less concerned about this than a private bank. When asked, many managers will initially say that any customer is a good customer. But when probed they will often change their minds. Who wants a customer who doesn't pay, or one who maliciously misuses the product or service for an illegal purpose? What are the characteristics of the customers you do want? Some will seek customers who are challenging, knowing that their demands will fuel the need to innovate. Others want customers who will reinforce the brand image they are seeking to develop.

Segmentation has long been a marketers' tool to help them better describe the customers they serve. Segmentation, according to marketing professor and author Philip Kotler, is the 'sub-dividing of a market into homogeneous sub-sets of customers, where any sub-set may conceivably be selected as a market target to be reached with a distinct market mix'. Segmentation has rarely been properly applied. Ask any marketing manager to name the segments they address and they will typically tell you about industry sector, life-stage, geographic region, income level, socioeconomic grouping or benefits sought. The problem is that these are of little value in identifying and reaching customers. They were fine in an era when the supplier had the upper hand, when there were enough buyers to go around. Increasing competition and choice, and the expectation of being treated as an individual mean that, to succeed, we have to be able to pinpoint the individual, or even better, to pointpoint the individual at a particular time when his or her propensity to buy is high.

Paul Fifield,[3] a marketing expert in the UK, has developed a novel, and I believe very useful, approach to segmentation. It is based on the simple premise that individuals and organisations operate in a number of different contexts (Figure 2.1). Let me use a simple illustration. I am an author, consultant, a family man, someone who enjoys travelling, football and wine. These are just some of the contexts within which I operate, and I share many of these contexts with other people. For effectively market targeting a supplier would need to identify these contexts and the circumstances in which a particular context is uppermost in my mind. That is the time when my propensity to buy is greatest. Calling me at home to sell me double glazing when I have just sat down to dinner with my family will make me antagonistic to double glazing salesman for a long time. Now imagine being able to identify a group of people all operating in the same segment at the same time. This is the power of context.

The context approach was used to help a group of colleagues better understand the consulting market. We spent almost a full day identifying and grouping together the possible contexts. We generated over 500,

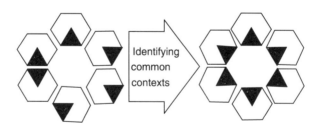

Figure 2.1   Context-based segmentation

which we distilled into 24 groups. We finally settled on three major segments:

- *The CIA*: these are the Complacent, Ignorant and Arrogant described in Chapter 1. We concluded that these were not prime targets as they perceived no problem or would not be open to new ideas. If we had chosen this group, we would have built a marketing strategy around generating FUD (Fear, Uncertainty and Doubt).
- *The Stuck*: this was the largest segment and was broken down into four subsegments depending on the nature of the reason they were stuck. This was also a crowded segment, that is well served by the existing consultancy companies.
- *The Pioneers*: this group comprised organisations who were leaders, the best-practice companies on the lookout for new ideas that would enable them to maintain their lead. Although the smallest segment, they were particularly attractive. They would keep us on our toes and help us to establish the reputation needed by a new group. They would also give us the opportunity to enter the 'stuck' segment at a later date with a proven track record.

Context differs from other forms of segmentation in that it is dynamic. Other approaches to segmentation are descriptive, classifying the customers. Once classified, they are stuck in that box until the next time the organisation revisits its segmentation approach. Conversely, context-based segmentation recognises the dynamic nature of individuals and organisations, describing the situation they are in at a particular point in time. Under the context approach the segments are constant (at least in the medium term) but people and organisations move in and out of them. In my example of the consultancy segments above, a single organisation might be a pioneer in one aspect of its activities but stuck in another. One customer, many segments. This forces the organisation to consider the customer's current context (or contexts) much more carefully and tailor the offering and the message to that context. It requires much more thought and, ultimately, processes of both communication and delivery to match the supplier's offer which the customer's context. In turn this greater understanding of the customer – for without greater understanding of the customer, context will not work – will be rewarded by more business opportunities. Context lends itself to organisations that focus on retaining customers.

This approach to segmentation is of course based on the number and quality of the contexts the organisation is able to generate. It demands a strong external perspective. The context approach points to the marketing messages and the channels through which the messages can be delivered. More importantly, it is an invaluable way of building a portfolio of products and services to address the chosen market. The existing portfolio can be mapped against the contexts and the needs they express; indeed context exercises provide a valuable source of ideas for new product development. Context segmentation does not stop at marketing. It informs the rest of the organisational design: the style of engagement, the tools and techniques needed, the type of people needed can all be different (significantly so) for the different segments.

Identifying the types of customer you choose to serve is only the first half of the picture. The picture is incomplete if you do not actually know the customers themselves. You might not expect a consumer goods manufacturer to know the end customer, but what about a bank? Surprisingly, a number of our leading financial institutions do not even know how many customers they have. They can tell you how many account holders they have, but cannot always identify the fact that three account holders are the same person. Unless you know individual customers, you cannot hope to answer the next question.

An increasing number of organisations, however, are realising the value of knowing who their customers are. For example, Heinz has launched a direct marketing campaign to get to know its customers better. 'Heinz at Home' is a magazine with product information, recipes and other food information delivered to named individuals. The coupons included with the pack are tailored to the known buying habits of the individual. The magazine is also used as a distribution mechanism for market research, further building the company's understanding of its customers. Of course this does not give total protection. The loss-leading strategy of supermarkets selling baked beans for 3p a tin shows that, in some cases, no amount of customer understanding can succeed. In the short term such strategies may gain market share. For continued success, however, there is no substitute for understanding the customer.

What are Customers' Needs and Aspirations?

The second question is the one that all organisations have to answer. Many businesses start by entrepreneurs spotting a need that is not being addressed, or is being badly addressed. Many come from within the industry and have often tried to get their existing organisation to adopt the new product or approach.

As the Swedish-based Asea Brown Boveri (ABB, see below) has identified, the basis of quality is the core product or service. Increasingly, however, that is not enough. Quality from the customer's perspective has two dimensions, as shown in Figure 2.2.

Much emphasis has been placed on developing the hard aspects of quality, which relate to aspects of the product or service. Indeed it is in this area that total quality management (TQM) has its roots. Led by the Japanese, who themselves were taught by Americans, the world as a whole has made significant strides in designing and building quality products. But in a competitive market the quality of the core product or service is nothing more than a table stake. When a product can be studied and copied in months, the sustainability of product-based advantage is usually limited. That is not to imply that organisations should not seek to develop and innovate their products – they must. But they must not assume that is all they need. Customers demand more than products. They want to be recognised as individuals. If they have a problem they want to be listened to, to have their problem recognised and solved. They assume that a level of knowledge exists in the organisation that is at least equal to what they have told any part of it. This has significant implications for managing contact with customers, which I shall address later in this chapter.

For organisations that offer complex products or services, the implications of the above model are even greater. Let me give you an example. If you hire a lawyer for advice (the core product), you have no way of assessing the quality of that advice unless you are trained in law yourself or if something goes dramatically wrong. You can however assess the soft aspects of quality. You will have a perception of the effort the lawyer is putting into understanding your problem, and the degree with which she

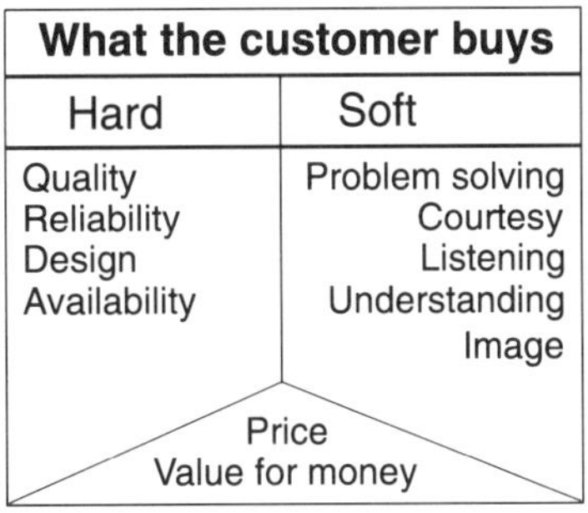

What the customer buys	
Hard	Soft
Quality Reliability Design Availability	Problem solving Courtesy Listening Understanding Image
Price Value for money	

Figure 2.2 The dimensions of quality

empathises with you. You can assess how friendly she is, the quality of the facilities and the way she explains the bill. These experiences, and here logic flies right out of the window, will significantly influence your assessment of the total experience. You will perceive her to be a good lawyer not because of the quality of her advice, but because of the care she has taken with you. And of course you will tell others about your experience and recommend her to them.

In a significant study in late 1995,[4] Mintel and Coley Bell Porter identified five factors as key to the perception people hold of a company: quality of products, fair pricing, service, complaints handling and attitudes of staff. The last three are all soft factors. Think about the suppliers you most enjoy dealing with: how many of them have excelled in the core product versus the care aspects?

There is another important point to be drawn from the simple diagram above. Excelling at the hard aspects of quality, with the exception of design, relates essentially to processes. Product quality, reliability and availability are process-based attributes. However the soft aspects of quality all rely on people. They are about relationships, respect for the individual and shared learning. They are rooted in the values and culture of the organisation. It is one of the main reasons why customer focus is an organisation-wide issue, with people, culture, values, vision and leadership at its core.

The Swedish-based engineering giant ABB has recognised the importance of organisational development and an external focus in the quest for competitive advantage, as Figure 2.3 shows.[5]

Source: Dr Arun Gairola ABB Germany, Customer Focus Program.

Figure 2.3   ABB's staircase of advantage

It is important to recognise that, like any staircase, the whole thing will collapse if the lower steps crumble. Product excellence is the foundation, requiring excellent processes to ensure they can be reliably and consistently created. In turn process excellence is a product of continuous improvement, which requires committed and capable people – a function of organisational design. All this has to be focused on an ability to identify the express and latent needs of the customer – marketing excellence. How all of these things operate is a function of the culture and values the organisation can instil. This takes immense and sustained effort, and cannot be copied, hence the greater sustainability of the advantage they deliver. It is also interesting to note how Figure 2.3 reflects the areas managements have focused on in the past twenty years. For those still struggling with problems of basic product quality, the diagram is a warning. Move quickly and decisively up the staircase or risk losing everything. The gap between the best and the rest is likely to widen.

How are we Meeting our Customers' Needs?

The third question is all about performance – from the customers' perspective. The dynamic organisation uses a range of techniques constantly to test how it is doing in meeting its customers' needs. No one technique is right. Surveys, comment cards, focus groups and customer panels all have a role to play. There are however two golden rules: (1) whatever research is undertaken, it should be linked to action in some way, and (2) listening to customers (monitoring performance) has to be a continuous activity that spans the organisation.

The butterfly model (Figure 2.4) is useful for understanding the range of opportunities there are to listen to customers. The three areas of measurement relate to three areas of action.

Every organisation deals with a number of events: the delivery of a product, a telephone enquiry, serving a meal. A sample of these are monitored and compared with the factors customers have determined to be important. The results are then fed back to the functions responsible for the event. It is important that this feedback is complete and rapid. This allows the function or team to do two things. Firstly, they can contact the customer with an appropriate message, for example the Birmingham Midshires Building Society issues an apology or a thank you for every survey or comment card returned by customers. Secondly, the data provides the organisation with information upon which further improvements can be built. Providing people with the statistical tools of

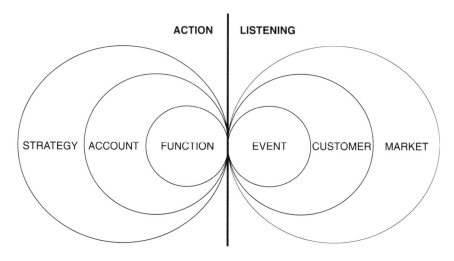

Figure 2.4   The butterfly model

quality can improve their ability to understand and exploit this data. Using event-driven mechanisms to monitor satisfaction is one of the reasons why Avis Europe was able to improve its productivity for 13 consecutive years. (For more information on Avis and the Birmingham Midshires Building Society, see the cases studies in Part II.)

The customer element of the model refers to the combined perceptions of an individual customer. This is of course more relevant to those organisations where the overall relationship between customer and supplier is important. A customer's perception of a supplier is more than the sum of the events, although these will influence the overall perception. Other factors such as word of mouth, press coverage, sponsorship and key individuals will have an impact. For large business-to-business relationships, this image is multifaceted because of the myriad of contacts.

In one partnership I was involved in planning, a number of overlapping teams – staffed by members of both organisations – were established to monitor the relationship between the two organisations. Each major project had a joint project board to follow the progress of that specific project. In addition to project performance, the team considered how the two organisations could more effectively share resources and expertise to benefit either or both parties. The operational team studied all the projects and considered issues such as simplifying administration, sharing information and providing opportunities for the development of individuals through secondment to the other organisation. The final team was the partnership strategy team, which comprised senior managers from both organisations and met either on demand to address particular issues or twice yearly. This team looked at the direction being taken by the two companies and how they could cooperate.

This is not something to consider for every customer, but it is a valuable way of improving relationships and therefore enhancing the likelihood of retaining major customers. The action side of this is customer (or account) planning. It is not a fix for poor performance, but it does provide a mechanism where by this can be discussed as well as being a useful in tailoring the organisation to the needs of an individual customer.

The final element of the butterfly model links the perceptions of the market place with direction. In my opinion the market place has to extend beyond the customer base to address lost customers, customers of competitors and people who do not buy that type of product or service. This mechanism seeks to tap into the trends of the market: what's new, what's losing popularity, what are the new issues out there? It should also allow identification of key buying criteria and reveal how the organisation is performing in comparison with its competitors against these criteria. The information gathered in this element of the model is used to inform product development, basic research and improvements in the effectiveness of the organisation.

The cycles of three elements should be tied to the rhythm of the organisation. Event sensing will have a much faster cycle than market place sensing. Whilst some of the mechanisms will be structured, planned events, it is important not to constrain the on-going collection of data.

MANAGING COMPLAINTS

An important part of building an understanding of customers is providing mechanisms to collect and address complaints. The value of complaints is well known. They provide instant feedback on how the organisation is performing and afford an opportunity to say 'Sorry, we messed up, but let's show you how we can do things well'. Unfortunately, unless the organisation makes it easy for customers to complain, most people will walk away and take their bad feelings and wallets with them. Research from TARP[6] suggests that organisations only receive complaints from 25–50 per cent of those experiencing a problem. Furthermore senior managers hear of only 0.5–5 per cent of incidents where people experience a problem. Successful complaint management centres on providing front-line staff with the authority and means to resolve problems and complaints on the spot without having to refer up the line. This, of course, assumes that the people operating on the front line have the skills and empathy to deal with a complaining customer.

CAPTURING THE VOICE OF THE CUSTOMER

Whilst there is no one approach to listening to customers, one technique – 'Voice of the Customer', a variation of quality function deployment (QFD), is both valuable and flexible.[7] QFD was developed by the Japanese as way of getting customer input into the product development process. 'Voice of the Customer' works at all levels of the relationship with a customer, not just with product development.

'Voice of the Customer' provides a way of making improvements through a process of listening, mutual learning and action. During the process we learn to listen to what invited customers have to say, by working with invited customers to understand their needs and to share knowledge and expertise. We then seek to make improvements based on that input. While this is not unique, the structure that QFD supplies is valuable in both guiding people through a proven process and making explicit the link between customer needs and the actions required to address them. The clear link between feedback and action is a powerful way of establishing a greater commitment from customers.

Quality function deployment was first brought to the widespread attention of the West in a *Harvard Business Review* article entitled 'The House of Quality' by Don Clausing and J.R. Hauser (1988). The title takes it name from the shape of the matrix used (Figure 2.5).

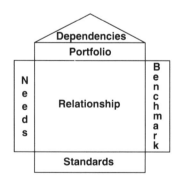

Figure 2.5   The house of quality

At its most simple, QFD is a matrix for relating a customer's needs to the features of a product or service and using this to bring about improvements. With 'Voice of the Customer' this use is extended to cover the overall relationship between a supplier and its customers. The 'Voice of the Customer' process provides a way of accessing information that would otherwise remain hidden. The power of the approach is limited only by the willingness of the organisation to act on the data and the ability of its people to develop answers to the problems and aspirations that customers express.

A guide to using 'Voice of the Customer' is included as Appendix I. This is based on the work of Nikki Alford, a former colleague.

BEYOND LISTENING

> 'When people are free to do as they please, they usually imitate each other.'   (Eric Hoffer)

Whilst listening to customers is vital, the dynamic organisation does not stop there. Anyone can listen and act on what they hear. Of course an organisation that has a stronger relationship with customers will have access to more information and therefore the opportunity to institute more improvements. However the 'listen–do' cycle is not enough; it can lead to and perpetuate a 'me-too' position. Real success comes from the cycle shown in Figure 2.6.

> 'Some companies ask customers what they want. Market leaders know what customers want before customers know it themselves.'
> (Gary Hamel and C. K. Prahalad)

Listening to customers is not simply a question of asking them what they want. It is often said that customers do not know what they want, indeed anyone who has carried out such studies will know that most companies express their future needs as extensions of their present knowledge and experiences. Often they cannot *express* what they want. Listening is an active process and involves watching, studying, talking to, arguing with and making developments with the customer as well as

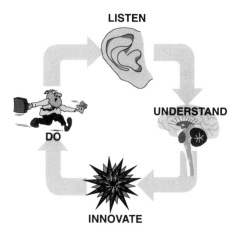

LISTEN

UNDERSTAND

DO

INNOVATE

Figure 2.6   The enhanced listening cycle

listening in the literal sense. In this way you can capture the implicit needs the customer is unable to articulate. There is an old saying 'If you really want to understand a person, you must live in their socks'. The arrogance I referred to above often manifests itself by people assuming they know what their customers want. They rarely if ever do. Customers do not buy on price and product specification alone. A significant part of the buying decision is based on the feel-good factor – the commercial world's equivalent of the political phenomenon of the same name. The customer feel-good factor is not to be found in figures, it is sensed during direct contact with customers. This partly explains the success of values-based enterprises such as The Body Shop and Virgin, and the problems established brands have had with values-based issues. Shell was hit particularly hard by the Brent Spar fiasco, even though it was proven right in the end. In the irrational world of customers, right is often not enough.

In Figure 2.6 I have used the brain to denote understanding for two reasons. The first is summed up in the words of Gore Vidal: 'For every complex problem, there is a solution so simple and incisive in its clarity and so blindingly wrong'. In his book *The Fifth Discipline*, Peter Senge (1990) shows how a solution that initially looks correct can actually aggravate the problem. He explains the need for systemic thinking in problem solving.[8] The second reason for using a picture of the brain relates to its structure and its relationship with innovation. The brain is a network of interconnected neurones. The more connections a neurone can make, the greater the thinking capacity. The same is true of the link between listening and innovation. The more sources of data, the greater the possibility of spotting a pattern or creating a new link. This of course depends on understanding. It also depends on an open mind. Many new developments are the result of the synthesis of previously separate technologies and ideas. Equally, many significant developments have been dismissed by those who are unwilling to think beyond their existing view of the world. The more sources of information coming into the organisation, the greater the possibility of innovation.

The final part of the cycle is doing. The Chinese can only express the concept of learning using two symbols. The first represents study, the second practise. The dynamic organisation recognises this and does much of its practice with customers. It develops its new products, services and ways of doing business with its customers, not just *for* its customers. This makes selling easier. The buyers have already bought into the idea – they are part of it. The Boeing 777 was a huge success at launch, due in no small part to the active involvement of staff from Boeing's leading customers. The plane that took off was not Boeing's plane, it truly was the customers'. The potential buyers all had enthusiastic disciples for the plane inside their own organisations. Many people are talking about the 1990s as the era of relationship marketing. I believe this goes beyond our current concept of marketing. To me, the dynamic organisation considers relationships to be a central part of its values system.

INFORMATION

The one thing about service to customers is that we are all experts because we are all consumers. There are three major reasons why we, the customers, are not receiving the level of service we have come to demand.

The first of these service glitches is that the people who are dealing with us just cannot be bothered. Service is a people business. Relationships are not built between organisations, they are built between people in organisations. A complaint levelled at some organisations is that they constantly change their front-line people. Relationship building takes time. Both parties have to invest time and effort to understand not just the business interactions but also the nuances of personal relationship. As one manager commented, 'it costs us money every time they change a salesman'. But this is a lesser problem than the grumpy, disinterested person we have all come across at some time as a customer. The indifference some employees show customers is by far the main reason for customers moving elsewhere.

The second reason is that the system prevents people from providing service. A research study a few years ago asked, 'If red tape gets in the way of providing good service, is it removed?'[9] A surprising 58 per cent of UK respondents said 'No, we stick to the rules', more than in the rest of Europe, Japan and the US. You have probably come across this type before: 'I'd love to help you, but it's more than my job's worth to break the rules.' Sometimes this is an excuse, but often it is a genuine grievance. The person wants to help, but the implications of breaking the rules are awesome; or at least are perceived as awesome. It is this factor that quality guru Edwards-Deming identified when he suggested that 90 per cent of quality problems are caused by the system.

The third common reason for bad service is an organisation's inability to put the right information in the right hands at the right time and in the right place. This manifests itself in organisations where the left hand does not seem to know what the right hand is doing; where you and I, the customers, seem to be filling in the cracks. Too often we are left hanging in the air by organisations that are unable to get their act together.

I experienced a classic case of information starvation when travelling to my parents for a weekend. I arrived at 5 p.m. at Kings Cross station in London on a Friday afternoon and waited patiently in line to buy my ticket. Then, ticket in hand, I surveyed the large departures board and proceeded to the allotted platform. It was only then that I discovered why there seemed to be more chaos than usual. At 10.00 a.m. that morning a major gas leak on the route taken by my train had resulted in severe disruption. The electricity supply to the train had had to be turned off and the whole train pulled past the leak by a diesel engine to avoid any sparks that might have ignited the gas.

Now even I could see that this was quite beyond the control of InterCity East Coast Trains. What was unforgivable was the complete lack of information. Why couldn't the ticket sales people have told me of the delay when I was buying my ticket? Then I had would have had a choice: trains departing from the adjacent St Pancras station followed a different route and were unaffected; a coach was another option, as was waiting until early Saturday morning to complete my journey. But I received no information and therefore had no choice that did not involve the risk of losing my money. The departures board continued to display the timetabled departures, even though many had been cancelled and others severely delayed. The few station announcements that were made were extremely difficult to hear. No special help points had been set up. When asked, most of the staff politely said, 'Don't ask me, I don't know what's going on.' At 6.50 I boarded the delayed 5.15, which was not scheduled to stop at my station, a fact I discovered when I fortunately overheard a member of staff talking to another customer.

You might think that all went well after that, but we suffered another round of totally inaccurate information on the train when we stopped just south of the affected area. Four times we were told we would recommence our journey in the next ten minutes – there was a 20 minute break between each announcement!

The train company was not to blame for the gas leak and by delaying the train it was acting in the best interests of customer safety. However, it was to blame for its abject failure to provide timely information that bore even a passing resemblance to reality.

Without underestimating the importance of people and the overall management processes of organisations, I now want to examine the role of information in the delivery of service – and it has a crucial role to play.

Technology certainly has had a major impact on our ability to run organisations. When the Roman Empire was at its nadir it stretched far and wide. The whole organisation was controlled from Rome using an information system that worked at the speed of a horse. There was no time to 'check with head office'. The Romans knew how to make empowerment work. They picked able people and inculcated them with the values and policy of the Roman Empire before sending them out into the world to conquer. Every now and then these generals were sent back to Rome for a refresher course in the doctrine.

Derek Prentice, formerly of the Consumers Association and once a chairman of the European Consumers Association, tells the story of a white goods manufacturer. Following a product fault that caused a fatal accident, the manufacturer instituted a recall programme. Derek proudly explained how his association had discovered that the manufacturer had succeeded in tracing only 8 per cent of the faulty machines, and knew it.

A similar example, but with a different outcome, is that of Whirlpool, also a major supplier of white goods. Its presence in Europe was consolidated in the early 1990s by the purchase of Philips' white goods business. Whirlpool invested heavily in tracking the end customer of its products by building a database of consumers. Now each appliance can be tracked from the time it leaves the manufacturing plant to its purchase by a customer. On one occasion a faulty hose clip was discovered on a new washing machine and the database identified the purchasers of machines bearing the faulty clip. Each individual was contacted and an appointment made for an engineer to effect the repair. Unlike the other organisation's 8 per cent, Whirlpool was able to contact each of the few hundred customers involved – just through having the information. Indeed the management was first alerted to the fault by a computer-generated analysis of complaints and warranty calls.

Such information is not kept just so that Whirlpool can more effectively operate product recalls. As it has no direct contact with the consumer, Whirlpool has to find a way of getting the message over to potential customers. Advertising is important, but to be effective it has to be targeted. And that needs information.

Now if you think that building up a picture of the customer is difficult for a washing machine manufacturer, imagine what is like for a firm that makes baked beans. No warranty information to collect here. But understanding the customer is just as important. Where the customers are, where they shop, what they buy, what they like doing, their eating habits; this is all important information for a firm that is fighting for a share of the baked beans market.

The Heinz magazine I mentioned above once contained a questionnaire. It was very detailed. Of course it asked about the Heinz products we use, but it also asked about what competitor products we use and where we buy them from. It asked what factors were important when buying food produce, what papers and magazines we read, how many children we have. It was very comprehensive. To encourage people to return the completed questionnaire, Heinz offered a Club Med holiday to a lucky winner. My wife returned the questionnaire.

With that sort of information to hand, Heinz can target its advertising more effectively, both geographically and in its choice of media. It can also begin to interpret trends, and see relationships between purchase patterns and events. More importantly it can reach the consumer directly. Lord Lever once said 'Half my advertising spend is wasted, the trouble is, I don't know which half.' With this sort of information he might have been able to make a far more informed guess. So lesson one is, get out and get the information that will help you buildup the all important pictures of your customers.

There are many more examples of how aggressive use of information is changing the way organisations operate. By collecting and analysing point of sale information on a daily basis, Bennetton is able to identify which lines are selling well in which areas. They use this information, coupled with a superb logistics system, to tailor deliveries to each store, thereby maximising the returns from each store. Other retailers are now copying Benetton's approach.

American Express is using a combination of high-speed printing and extensive data on its customers' needs to tailor the service delivered to each cardholder. Using advanced data technologies, Amex analyses the buying patterns among the millions of transactions held in its huge database. Because of the information this analysis provides, statements can include special offers to match the member's spending pattern. For the merchants who accept Amex cards, this provides a minutely targeted group of potential clients, reachable at fraction of the cost of traditional direct mail. One wine merchant calculated the cost as 28p per response compared with £42.16 using traditional direct mail.[10]

But point of sale and point of service are two different things. Service occurs at many points in a relationship, sale only on a few occasions – and if the service is bad, probably only once.

Ritz Carlton operates hotels for the discerning business and leisure traveller in the higher price bracket. It was the first hotel operator to win the Baldridge award, America's prestigious quality prize. If you ask for four, non-allergenic pillows in your room, you can guarantee that the next time you stay in a Ritz Carlton hotel you will have four non-allergenic pillows. Each little detail of your desires and nuances are captured by Ritz Carlton staff and kept on a customer database.

Of course this information is not being put to full use if it is not available to everyone who can take advantage of it. Many organisations are still working on the premise that access to information should be on a need to know basis. Under the guise of security, they perpetuate a 'knowledge is power culture' in order to reinforce the hierarchy. A research study[11] showed that only 15 per cent of organisations thought they were totally effective in absorbing information from the field into corporate decision making. Are information systems at fault? Well in part yes. But more significantly it is the paradigm of management in those organisations that is at fault. The front line is the closest part of the organisation to the customer. The staff are aware of many of the issues facing the customer because they deal with them day in, day out. But no one listens; specifically, their bosses don't listen.

Instead they rely on market research, which often gives them answers to only those questions they want to ask. Ken Olsen of Digital is reputed to have said in the early 1980s 'I cannot think why anyone would want their own computer on their desk.' Estimates suggest there are over 150 million PCs in use today – and the number is still growing. Instead of listening to customers, these organisations create a research brief, often based on outmoded views of the market. It is difficult to construct questions that ask about what customers do not know or do not realise. If asked 'Will you spend £1000 on a machine to send a document at a cost of £1.00 per page when the Post Office will do the same thing, albeit more slowly for 30p?', most people would reply no. But the fax machine is in use in nearly all businesses today.

> 'In the end, the abundance of information can paralyse, just like the excess of food, sleep or love. The future will consist in telling people how to select or reject information.'   (Umberto Eco)

Let me issue a word of caution about market research. It is not without its dangers. In 1900 Mercedes used market research to identify the size of the world's car market. It stated that the market would not exceed one million cars. Why? Because the availability of chauffeurs would be a limiting factor. By 1920 there were eight million cars in the US alone, when Henry Ford changed the paradigm of car transport and ownership. A study of computing demands in the late 1940s said that the *world* market for mainframe computers would never exceed twelve.

My message is a very simple one. You have to go beyond market research. It is an important weapon in the armoury of the modern business, but it has its limitations. It cannot tell you what customers do not know. Only close and regular contact can tell you that.

Having the information is one thing, but there is no point in having it if it cannot be used. Information is like manure. Keep it in a pile and it just festers and rots. Spread it around and it encourages growth. But information that is of use is that which people need to do their jobs. IT departments have confused data with information, and have been reasonably good at supplying the former but not the latter. They have, quite naturally, developed systems that suit the way the organisation was, and in many cases still is, organised. Finance information to the finance department, sales information to the sales department, production information to the production department, and so on. A salesman who wanted to know the production schedule for product X often had no access to that information. And if he was allowed access to it, he had to use the production system to get it, which was structured around manufacturing schedules, not product options.

The 1980s saw massive investment in systems integration to correct this. Links between the different systems were built in. Some companies, SAP for example, even began to market integrated systems. All singing, all dancing systems that did everything; provided you did it their way of course. The problem is that customers' needs change. No sooner has the bank integrated the current account information with deposit account information than we start asking questions about the Visa account. Once that is roped into the information system, the bank has to start offering mortgages, in an attempt to take a greater share of a customer's financial portfolio. Where will it end? Just to put another twist on it, we want to be able to arrange a loan over the phone. And on and on. What is needed are information systems that can be quickly changed to meet these needs.

Integration within the organisation is only part of the picture. As more organisations use alliances and partnerships to offer the increasing level of service demanded, they have to integrate across a number of organisations.

Let me give what is becoming an everyday occurrence as an example: buying a mobile phone. You buy a mobile phone and, quite rightly, you want to use it as soon as possible. No problem you might think. But what you see as one transaction often involves five or more different organisations. You buy your mobile phone from a dealer – it might even be Ford! It has to set up a contract for air time to give you the right to use the cellular network. You need a number of course. So the dealer has to allocate a number to you and notify the network. The network operator has to incorporate your number into its network and update its systems to recognise you. Because of the very high theft rate for mobile phones, you buy a package that includes insurance; another transaction with another company. You also opt for a maintenance package, which provides you with a replacement phone should yours be damaged. To get you to buy from them, the supplier has a special deal – interest free credit: nothing to pay until spring next year. Now that needs a call to the credit checking agency to make sure you are creditworthy. Then a call to the finance company to set up a credit agreement. With all this complete, you can have your phone. Phew!!

But wait, you are a vigilante customer. Not only do you want the phone, you want it *now*. Not tomorrow when the credit company has checked you out; not next week, when the phone has been delivered; nor this afternoon, when the network company has set up the line. No, you want it *now*. And you will complain about poor service if you don't get it now. That is exactly what an increasing number of companies can do for you. While you are giving them details of what you want, their computer systems are dialling the computer systems of the network operator, the credit company and the insurance company. By the time you have filled in all the details. The answers are back and you can walk out with your phone.

This cannot be done by simply integrating the systems within one organisation. If you are at the point of service, you have to look to integrate information across the entire supply and service network. Nothing less will satisfy the vigilante consumer.

Now this might have some of you sweating over the thought of having to scrap all your existing systems and installing these all-reaching systems. You might be reminded of the words of French President Georges Pompidou: 'There are three ways to ruin, women, gambling and technology. Women are the most enjoyable, gambling the fastest, but technology is the most certain'. Systems to deliver that level of service do need investment, but it does not have to be the Pompidou way.

Here is my next beyond. To construct information systems that deliver exceptional levels of service and are flexible enough to change in line with changing business needs, requires us to go beyond our existing way of thinking about how we develop information systems. Projects that cost the earth and take an eternity to develop have to give way to systems that deliver business results quickly, and can be changed as the business changes. We have to move beyond the plan, design, implement and manage approach where all the thinking and design was done at the beginning, by a select group of – usually IT – people (see Chapter 6 for more on this topic).

So here are my interpretations of 'beyond' – they are my checklist for those looking to exploit the information perspective of their organisation:

- You have to go *beyond* customers – you have to understand your customers' customers.
- You have to go *beyond* transaction information into relationship information.
- You have to go *beyond* your organisation into the whole service delivery chain.
- You have to go *beyond* the traditional thinking that has dogged most information technology developments.

CUSTOMER CONTACT MANAGEMENT

All the information in the world is of no use if people cannot access it, particularly those dealing directly with customers. The style and ease with which a customer is able to interface with an organisation is key to customer satisfaction. Surveys from numerous organisations show the importance of ease of access, which is often placed ahead of price and product range.

There are a number of important aspects of the interface between customer and supplier:

- *One stop*: studies in Canada show that satisfaction levels drop dramatically as soon as the customer has to deal with multiple points of contact in any interaction. Whilst I do not know of studies that have proved this to be true in the UK, personal experience suggests the results would be little different. We have all had contact with organisations who pass us from pillar to post, or insist we deal with different sections for different issues.
- *People*: relationships are key to long-term loyalty. Having people with the right skills, knowledge and behaviours at the right place is therefore critical. This includes the much abused word, empowerment. Problems with customers are bound to arise. How an organisation resolves these, notably the immediacy and appropriateness of the solution, is key to converting a complaint into customer retention. Studies have shown the very positive impact a complaint quickly and effectively dealt with has on repurchasing decisions.
- *Individualised responses* – the segment of one has always been a reality, it is only market segmentation techniques and our ability to deliver to them that has been lacking. Segmentation is increasingly impacting on the processes and approach the organisation uses to respond to individual customers. Individual customers need an individual approach. This presupposes a detailed knowledge of customers, and that the organisation has selected its preferred segments. No organisation can be all things to all people. A natural extension of this is having different forms of interaction to match the different segments, requiring flexible processes – not fixed, standardised ones.

Customers' increasing choice is also shifting power away from suppliers. One manifestation of this is the desire of customers to exert greater control over the relationship. Paradoxically those organisations that give customers what they want and more freedom to move, are likely to generate greater loyalty by demonstrating a genuine concern for the interests of their customers.

Effective customer contact management has to operate in this environment. On top of this, organisations cannot dictate the purpose of a contact initiated by a customer, or how much the customer will request in a single interaction. Indeed seeking to limit the contact will damage satisfaction and limit the opportunity to cross-sell. Trying to control this by imposing multiple telephone numbers for different purposes will also reduce customer satisfaction by making the organisation more difficult to do business with. This demands a contact management capability that can address a wide range of functions and information.

The broad view of contact management, defined from the viewpoint of the customer, has a bottom-line benefit. There is a wealth of research showing the financial payoff of customer retention. In addition, recent research reported in the *American Banker* magazine[12] shows that access to customer information supports retention. In banks where customer retention exceeded 90 per cent, access to customer information was considered 'extremely easy' by 46 per cent of the companies surveyed. This compares with an 'extremely easy' access rating of only 13 per cent where retention rates were lower. Providing a contact management capability that supports such breadth and ease of information access clearly pays off.

The same study asked what information the banks lack in their customer records (Figure 2.7). As organisations seek to encourage greater empowerment at the front line, this lack of information will be a serious problem.

This outside-in view of requirements suggests that, to achieve customer satisfaction in this challenging environment, contact management must support the range of interactions a customer wishes to initiate. This will require the following activities (see also Figure 2.8 on page 52):

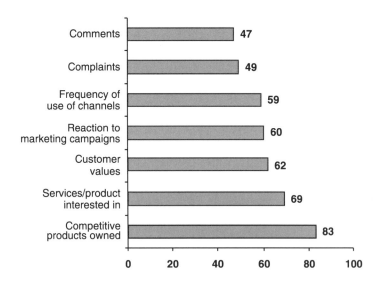

Source: *American Banker.*

Figure 2.7   Information not included in customer records

- *Log contacts*: record the basic details of each contact.
- *Schedule activity/further contacts*: diary management for further calls or actions. This will need to extend to all those in the organisation who deal with customers.
- *Customer calendar*: a calendar of events for the customer showing information such as birthdays, renewal dates, payment dates.
- *Collect non-transaction information*: collecting customer information has to be an on-going activity if it is to fill the gaps identified in the study of US banks. Providing a mechanism for this is essential. One Belgian bank collects snippets of information about customers, for example a new baby, which are then sorted by a simple expert system and passed on to the appropriate people for follow-up.
- *Provide customer circumstance information*: circumstance information is that which describes the customer's worth and risk. It will include segment data, products purchased and purchase of competitors' products. This is essential to support-cross selling opportunities.
- *Complaints manager*: complaints are a valuable source of data – collect complaint details and monitor the progress of complaint resolution. This should link back to complaint reporting and root cause analysis.
- *Access other information sources and functions*: the contact manager should be able to access other functions and information. This will include product data, transaction functionality and market campaign data.
- *Support customer, and supplier initiated contact*: the contact manager should be able to deal with inbound calls initiated by a customer or outbound calls from the supplier.

In effect, contact management provides a customer-oriented window into the organisation to support front-line staff. (See also the WIZARD system in the Avis case study in Part II.) The face an organisation presents to its customers is key to customer satisfaction, and therefore to retention and the associated financial rewards. Unless organisations take an outside-in view of contact management and build contact management capabilities that meet the breadth of customers' needs, they cannot claim to be customer focused.

Whilst a contact management capability of the type described above is of great value, it is important to remember that people are the most important element of customer contact. People can cover up for bad systems, but this is rarely true the other way round. Relationships are a personal thing. Organisations don't buy things, people do. Organisations don't build relationships, people do. A customer spending an annual six

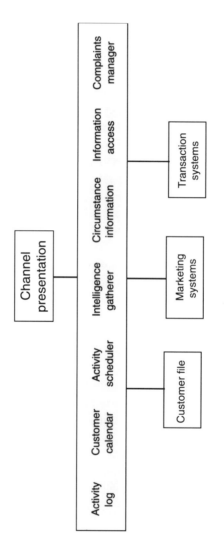

Figure 2.8 Contact management system

figure sum with an organisation said 'The reason I buy from one supplier versus another, probably boils down to my perception of one or two people.'

As the innovation of IT continues, cheaper and more sophisticated systems are making it easier to manipulate the mass of data about customers. Data warehousing and data mining are now commonplace terms in the vocabulary of marketers. Financial service companies are using these techniques to build profiles of customer profitability and worth. Supermarkets are examining the buying patterns of consumers. This is perfectly illustrated by the US supermarket chain Wal-Mart. Analysis of sales data identified a relationship between nappy and beer sales on Friday evenings. Further investigation revealed that the shoppers in question were men with young children. As a result the organisation now stacks the two products in close proximity. Airlines have long used data about travel patterns and habits to determine the mix of seat classes on each flight.

'Information is no substitute for thinking and thinking is no substitute for information.' (Edward de Bono)

The interpretation of data is an important element of understanding customers, but it is vital to remember that such data forms only part of the picture. The past is no guarantee of the future. Whilst we can learn from it, we must not be bound by it. Data of this type is historical and, to date, based on transactions. If we are truly to understand our customers, and through that understanding build up relationships that can be sustained, we have to understand what drives them; their values and beliefs, likes and hates, aspirations and worries. This relationship data is much harder to collect and analyse, but I believe it is the key to successful customer focus. Having this data means greater emphasis will be placed on thinking about customers. This in turn will place more importance on the people who work in our organisations. Information technology might help us to collect and analyse the data, but it is people who generate the insights upon which business is built. Again it comes back to people.

'I believe the fundamental strategic battle for the coming century will be the battle for the customer.' (John Neil)

Getting close to customers is the foundation on which the dynamic organisation is built. Its importance cannot be underestimated.

3 A New Approach to Change

If it was so, it might be; and if it were so, it would be; but as it isn't, it ain't. That's logic.

(Lewis Carroll, *Alice Through the Looking Glass*)

'The only legitimate goal of organisation design is to shape, facilitate or alter the behaviour of individuals within that organisation in order to meet the demands imposed by changed circumstances.' (Yoshinori Yokoyama)

'Progress was all right, only it went on too long.'

(James Thurber)

If change is what we have to get used to, we had better look for a new way of building and managing our organisations. Many of our organisations are like tin sheds in the face of a hurricane. As soon as the wind blows they fall apart, they cease to function. Although much has changed, and is still changing, there is one thing we stubbornly refuse to change – the way we manage. We might take on fads such as TQM, business process reengineering (BPR) and the rest, but they have had little impact on the fundamental processes by which we manage organisations. The dynamic organisation however focuses on a different set of management processes. This chapter begins by looking at how most organisations are managed and then suggests a different approach to the process of management; one that focuses on building change into the organisation.

This chapter does not contain a recipe for continuous change. Whilst I have long toyed with the idea, I have come to the conclusion that continuous change is neither desirable nor practical. We all seek some continuity, and not all change is progress. But equally the approach to change practised by most Western organisations is no longer tenable. The pace of the changes in our environment does not allow for the thawing and refreezing of our organisations.[1] What is needed is what was advocated by Klaus Jacobs, former chairman and chief executive officer of the confectionery giant Jacobs. Drawing on his personal experience, he suggested 'that the secret is to accept spurts of renewal as a fact of life – but never to allow the accumulated need for change to become so great that managers cannot cope with it, for this is the point that more drastic and usually painful changes are required'. The dynamic organisation is one where the mechanisms and culture to anticipate and introduce change are heightened; where the need for drastic change is reduced.

Not all organisations have the benefit of leaders with the wisdom of Jacobs. And we cannot rely on one person to provide that; although one person can and often does make a difference. Rather, what we need are mechanisms that help put the organisation in closer touch with its environment and convert signals into action.

TODAY'S METHODS FAIL US

Whatever the industry, walk into any organisation and 99 times out of 100 you will find two processes (and they usually are quite separate) at the heart of the organisation: strategic planning and budgeting. Strategic planning sets the company's direction. Budgeting provides the figures for revenue and expenditure. Let us take a brief look at some of the problems with each, starting with strategic planning.

Strategy has become a much abused word in business circles. At its simplest it is about how things are done, and as such always follows a decision about what should be done. Purpose is about what the organisation is there for, its *raison d'être*. Answering 'how' before agreeing on 'what' results in aimless wandering. The first action when choosing a route is determining the destination. Having a destination is what constitutes the difference between being on a journey or a ramble. Unfortunately too many organisations are still rambling. Occasionally, of course, a rambler will stumble across a gold mine. By all means take advantage of luck when it comes your way, but would you like to base your business on luck alone?

'There is no expedient to which man will not resort to avoid the real labour of thinking.'   (Sir Joshua Reynolds)

Even where a sense of direction exists, most approaches to strategic planning are fundamentally flawed. Many believe strategy is about what happens in the future. In fact, strategy is about what you do today to create the future. Strategy is here and now. This misconception leads people away from action into interminably long planning cycles. Numerous strategy methodologies talk about lengthy research, planning and decision cycles, but say little about doing. Remember that the Chinese express the concept of learning with two symbols representing study and practise. Proponents of strategic planning seem to have got stuck on the study (planning) and ignored the practise (doing). I believe most organisations suffer from too much strategic planning, not enough strategic thinking and far too little strategic action.

Many managers do not believe people have an interest in strategy *per se*. I suspect those who perpetuate this indulge in some form of intellectual apartheid. In fact people seem to have an innate need to understand the big picture and indeed produce better results when they have had a hand in shaping it. We all seek control over our destiny. I will return to this later in the chapter when I discuss the change process. An important part of strategy is the rationale behind the decisions. How many times have you heard people in organisations say 'I wish they'd tell us why.'

'When the planners run around like Chicken Little crying "The environment is turbulent", what they really mean is that something has happened which was not anticipated by their inflexible systems.'   (Henry Minzberg)

In the functional organisation, strategic planning became another function. Being a head office function, and being strategic, it was of course staffed by the brightest people the organisation could hire – very expensive people because this was an elite activity. All too soon strategic planning moved from the realm of an important management process to a self-serving bureaucracy. The strategic planning department researched the market (or at least the figures on the market produced by analysts), devised the plans and oversaw their implementation. If anything went wrong, and it often did, it was because the strategy was not properly implemented.

Strategic planners (and other planning zealots, for they exist in other guises) assume that it is possible to foresee and plan for all eventualities that will arise during the life of the strategy. This of course is not true.

Too much emphasis has been placed on analysis and logic, whereas the world and its people are unpredictable. Politics is an important part of organisational life. Even science, the self-appointed guardian of objectivity, usually starts with a hypothesis – which you and I call a hunch. The results of analyses, no matter how well researched, will never generate commitment in the way that a dream, articulated by a respected and enthusiastic leader can. Kennedy had few facts and figures to support his vision of the US putting a man on the moon. Indeed many of the technologies and ideas that eventually led to Neil Armstrong stepping out onto the Sea of Tranquillity had not been developed when Kennedy expounded his vision.

I recall developing a proposal for an important piece of consulting work. We had never done work of that kind, but we knew what needed to be done and we had some of the tool kit in place. But we knew we *could* do it. Our determination and commitment was what sold the work, and because of our determination to succeed we were able to work out the steps along the way. We delivered to the customer's satisfaction.

'By actually trying, various problems became known. As such problems gradually became clear, they taught me the direction of the next move.'   (Tai-Ichi Ohno)

A further problem is the lack of understanding of the recursive effect of action on plans. Plans direct actions, which in turn shape the plans. What you do affects the results, which in turn guides what is done. This is a perfect description of a closed loop system, a bit like a thermostat controlling temperature in a central heating system. The action is dynamic, based on the environment. The problem is that the environment of an organisation is vastly more complex and less predictable than that of a central heating system. A simple cause and effect loop is replaced by a multivariate model where cause and effect are remotely linked. Sometimes the link is so remote that it is not perceived. This is the important point that Peter Senge makes[2] when describing systems thinking as one the five disciplines of a learning organisation. But strategy planning methods, like most methodologies, have become locked into reductionist, linear processes that work perfectly in theory but hardly ever in practice. It is no more possible to understand how an organisation works by looking at individual functions and processes than it is to understand how a motorbike works by looking at its individual components.[3]

Strategy is not alone. Other activities that have taken a similar, structured and reductionist approach have also failed. The world is littered with stories of major IT projects that have horribly failed to meet time and cost targets, despite the most rigorous project management and sophisticated computer planning and management tools. In business too we can see parallels. Companies in Japan and Germany have relied much more on continuous improvement than the stop–start, big bang, megaplanned approach to change so popular with many US and UK organisations. Financial service institutions have long understood the power of compound interest. Unfortunately few have applied the concept to the management of their organisations.

I believe that strategic planning of this ilk, still used by many companies, epitomises the ultimate separation of thinking and doing – Taylorism at board level. One of Jack Welch's early actions after taking over at General Electric was to dismantle the corporate strategic planning group. He has since stewarded the company through unprecedented growth and change.

> 'Loyalty to a petrified opinion never broke a chain or freed a human soul.'
> (Mark Twain)

So if we are to dispense with strategic planning as we currently know it, what is to take its place? The first step is to recognise that at least two, interacting cycles are in operation. The first cycle is the process of fine-tuning the organisation so that it can better meet its purpose. This is the change that regularly concerns most organisations and the change that I will describe below. The second cycle is about much more fundamental shifts; significant discontinuities in the environment that demand an equally significant rethinking of the organisation's fundamental purpose and values. This type of change is much less prevalent. In his excellent article 'Crafting Strategy',[4] Henry Minzberg explains how infrequently the organisations he has studied are involved in strategic reorientation.

The two cycles are of course interrelated. The less adaptation an organisation undertakes, the quicker it is likely to become out of step with its environment. This is because the organisation has failed to adapt, within its purpose, to the environment. Like King Neptune on the beach, the arrogance of many organisations blinds them to the need for continuous adaptation and forces them into major change. Years of minor shifts in the environment leads to major disconnections, which requires major change. Anyone who has stood on a beach has experienced this. As you stand still, the currents and tides change the environment around you. Where you were once putting a toe in the water, you are now either drowning, or high and dry.

> 'Effective strategists are not people who abstract themselves from the daily detail but quite the opposite: they are the ones who immerse themselves in it, while being able to abstract the strategic messages from it.' (Henry Minzberg)

I believe that leadership of an organisation is about creating an environment in which adaptation is driven by people who want to give of their best and where leadership is encouraged and practised right across the organisation. The focus on environment is important. It is about shaping the organisation rather than managing the detail. Like an architect, who also focuses on creating an environment suited to the purpose of a building, the leader must also be concerned with the materials and method of construction. Details matter.

Establishing the organisational environment requires a focus on three major areas:

- Developing a shared vision.
- Shaping a core culture.
- Developing the processes of management.

The three are closely intertwined. An organisation's values and vision have to be compatible with each other. The management processes shape the culture, which in turn can enable or inhibit an organisation's pursuit of certain visions: its beliefs blind it do certain paths. This is the holistic nature of change in organisations. It is not possible to act on a single front. It requires what one major pharmaceutical company calls an integrated change agenda. It is because organisations do not recognise this interconnectedness that so many attempted changes end in failure. It is also why most fads do not work. They address one aspect of change but fail to consider the others. It is also why meaningful change takes time. Quick wins might be possible, but they should not divert attention from the real goals of the change. This is very difficult when the short-termist rulers of the City are baying for jam today. It is important to note that the two most successful postwar economies – Japan and Germany – both have substantially different patterns of shareholding[5] that support the longer-term views of organisations.

DEVELOPING SHARED VISIONS

'When there is no vision, people perish.' (Franklin D. Roosevelt)

For me, shared vision is nothing more than a sense of direction that is felt across the organisation. It is not blind allegiance to a set of words, nor is it one person's view of the future, although it might start that way. And the word vision is not important. Many organisations use mission, strategic intent or purpose to express the same thing; some have all three! Whilst some would argue the important differences of these things, I would settle for a shared sense of purpose and direction, even if it were called a fantasy. What is important is that people understand it, that they consider what it means for them and their work, and that they translate that understanding into action – doing something different. This of course means that they have to be involved in some way in shaping it, or at least their part of it.

'The world stands aside to let anyone pass who knows where he is going.'   (David Starr Jordan)

True visions seem to be of benefit, as a US study shows[6] $1 was hypothetically invested in 1920 in 20 companies that a sample of senior managers considered the most visionary. If the company did not exist in 1920, the $1 was invested in an interest bearing account. On average these 20 companies outperformed the Wall Street index by a factor of 50. The study does not prove that vision was the cause, but the relationship says something about the power of vision. This is not in the least surprising if you consider visions more carefully.

Much is written about visions and values. Many organisations have mission or vision statements, and values statements are also popular. Research shows that 80 per cent of UK companies have written statements of values, although only 22 per cent believe they constantly influence day-to-day decision making.[7]

'This is the true joy of life, the being used for a purpose recognised by yourself as a mighty one.' (George Bernard Shaw)

Everyone in an organisation wants to be informed of the big picture. What's the strategy? Where are we going? How do I fit in? These are common questions in organisations. People are not satisfied with just knowing their own patch. In a flatter organisation, knowing how the different pieces fit together is essential for everyone. There will be no hierarchy to settle boundary disputes, although this might be less of a problem with fewer managers to create these in the first place.

Let me begin by differentiating between a true vision and a visioning process. As visions became *de rigueur* in organisations, management teams began to believe they have to go away every couple of years and spend a few days thinking about the future of the organisation, after which they produce a vision statement. They are urged to make these statements aspirational and challenging, in an attempt to motivate people towards greater effort. To achieve this a communication exercise is implemented across the organisation. Plans are put in place to achieve the vision. Whilst this has some benefit, it is a false exercise. Change for change's sake is unnecessary; it does not always equate with improvement, which is the real goal.

'Genius means little more than the faculty of perceiving in an unhabitual way.' (William James).

Leaders are told they have the responsibility of creating the vision. I would say that leaders should be responsible for ensuring that a shared vision emerges. They do not have to think it up themselves. Indeed that would vest the future of the organisation in the mind of one person. Few organisations are blessed with a chief executive officer who can conjure up a vision just when the organisation needs it. Visions are often built upon the failure of a previous vision – failure that resulted from resisting change for too long. The success of the previous path imbues a sense of belief that is essential at the beginning but downright dangerous towards the end of its life. This does not however abrogate the leader's responsibility for ensuring a vision arises and is truly shared. It is central to the role. It also recognises that the person taking up that role often leads the pack in recognising the future. Indeed it is this foresight that forms a central part of leadership.

I personally have never been inspired by a set of words. I have been inspired by hearing people expound their dreams, explain their views of life and the future. I have joined organisations and sought to work with others because of the way they express themselves. But in every case I have been impressed by people. As a conference organiser I have had the privilege of listening to many great leaders. I know when I have heard a truly great one because I find myself thinking 'I could work for that person.' Jan de Soet of KLM, Bob Galvin of Motorola, Lesley Colyer and Alun Catchcart of Avis, Ib Lund Jensen of Lego and Bill O'Brien, formerly of Hannover Insurance, are all leaders who have inspired me. Not all fit the view of a leader as a charismatic personality, but all have the ability to describe a vision and espouse personal values that I can (indeed want to) relate to. It is this personal relationship that separates a vision shared from a shared vision. The former is an individual's thoughts, which are then communicated – one person's view imposed on the organisation. The latter begins with one person's view but then develops through conversation.

Whilst vision always starts with an individual's view, building a shared vision is, by definition, a dialogue as opposed to a monologue. No matter how well delivered, a monologue is just that. This concept of using conversation to form shared visions is not well understood. But it is how shared visions are formed. The conversations serve several purposes. They expose people to the ideas and get them to consider and ask about what it means for them. They create an opportunity to test the validity of the vision in different parts of the organisation and among other stakeholders. They also enrol people in the thinking and development process, particularly in relating the vision to the local context and circumstance. This is an important new role in the work of middle managers.

In trying to move forward the European operation of the Digital Equipment Corporation, the then President for Europe, Pier-Carlo Falotti, conceived his Lego vision. He was head of an organisation spanning all the functions of the company, from research and development to sales and marketing. He knew that what excited a research engineer was finding new ways of doing things, whereas a top-notch salesman loved the thrill of the chase and the scent of the sale. In order to encourage the whole organisation, Falotti put the core attributes of a vision within Digital into a series of short phrases. He encouraged people to use these phrases to build a vision for their own operation, and even for themselves. It was an attempt to encourage the conversations referred to above. It was a good idea but it failed. It failed because there was no unifying core around which everyone could gather. It failed because there was no concerted effort to support the different parts of the organisation that wanted to create their own visions. It also failed because there was no effort to build a management process that embedded this idea into the organisation. It was in effect a seed cast on infertile ground.

The true process of forming a vision starts with a pattern in the external environment that someone identifies as presenting an opportunity for the organisation. This pattern may be seen by several people at about the same time. It does not have to be, indeed it is unlikely to be, spotted by the top manager. The idea of the senior executive being solely responsible for the organisation's future is wrong. No one person, or even a group of senior managers, can be sure of spotting all the right trends. Patterns emerge as and where they emerge; although they will never be seen by people who are not looking for them. They can however set up mechanisms that allow ideas to surface, where challenging the *status quo* is welcomed, and where trying something outside the norm is encouraged. These areas will be addressed later in this chapter when I discuss culture and management processes.

An external perspective is key to the formation of visions, for it is in the outside world that most change begins. This is one of the reasons why everyone in the organisation, especially managers, must spend time with customers, for as a key constituent of the outside world the changes impacting on them are an important manifestation of the patterns. It is also the reason why visioning is an activity that cannot be driven by a calendar. Patterns in the outside environment happen when they happen. They do not wait for the right time in a company's strategic planning cycle before emerging. For this reason organisations cannot tie themselves to rigid planning cycles. Acting when the moment is right is the key.

Whilst I have no favourite vision, I do believe that good visions have certain characteristics. Firstly, they focus on something that is itself dynamic, such as the needs and aspirations of customers. Secondly, they should relate to some higher value. Bill O'Brien, former chief executive officer of Hannover Insurance, once described how he set himself the personal challenge of 'building an organisation where people wanted to come to work'. Finally, visions should be imprecise, thus leaving room for interpretation, discussion and diversity. This is important, because it is in the gaps that people can be creative. Most importantly, a good vision may be described in many ways but always conveys the same meaning and intent. That is why the best visions are more talked about than written down.

There is a magic secret to creating a shared vision. It is conversation.

CULTURE AND VALUES[8]

> 'Whenever I hear the word "culture", I reach for my revolver.'
> (Herman Goering)

IBM staff are known as 'the blue suits', whilst people working at Microsoft, including boss Bill Gates, are renowned for their casual dress. Any two organisations in the same business and serving the same customers never do things the same way. Why are some organisations known as stuffy and others as friendly? Does it matter? I believe it matters a great deal. Speaking of the role of culture in a modern organisation, Jack Welch, mastermind of the change at General Electric, said 'Every organisation needs values, but a lean organisation needs them even more. When you strip away the support systems of staffs and layers, people need to change their habits and expectations or else the stress will just overwhelm them. Values are what enable people to guide themselves through that kind of change' (Slater, 1993).

If vision provides a view of what the future involves, values, manifested in the culture of an organisation, create the boundaries of acceptable behaviour while getting there. We have all experienced the power of cultures – the rules of an organisation, often unwritten, that encourage people to behave in a certain way. Some of these rules are explicit, embedded in statements of procedure and rules. But so much of how an organisation behaves is unwritten: who the winners are, who is respected, how priorities are set, how communication works, how rules are set and followed. These are all things where the unwritten rules are more powerful than any procedure manual. Anyone who has moved from one organisation to another will have experienced culture shock to some degree.

The Importance of Culture

We also experience organisational culture when we do business with an organisation. People have a different perception of Marks and Spencer than of C&A, of First Direct than of Barclays, or of British Rail than of

British Airways. As customers we are influenced by our perceptions of an organisation's culture, is manifested in its image, its people and its style of doing business. Most of us have chosen to buy from one supplier rather than another for reasons other than price, quality or availability. We do business with companies partly because of what we think of them and how they relate to our personal values. This is one of the reasons for the success of values-based companies such as Virgin and the Body Shop. We buy what they stand for as much as the quality of their products. Even when specific value stances have not been taken by organisations, culture still plays a large part in the buying decision. Where quality of the core products or services is the entry price of being in business, more emphasis is placed on the quality of the organisation, its people and their ability to focus on the customer. Much of this feel-good factor is about the customers' perceptions of the attitudes and beliefs of the people inside the organisation, which, together with the organisation's systems, structures and communications, create an image in the customers' minds. Culture lies at the heart of the customers' feel-good factor.

Organisations often fail to recognise the pervasive nature of culture and values. Processes are reflections of a company's culture. An organisational culture that lacks trust and openness reflects a system where control is paramount and information is only available on a need-to-know basis. Customer-focused cultures mean systems that make it easy for the customer to do business with the company. Cultures also reflect the type of people a company hires. Avis clearly expresses the customer-focused nature of its 'We try harder' culture when advertising for new recruits. In this way cultures are often self-reinforcing: like attracts like.

This of course is good if the culture is right. In a long-term research project Harvard Professors Kotter and Heskett (1992) examined the relationship between financial performance and corporate culture. Kotter and Heskett[9] measured over 200 large US firms against a culture strength indicator developed by them. Correlating this indicator with economic performance over 11 years showed a clear link between strong culture and long-term economic success. But a strong culture that is out of step with its environment, notably the requirements of customers, employees and shareholders, can restrict an organisation's ability to make the changes needed to succeed in a changing world. This is depicted in Figure 3.1.

The Cultural Onion

Think of culture as an onion (Figure 3.2).[10] At its heart is a very personal element – the individual's and the organisation's core values. These

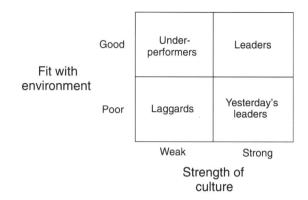

Figure 3.1   Culture and the environment

beliefs, which we all hold, guide our lives. We cherish them dearly and fight for them when they are threatened. The values of many organisations can be traced back to the beliefs of the organisations' founders. The next two layers are about the people who succeed in the organisation, the winners and their competencies. Competencies in this context are not traditional skills, but the behaviours of the winners. Every organisation has its champions and heroes. These people exert a great influence in the organisation, sometimes far beyond their formal powerbase. Others in the organisation look to them for guidance and inspiration. These three inner layers together make up the organisation's management style. Surrounding this are three layers of the more overt signs of culture: rituals, symbols, and structures and systems.

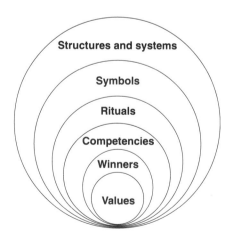

Figure 3.2   The cultural onion

Rituals are the mannerisms and social habits of the organisation: the style of meetings, the approach to hiring and firing and the office party are all elements of an organisation. Some organisations have wild extravagant parties involving the whole 'family': employees, spouses, customers and suppliers. Other organisations are much more reserved. Symbols are the outward signs of the organisation. The style and consistency of the corporate image, the annual report, car parking, style of communication and advertising – these elements of culture shape the public face of the organisation. The final layer of the cultural onion comprises the structures and systems of the organisation. These are the control and guidance mechanisms of the organisation, which dictate how the organisation's activities are planned and coordinated. This is the layer at which many of the people who dabble with organisational change operate. But real change has to cut right through the onion – and of course that often leads to tears!

Measuring Culture

In a landmark study, Professor Geert Hofstede, professor of organisation at the University of Mastricht, Holland, identified six universal dimensions of organisational culture (Figure 3.3).

But in managing change, building up a shared picture of where you are and where you want to be is half the battle. The ability to provide a common vocabulary for understanding culture across multiple perspectives is one of the great values of the tool developed from Hofstede's work.[11]

Changing Culture

Having a common view of the organisation's current and desired culture is a useful starting point, but having a map is not the same as completing the journey. Indeed getting the map is by far the easiest bit. Patience and perseverance are essential for what will take several years for most large organisations. So long term is this, that some organisations question the value of doing it. But culture is so much at the heart of what the business is and what it does that there is no option but to change it, if that is what is needed. Shaping the culture is at the heart of the leader's job. It is vital to know the strengths of the organisation's existing culture, as destroying these would be disastrous. Equally, trying to copy someone else's culture is pointless – cultures are unique. That is not to say there is no value in studying and understanding the cultures of organisations you admire –

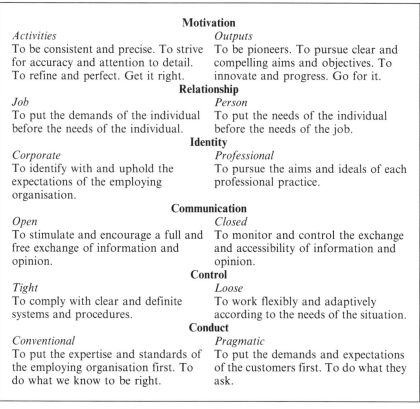

Motivation

Activities
To be consistent and precise. To strive for accuracy and attention to detail. To refine and perfect. Get it right.

Outputs
To be pioneers. To pursue clear and compelling aims and objectives. To innovate and progress. Go for it.

Relationship

Job
To put the demands of the individual before the needs of the individual.

Person
To put the needs of the individual before the needs of the job.

Identity

Corporate
To identify with and uphold the expectations of the employing organisation.

Professional
To pursue the aims and ideals of each professional practice.

Communication

Open
To stimulate and encourage a full and free exchange of information and opinion.

Closed
To monitor and control the exchange and accessibility of information and opinion.

Control

Tight
To comply with clear and definite systems and procedures.

Loose
To work flexibly and adaptively according to the needs of the situation.

Conduct

Conventional
To put the expertise and standards of the employing organisation first. To do what we know to be right.

Pragmatic
To put the demands and expectations of the customers first. To do what they ask.

Figure 3.3   Dimensions of organisational culture

there clearly is. Putting too much structure into cultures – making the behaviours explicit – only creates sterility. The dynamic organisation trusts in people to interpret the core values in a way that is consistent in intent but rich in the variety of ways they are implemented. This is one of the keys to adaptive cultures.

The journey can only be undertaken by someone who has an over-whelming sense of principle. Saying one thing but doing something else is a recipe for failure. Unfortunately that is just what too many do. They preach the need to be customer focused, but do not include customers in their constituency. They expound cost-consciousness, but award them-selves salary and benefit increases far in excess of anything they deem reasonable for the rest of the staff. It is not that they speak with forked tongues, it is that their words and actions do not match. They do not see action as a powerful form of communication. Tom Reseigh of the Nationwide Building Society gave a presentation in which he had misspelled the word 'communication'. He had written 'communiaction'.

What type of company are you?

The diagrams below depict organisational cultures. Can you spot your organisation?

The Perfectionist

Activities		Outputs
Job		Person
Corporate		Professional
Open		Closed
Tight		Loose
Conventional		Pragmatic

Consistency and attention to detail are the hallmarks of the perfectionist culture. These organisations are inward looking, ever seeking precision and smooth, predictable performance. They are conservative, and strive to master their speciality. The pace is steady and even, each day is much like another. They are formal and structured. Decisions are made at the top, after due process. Activities are carefully monitored and reviewed. There is a strong emphasis on standards and procedures. Mistakes are quickly spotted and investigated. If in doubt, people stick to the rules. These organisations do not try to adapt to the individual needs of customers. They are consistent rather than responsive. They change slowly, almost imperceptibly. They stick to what they know, refining and developing their core competencies.

The Driver

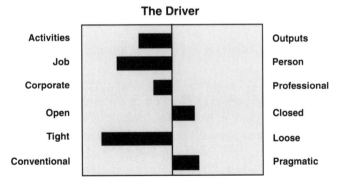

Activities		Outputs
Job		Person
Corporate		Professional
Open		Closed
Tight		Loose
Conventional		Pragmatic

In driver cultures, getting the job done takes precedence every time. The needs of the organisation dominate all else. Good people are kept in positions where they are most effective. Tasks are clearly defined, unilaterally apportioned and exactingly monitored. No one is any doubt what they have to do and what the consequences might be if they don't. There is little room for excuses, few allowances are made for extenuating circumstances. This culture is all about work and the demands of the minute. There are structures and systems to match. Every aspect of the operation is closely scrutinised and carefully calculated. There is little waste, few distractions and no unnecessary baggage. Driver cultures distinguish themselves by their tough uncompromising and fully focused concentration on the job at hand.

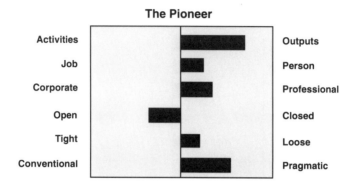

The Pioneer

Activities		Outputs
Job		Person
Corporate		Professional
Open		Closed
Tight		Loose
Conventional		Pragmatic

Results are what count in pioneer cultures. These organisations are customer focused and future oriented. They strive to be different and to distinguish themselves from the competition. They are bold, adventurous and innovative. The pace is fast, the structures flat and fluid. The atmosphere is informal, people know what is expected, take responsibility and rise to a challenge. When in doubt they use their initiative. Mistakes are tolerated and everyone gets recognition as long as they perform. Customers are the people that matter most, and great attention is paid to their individual needs. These organisations continually adapt. Major and minor changes are a fact of life. Their most distinctive characteristics are energy, the desire to achieve and an opportunistic outlook.

He left the word in, believing it described something that organisations needed more of.

There are no hard and fast rules about changing culture, but experience provides some useful pointers. The first is to be clear about the culture you currently have and a view about what you need. The preferred culture should be tested against the needs of customers, the aspirations of employees and the thoughts of shareholders. The initial statement of this should be just that – initial. Conversation is equally important here. Jack Welch of General Electric used any avenue available, but notably the company's management development centre at Crotonville, to exchange views on the emerging value and culture. I use the word conversations because it implies a degree of intimacy and exchange that other words fail to capture. Through conversations, people can test their understanding, but more importantly they can test commitment, belief and understanding. We all know how important it is to 'see the whites of someone's eyes' when assessing their intentions. The same is true here. I was once fortunate to have lunch with Jan de Soet, then chairman of KLM Airlines. We were talking about change and building customer focus. I remember his advice: 'If you cannot look into the eyes of the CEO and see commitment, don't get involved.' You cannot see that commitment in a company newsletter or even a corporate video. People have to touch it, probe it and test it. Like the doubting disciple, Thomas, they are not convinced unless they have seen it for themselves and put their hand in the wound.

Throughout the period of developing the core culture it is important to act and make decisions as though the culture were already in operation. Living the values and culture in this way not only reinforces the commitment to change, but actually helps people understand how the changes are manifested. Talking vaguely of culture change is meaningless. Describing how things will be different and, more importantly, doing things differently sets a visible example. The art of changing the culture is transferring the broad principles into specific actions.

To change culture you have to work through the layers of the cultural onion. Some of these are easier to change than others. It is very difficult to change a person's core values and beliefs. But it can be done, and the results are remarkable – much like a former smoker who becomes evangelical about the perils of smoking. Values can be changed if they are constructively challenged through assignments and experiences specifically designed to force the individual to question those values. Even then there are no guarantees of success. Organisations more typically change the values of key individuals by changing the key individuals. This is why significant change is often associated with a change in the leader and the management team. This is not an easy task, particularly when dealing with people who have been colleagues, even friends, for many years. Changing managers injects life into the new values quickly by creating new heroes.

Building a cadre of heroes can also be done by publicly and repeatedly recognising acts that support the new values. One financial services manager told the story of an employee dealing with a customer who at the time was in New Zealand. To provide the service he called the customer from home and subsequently put in a claim for the phone call. The expenses department rejected the claim, but when senior management got to hear of the story they not only paid for that phone call, but his phone bill for a whole year. The story circulated around the organisation and became part of the folklore. Whilst actions such as this seem relatively small in themselves, the halo effect of management attention ensures that these people exert an influence beyond their position.

The third aspect of the mechanisms to replace traditional strategic planning, is a focus on management processes.

FOCUS ON MANAGEMENT PROCESSES

Many companies have reengineered. Most, however, have focused on the processes by which the organisation delivers products and services to customers. This has been a necessary change as organisations had become bureaucratic, slow and totally unresponsive to the needs of the customer. They had built a degree of fat that threatened their health. As anyone who has been overweight knows, there is a difference between dieting and staying healthy. The latter requires action beyond diet, notably exercise. Staying healthy requires a change in lifestyle.

For most organisations, however, the reengineering revolution has not touched the management processes, the mechanisms by which the organisation translates its vision and values into reality; the mechanisms that truly determine long-term health. The four key processes are:

- Delivering change
- Competency development
- Reward and recognition
- Measurement

What is vital is not just the quality of the individual processes, but the quality of the fit between them as a set, and the values of the organisation. It is the beliefs and principles embedded in the values that should shape these processes. Not to do so is to admit to organisational schizophrenia. I have not included communication as a key management process because, in this context, it is a competency of leadership.

Delivering Change

I referred earlier to the two cycles of change – adaptation and fundamental business reorientation. Here I will address the adaptation cycle. It is by far the more prevalent form of change in organisations.

'The Apollo spacecraft had travelled the 240,000 straight-line miles to the moon while being off-course 80 per cent of the time. And yet it landed within a few feet of its target.'
(Dudley Lynch and Paul Kordis, 1988)

There are many models for managing change, most of which follow a similar path: figure out where you are, where you want to be and how you are going to get there. I have depicted my version in Figure 3.4. It can be used at any level of the organisation.

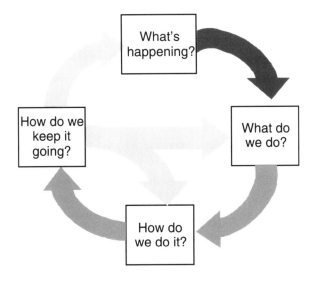

Figure 3.4   Delivering change

What's happening out there?

- What market and environmental data have we got/do we need?
- How does/will this affect us?
- What opportunities or threats exist?
- What are others doing?

What do we do?

- What's the current organisation like?
- How do we want to operate?

- What's the scope of the change?
- What are the key principles guiding the change and how do they reflect the organisation's values?
- What are the priorities?
- Do the numbers add up?

How do we do it?

- What skills and resources do we need?
- When do we make the change?
- What are the key stages?
- Have we addressed all the angles?
- How will we measure success?

How do we keep it going?

- Have we changed our behaviour and underpinning beliefs?
- Do our measures reflect our intent?
- What skills need to be embedded?
- What feedback loops are needed?
- What does this mean for our values?

There is nothing unique or magical about it, but a number of important principles are embedded in the model:

- Change has to be founded on what goes on in the outside world. Information about changes to customers, competitors, the socio-economic environment and innovation should drive change in an organisation. Organisations fail to tap into the energy this information represents at their peril.
- Involvement in the change process is key. People do not resist change; they resist being changed. Involvement is an often overlooked but very effective form of communication and the key to effective change.
- Change cannot be planned in minute detail. Time changes the situation, as does the action of change itself. Detailed plans too often become the driving force, rather than the goal itself. Means become more important than the end. Good project management is not good change management, but good project management is important.
- 'Why' is as important as 'what' and 'how'. People have an innate need to understand why things are being done. It satisfies their curiosity and addresses their concerns. It is an important element of generating emotional commitment.

- The values of the organisation are embedded in the change process. Action has to be consistent with the values, or the values have to be called into question. This process of embedding and testing values is vital if they are to remain relevant to the organisation and its environment.

> 'Whatever the formal plans, people will find the best routes to follow and make any adjustments they need to make.'
>
> (Yoshinori Yokoyama, 1992)

The change process should be widely understood and put into practise. Only then can the skills needed to support the culture of adaptation be developed. To ensure this approach to change was embedded in the organisation, the National and Provincial Building Society educated all its managers and most of its staff in the techniques and process of change. In this way, the change process became embedded – a natural part of work. The National and Provincial published extensive guides to activities such as process change, appraisal, team design and other skills of managing change. These guides supported a clear process of change that everyone understood, and was part of (see the case study in Part II).

Developing the skills for change is something many organisations overlook. These skills can be learned and should exist across the organisation. The essential set are:

- Leadership
- Facilitation skills
- Team dynamics
- Systems thinking and organisation modelling
- Learning skills

When describing the turnaround at Hannover Insurance, chief executive officer Bill O'Brien commented that one of the most important things they did was to send a large number of people on a one-week course 'to think about thinking'.[12] The course, which was run by a professor of philosophy, helped people understand their process of thinking, and how different cultures think. It helped them understand their actions and how they could think 'outside the box'.

Making the change process explicit and well understood is the first step towards making it implicit – a natural act within the organisation.

Someone learning to drive a car at first has to think consciously of the processes and steps involved in turning at a junction, reversing or joining a motorway. Through constant practice these routines become natural – they become implicit in our skill of driving. What was explicit, becomes implicit. The same is true of an organisational change process. Few organisations take the trouble to work out a change process to suit their organisation. Fewer still embed it throughout the organisation.

Competency Management and Development

One of the most important processes supporting a culture of adaptation is the competency development and management process. Forming and developing teams is only effective if the right competencies can be combined. Skills alone are not enough; knowledge and behaviours must also be considered. We have all been annoyed by people who clearly have the right skills and knowledge, but whose behaviour leaves much to be desired. Equally we have met people who are truly genuine, but lack the skills or knowledge. These three elements — skills, knowledge and behaviours – form the basis of a comprehensive competency framework.

Competency, knowing who can do what, underpins the dynamic organisation. As new information comes into the organisation it highlights problems and opportunities. Solving problems and exploiting opportunities quickly is what separates winners from losers. Each problem or opportunity can be expressed as a series of competencies needed to address it. This competency requirement can in turn be used to identify the individuals needed. Equally, opportunities and problems create circumstances that individuals can exploit to develop their competencies in a way that relates directly to the work of the organisation. This connection between development and work is only possible through the competency approach. Competency management is a prerequisite of the flexibility needed to operate in a repidly changing world. This of course is a constant cycle, embracing development opportunities for individuals. Again we see the interconnectedness of change and organisations (Figure 3.5).

Information, the energy source of an organisation, highlights opportunities or problems. Dealing with these requires a number of competencies, provided by individuals who are teamed together to produce results. And so the cycle goes on.

The opportunities or problems may be the result of customer or employee feedback, process measurements or simply someone's bright idea. The teams may be within one function or, more typically, cross-

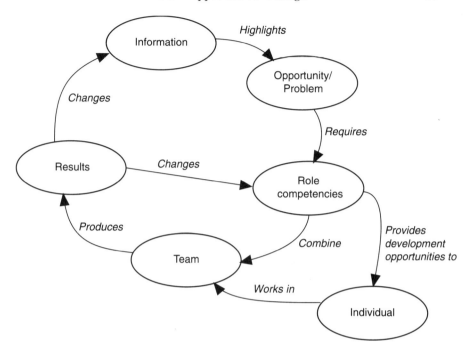

Figure 3.5   Opportunity, work, and teams

functional. Membership is based on ability to contribute rather than position. The underpinning mechanisms are role and individual competency. The National and Provincial Building Society has defined a series of 'capabilities': a combination of process elements, competency and systems. These capabilities are teamed to address business-as-usual and *ad hoc* work. This is distinctly different from the traditional approach to organisational design, where the organisation is broken down into functions and work is broken down into jobs. Job descriptions define who does what. The problem is that the effort involved in effecting any change is so great that people don't bother. The organisation ossifies, often despite the best of intentions. It is the mechanisms that are at fault.

This approach is not restricted to the *ad hoc* work of change. Business-as-usual, as expressed in the processes of an organisation, can provide role competence profiles, as can project plans. Indeed for such organisations the teaming of competencies is much more important. Organisations that are project based are continually having to team competencies to address an opportunity. Every time an invitation to tender or a project plan arrives, the organisation has to examine its database of available competencies and build a number of teams to address the opportunity. Of course this is not restricted to competencies within the organisation. Contracting in competencies is increasingly popular as companies seek to focus on their core business. Whilst the complexity increases, the nature of the problem and its answer do not. I believe competency is an essential element of what some people call the virtual organisation.

One effect of this approach to managing an organisation is the need for much more sophisticated and flexible management tools. Many organisations have defined competency sets for some elements of their work. Keeping this information up-to-date is a major task, as is making it available in a form that can be used by busy managers. There is a new generation of software tools to help with the management of complex, interrelated information, such as National and Provincial Building Society's organisation design facility (ODF). Using this tool, staff across the organisation can explore how their work interacts with that of others and what impact changes will have. (For more information on ODF, see Chapter 6.)

Development of the competencies of the individual and the organisation is a continuous process. Too many organisations lock themselves into fixed cycles, typically annual ones. What is needed is an appraisal process thath brings together the views of a broad constituency – self, peers, bosses and customers – when a particular piece of work or assignment is completed. This might mean some people being appraisaled several times a year, others just once or twice a year. It is the circumstances not the dogma that determines the timing. This will require organisations to rethink their personnel policies, which are all too often devised to suit the needs of the organisation and not the needs of the situation. More appraisals also demand a less bureaucratic approach, and more decision making power at the level of the team. If teams and teamworking are central planks of the organisation, then they should be the people to carry out the appraisals. After all it is the people who work closely with the individuals who are most familiar with their strengths and weaknesses. Thus appraisal becomes a continuous process rather than the meaningless paper-based exercise that is all too common. The dynamic organisation develops and taps into this knowledge. The facilitation and team dynamic skills I talked about above are key to the success of this approach.

Reward and Recognition

There has been much discussion in the press and academia about the importance of rewards, a subject I do not intend to spend much time on.

Rewards are important, but are well known to be a hygiene factor, although largely ignored by many organisations. There are two important principles I would counsel. The first is that payment should be equitable: the principle of allocating rewards should be applied throughout the organisation. The 'fat cat' mentality we have seen from some top managers has done much to undermine the integrity of their breed. I also fail to see how many can claim to be living according to the values of their organisations. The second principle is that grade systems should be simple. Nissan has just four job classifications, as does the National and Provincial Building Society. This provides much more flexibility in rewarding people without having to promote, which is essential for a flat organisation. (See also the National and Provincial Building Society case study in Part II.) But it is also a problem when the key determinant of success in an organisation has been movement up the ladder.

Much less has been said about recognition. In a study of the practices of companies recognised for their excellence in focusing on customers, recognition was highlighted as a common and vital practice. Awards are not just given by management. In a people and team centred culture, awards are given by everyone. 'The Spirit of Avis' recognition programme encourages submissions from employees, customers and suppliers (see Avis case study in Part II). 'You Make The Difference' is another example of a recognition scheme where employees send each other award certificates if they see someone exemplifying the company's values. The certificates have a space for employees to sign their names and add a short note. The certificates can be redeemed for items from the company's gift catalogue, although most employees prefer to display their certificates rather than redeem them. The value of being recognised and pride in having their achievement acknowleged often exceeds the value of any gift associated with it.

Whilst formal programmes are helpful, it is important not to overlook the little things. A kind word here, a thank-you note there, praise in a public arena, these are forms of recognition that are much appreciated, especially when they are made publicly. It builds a cadre of heroes and role models, further reinforcing the organisation's values. Recognition is one of those day-in, day-out things that the dynamic organisation does naturally.

Measurement

What gets measured gets moved. An organisation measures things to ascertain the state of its activities. Peter Drucker[13] identifies four types of information to inform and direct the tactics of a business focused on wealth creation.

> 'Financial accounting, balance sheets, profit and loss statements, allocation of costs etc. are an X-ray of the enterprise's skeleton. But much as the diseases we most commonly die from – heart disease, cancer, Parkinson's – do not show up in a skeletal X-ray, a loss of market standing or a failure to innovate do not register in the accountant's figures until the damage has been done.'
>
> (Peter Drucker)

- *Foundation information* concerns the financial health of an organisation. This type of information may be needed to comply with external standards and legislation. Apart from informing, this type of information may indicate a problem, but does not suggest what the problem might be.
- *Productivity information* grows from the focus on labour productivity. This is now recognised as too narrow and has led to developments such as economic value added, which measures value created above all costs (including the cost of capital), and benchmarking, which measures comparative productivity performance.
- *Competence information* focuses on the unique or special abilities of an organisation. These new measures focus on performance *vis-à-vis* competitors and the marketplace and help identify what the market currently values and what it is losing interest in. Innovation is a core competence for many organisations.
- *Resource allocation information* guides the allocation of scarce resources – capital and people. Investment appraisal is not new. However most organisations either fail to ask, or attach little importance to, two questions as part of this process: what is the effect of not investing and, post-investment, did the investment deliver the promised results? The UK Treasury acts on the latter by automatically reducing the department's operating budget based on the anticipated returns included in capital investment plans.

In addition to the tactical information needed to manage the business operations, an organisation needs strategic information to help it assess its future. This information is almost wholly external, for that is where change occurs. Information about how the environment is changing focuses on two questions: what business are we in, and how is business changing?

> 'Long before the bottom line indicates that the organisation is in trouble, everything inside has gone to hell in a hand basket.'
>
> (James Reiner)

The concept of a balanced business scorecard was developed by Robert Kaplan and David Norton.[14] They suggested an organisation needs to review four perspectives of its activities, combining both operational and financial performance. This combination covers both the drivers of performance (customer satisfaction, processes and innovation) and re-sults – the financials so common in organisations. The starting point for the scorecard is how customers view the organisation, which in turn guides what the company must excel at (internal perspective) to deliver results to the shareholders. The customer and internal perspectives have to be coupled with an ability to innovate – this is essential for securing tomorrow's results, which in turn are funded by current results.

The key entry point to the scorecard is how customers see us. Initial efforts focused on measuring customer satisfaction, although this alone is not sufficient. What satisfies a customer is not always sufficient to keep a customer. But not all customers are worth keeping. A truly customer focused organisation knows which customers it serves – and makes conscious decisions about those it does not wish to serve (see Chapter 2).

The internal perspective focuses on operations that are vital to meeting the customers' needs. In some respects these are the internal mirror of what customers want, and measure the processes that deliver the things customers value. To date these measures have focused on the delivery of the core product or service. But increasingly customers are viewing delivery of the core product/service as a table stake and are focusing their attention on other factors. Measures impacting on service quality are increasingly important. The other factors that have received little attention but impact on performance are management processes. These measures are the only real-time indicators an organisation has; customer and financial measurements are made after the event.

The innovation and learning perspective looks to the organisation's future ability to create wealth, and this is the area where least work has been done by most organisations. Pockets are beginning to appear. 3M measures the percentage of revenue it receives from products introduced in the last three years; indeed a target is set. This is based on the premise that it is better for organisations to render obsolete their own products rather than wait for a competitor to do it for them. Competency measurement and development of both the organisation and the individual are central to the development of learning. This measure of an organisation's additional learning is valid, provided there is a link between development and direction. The UK's Investors in People scheme provides an excellent framework for assessing and maintaining this link for individuals. Drucker's competence information (see above) also fits this category at the organisation level. Several organisations monitor product developments and compare the number introduced/ adopted by their organisation against the total. This also allows market-place developments to be identified.

The Kaplan and Norton (1992) framework does not have to be adopted as it stands, for example some organisations have replaced the learning perspective with employee satisfaction and turnover as the key indicator. This reflects increasing recognition of the link between employee satisfaction and customer satisfaction. Others have included in the scorecard milestone achievements for key corporate change programmes. What is important is that an organisation carefully changes the indicators that show how well it is fulfilling its purpose.

An increasing number of the world's leading companies are focusing on the measurement of operational performance indicators, arguing that getting these right means the financial performance will follow. This theme was evident at a recent conference on business performance measurement, with Xerox, Milliken, Hewlett Packard and American Express all extolling the importance of operational measures. Note, that all are leaders in their industry.

Strengthening the link between strategy (direction) and performance is what a balanced scorecard is all about, as Figure 3.6 shows. The scorecard should inform both the direction of the company and the pursuit of that direction. To strengthen this link, users of balanced scorecards are cascading them down through the organisation, in some cases right down to individual performance, with achievement of certain levels of performance within the scorecard being linked to bonus payments.

Mitsubishi Heavy Industries of Japan has used a simple mechanism to inform everybody in the organisation about its direction and corporate targets, and to link individual activities to these. When I visited the Mitsubishi plant at Sagamihara several years ago, posters were displayed all around the shopfloor (Figure 3.7).

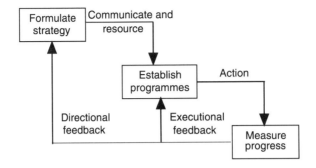

Figure 3.6 Linking direction through measurement

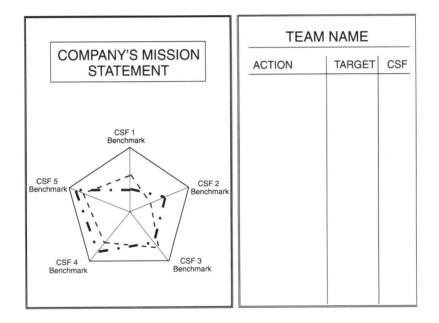

Figure 3.7 Mitsubishi Heavy Industries – Pentagon Campaign

The left-hand side of the poster was printed, the right-hand side handwritten. Managers explained that the posters were about the company's 'Pentagon Campaign'. The left-hand side portrayed the company's mission and critical success factors (five). These were presented as a polar diagram, the end of each arm showing the world leading benchmark, the company's target for the year, overall performance and actual results for the section of the plant. The right-hand side showed the activities work teams had devised to improve performance. This simple mechanism combined direction, goal setting and performance in a simple chart – an excellent example of what the Japanese call visible management. It was also a simple way of uniting the organisation while leaving a significant degree of freedom for people to identify and shape their response to the company's competitive challenges.

Scorecards are an important management process and an integral part of the direction setting process. Whilst long-term direction may be relatively stable (although even this is increasingly less so), the actions needed to achieve that direction will change as the organisation and its environment changes. This must be reflected in the scorecard. If it is not, the all-important link between strategy and performance will be weakened. Some of the measures may therefore be more transient.

One of the real benefits of a balanced scorecard is the support it gives in connecting strategic and operational management. As I have already said, strategy is not about tomorrow. It is about what is done today to create tomorrow. The balanced scorecard uses direction as its starting point, and by translating this into specific goals with specific measures it, directs the actions and investments of the organisation. This is not new, but traditional financial measures alone have been relied on to inform the decision making process. By building in operational measures, the scorecard creates a powerful link between people's daily actions and the organisation's direction.

Scorecards will not work if they are not used or are not seen to be used by senior management. All too often senior managers pay lip service to customer focus and employee satisfaction. They review the figures when the annual survey arrives on their desk but then revert to their normal agenda. Only when the same importance, time and energy is given to measuring, reviewing and acting on the broader scorecard will real change work. And remember, adopting a scorecard is *not* about dumping the financial measures of an organisation – these are a vital component of the scorecard. The broader perspective helps people throughout the organisation better to understand how the different elements and actions relate to each other.

An important point to remember here is timing. As change speeds up, so must measurement. Take customers as an example. If we only measure customer satisfaction once a year, it can be 12 months before we have the opportunity to learn what is going on, by which time the customer may well have gone elsewhere. When the speed with which we turn learning into action is a factor of our success, measurement cycles become important. The more often we measure, the more learning opportunities we create. Monthly measures give us 12 times the learning opportunities of annual measures. Can we really afford to wait 12 months to find out something is wrong? Of course we have to beware of a knee-jerk reaction, but more measurement provides better quality information and improves our ability to differentiate between blips and trends. More measurement means finding smarter ways of collecting the data. Whenever possible, measurement should be built into the process.

In a devolved organisation there is a danger that good ideas will not be shared. The scorecard, focusing as it does on the key areas of operational performance and strategy deployment, helps us identify best practices and spread them around the organisation. The regional management team of a major pharmaceutical company I have worked with see the identification and sharing of best practices as a core part of their responsibilities. The scorecard facilitates this.

The final point to remember is that measurement is only of value if it is used as the basis for action. Customers will gladly tell you what they want and how well you are meeting their needs. They will also be a great source of ideas for improvement. But they expect action. The same is true of employees. The golden rule is that if you do not intend to do anything, do not measure it – you will only waste your time and money and destroy your reputation in the process. But also understand that successful organisations measure more factors than the less successful ones. Motorola's Bob Galvin once told a conference 'If it can be measured, we measure it. The insights we get from what might often seem trivial are great'.

The impact of measurement on people is also important to bear in mind. Too often, measurements are imposed from on high. This leads to resistance. They argue that the measurements are inappropriate; they question the validity of the data. If however people gather their own data they will not dispute its accuracy and will be more likely to act on its findings. Bear this in mind when developing your scorecard. Allow people the freedom to shape their own scorecard around a number of common themes and core measures. In this way each scorecard can be constructed to meet the objectives and local operating conditions of the business unit concerned. Indeed providing a strong local element coupled with the core common measures is an essential feature of an empowered organisation.

Remember that the most successful organisations, the ones that survive in the long run, have a clear and compelling core ideology coupled with a strong culture. Together these form a powerful beacon to guide the people inside the organisation and create a clear image that customers readily associate with. Successful organisations also have the ability to balance self-confidence with self-doubt. They revel in their success but are not arrogant enough to believe that success is theirs by right. They are open to new ideas, whenever and wherever they arise. They reinforce and refresh their vision and culture by regularly testing them with staff, customers, shareholders and the world at large. Their management processes are built both to test and to reinforce this core ideology and to translate the understanding generated into change.

4 Leadership in the Post-Industrial Era

Fail to honour people, they fail to honour you; But of a good leader, who talks little, when his work is done, his aim fulfilled, they will all say, 'We did this ourselves.'

(Lao Tzu)

Gerard Langler, president of the Mentor Graphics Corporation says 'Followers want their leaders to take them on increasingly inspirational journeys. In fact they judge leaders on the basis of this ability'. But he warns of grand visions that may become masterpieces of poetry but not of profit. The most powerful visions are not those which are handed down from above, but those which come from inside. Helping people develop their own dreams for their work and personal lives is the major task facing leaders today.

Staff of the UK subsidiary of a major multinational were asked what they believed to be the essential qualities of a good people manager. Their answers were as follows:

- Honesty/trust/integrity.
- Communicator.
- A people person: time and concern for individuals.
- Available and approachable.
- Professional: has the appropriate knowledge and skills.
- Leadership: inspiring and motivating.
- Supportive.
- Decisive.
- Team player: fight for the team.
- Listener.

I am intrigued that 'communicator' and 'listener' were perceived as two separate qualities. It says much about how people perceive the act of communicating. God gave us two ears and one mouth in an attempt to set the standard for communication. He has evidently failed.

87

These characteristics differed significantly from what managers viewed as their essential qualities. Managers thought their work was about appraising, setting plans and managing budgets. Whilst managers thought of themselves as administrators of people and work, the people themselves were yearning for leadership. What I have described so far cannot be achieved without strong leadership. The role and duties of a leader in a dynamic organisation will be examined in this chapter, which will also show how this requires a change in the role of that much maligned individual – the middle manager.

James Watt's invention of the steam engine in 1769 heralded the dawn of the industrial era. Arkwright's Mule, the Spinning Jenny and Stevenson's Rocket were all inventions that generated enormous returns for their exploiters. The new money came not as the result of land ownership (though that continues as a source of wealth to this day) but from investment in machinery that supplemented and replaced human effort. Thus began the focus on production that we know as the industrial era.

Not everyone agreed with the changes that were happening. The Luddites destroyed the new-fangled machines because they believed they would damage the well-being of people by putting them out of work. In one respect they were right – the demise of rural communities began when people moved to towns to work in the factories.

'. . . a radical separation of thinking and doing.'   (F. W. Taylor)

To support the machine age, people such as Charles Babbage, Henri Fayol and F. W. Taylor later extolled a new theory of organisations – scientific management, which applied scientific and engineering thinking to the problems of managing. Henry Ford's production line and product standardisation and Alfred Sloane's divisions and hierarchies put scientific management into practice, with outstanding results. The model for the organisation of the 1900s was cast. Work and organisations were broken down into their basic components. Improvement was focused on optimising each piece. The quest for efficiency has driven our organisations ever since. But engineering and technology in the workplace, exploited further by scientific management, have brought us to a point where the basics have changed.

'The world that we have made as a result of the level of thinking we have done thus far creates problems that we cannot solve using the same level of thinking which created them.'

(Albert Einstein)

Fewer and fewer people are employed in the *physical* task of production. Even in manufacturing the majority of people do not actually make anything. That is not to say they do not have an important role. Most do, though I suspect that too many are serving the bureaucracy from which many organisations suffer. Alongside the shift in the pattern of work are changes in society. The money we have made, individually and corporately, has financed investment in people. The growth of the welfare state and state education has been made possible by the wealth created from the fruits of production, which in turn has created much of the demand for a better educated and skilled workforce.

It is well known that people learn more in their first three years than they do during the rest of their lives. As they learn more, they probe and push more. Anyone with children can remember saying 'no' to a child and being asked 'why'. The initial explanation is followed by 'yes, but why?', a conversation that after several iterations often ends up with an angry 'Because I said so.' Improved education has given people the confidence to ask why; to question the instructions handed down from on high.

People are now better educated, and they know more than their bosses about the work they do. How many bosses, even junior managers, know how to do the work that produces the core product or service? They may have done that work in the past, but the chances are that technology and thinking has moved on since then. Now consider what managers actually do. For a start they decide. They decide how the work should be done. They are involved in decisions about shop floor layouts and service delivery methods. So much of management is about deciding how to do things when managers are probably the least equipped to make such decisions.

'Action is of little use without control which should be all embracing.'

(Henri Fayol)

One of the pervading roles of traditional management is control. Look at what most managers do. They stop people doing things. They stop people doing something different, breaking the rules, changing things – even when change means improvement (which it doesn't always). Much of this is done in a different guise. They don't control, they authorise or approve. They design work and develop operating policies using their experience as the basis of judgements. They set objectives and measure progress against them. They measure performance and reward accordingly.

But how capable are managers of doing these tasks? Is the experience they have of doing the work really suitable for designing work for tomorrow? How many managers have actually done the tasks they are now designing? As managers do we ever consider our performance and influence on staff when we are assessing their performance? In situations of hierarchical control people are obliged to do what they are told, and little else. Creativity, then is all too often, applied to avoiding the need to follow instructions.

This is not to suggest that control is an unnecessary aspect of management, but how we exercise that control is increasingly inappropriate; a point I will return to later. There is also a danger that in seeking to build empowered organisations, we will throw the baby out with the bath water and destroy some of the necessary controls.

> 'The inevitable result of improved and enlarged communication between different levels of a hierarchy is a vastly increased area of misunderstanding.'   (Thomas Martin Jr)

When they are not controlling, managers communicate. They pass down messages from on high and pass up details of results, issues and intelligence. In communicating from the top down, much of the communication is formal and periodic and relies on the hierarchy to disperse the message. Great effort is put into explaining what the organisation is going to do and how this is going to be done. Little effort is put into explaining the concepts, thoughts and intuition that lie behind the decisions. Directions are passed down, and middle managers are left to field the questions about the thinking behind the ideas – a difficult task considering they have not been privy to the thinking.

Upward communication is also fraught. Intent on looking good and fearful of what will happen to the harbinger of bad news, too many managers 'massage the facts' to hide the mistakes they or their subordinates have made. This deception removes any opportunity for the organisation as a whole to learn, the one thing of value any mistake brings.

The hierarchy all to often comes into play when peer-to-peer communication is needed. Instead of just seeking out the person needed, the politics of hierarchy makes communication akin to travelling from London to Amsterdam via Calcutta. This is again a result of the scientific management thinking of the turn of the century. One of Henri Fayol's 14 principles of management was the concept of the chain of command. Coordination across the organisation, he said, should be effected by weekly conferences of departmental heads. He goes on to explain that this action is of little use without control, which should be all-embracing. I am sure many managers have this maxim tattooed on their hearts.

'No great improvements in the lot of mankind are possible until a great change takes place in the fundamental constitution of their modes of thought.'   (John Stuart Mill)

So what does all this mean for leadership? How can we change our approach to suit the emerging paradigm of the knowledge era? I find it interesting that in the new era we talk about leadership rather than management, which was the term used in the industrial era. I also see a danger, that, in an effort to correct the excesses of mechanistic management, we will swing the pendulum too far. Control will remain important to an organisation's success, but not in the way we currently envisage. We will need new ways to communicate direction in order to replace the hierarchical baton passing. In an excellent article, John Kotter said 'leadership and management are two distinct and complementary systems of action. Each has its own function and characteristic activities. Both are necessary for success in an increasingly volatile business environment.'[1] He went on to add that most [US corporations] are overmanaged and underled. This is not such a fundamental change. Alfred Sloane believed top managers had three responsibilities: to set the company's strategy, design its structure and establish control systems. I do not see a fundamental change in what top managers are doing. I do however believe that the way these things are done, and the beliefs underpinning them, have to change considerably both what Sloane proposed and from what most organisations, including his own, practice.

What follows are my observations on and prejudices about the necessary changes from management to leadership. There are no right answers and little practical experience to gauge their suitability. The ideas draw on the academic work of Senge, Forrester, Argyris, Kotter and Ackoff and the experiences of Avis Europe, Hannover Insurance, the National and Provincial Building Society and Cigna. Many of the concepts are not new, although they have rarely been put into practice. Unfortunately, while extolling the virtues of a free enterprise economy, many chief executives run the largest centrally planned and controlled bureaucracies around.

If there is anything new it is perhaps the insight of the interrelationship between individual ideas and their application as a cohesive approach, forming a new paradigm of organisational leadership. It is difficult to choose items from this menu because of the complex interrelationships involved.

I believe there are seven fundamentals to leading an organisation where the key assets are the skills and knowledge of its people. These are:

- Exploiting ideas.
- Encouraging shared visions and values.
- Fostering self-discipline.
- Building commitment.
- Fostering teamwork.
- Dispersing power and leadership.
- Championing a new approach to change.

Much is written about the role of the chief executive as a leader. Whilst this is extremely important, leadership is not exclusive to top management. In the dynamic organisation, change will be initiated throughout the organisation and leadership is required wherever change is needed. Indeed, with the wind of change becoming a constant hurricane, the skills described are as important for people on the shopfloor as they are in the boardroom. Only through their widespread adoption can an organisation hope to keep pace.

EXPLOITING IDEAS

'Man's mind, stretched to a new idea never goes back to its original dimension.'   (Oliver Wendell Holmes)

What makes the difference to any organisation is its ability to generate, capture and exploit ideas. The late Konosuke Matsushita, head of one of Japan's largest industrial enterprises, believed this is where the Japanese have a significant edge. In 1979 he said:

> We are going to win and the industrial west is going to loose. There is nothing you can do about it, because the reasons for your failure are within. Your firms are built on the Taylor model: even worse, so are your heads. With your bosses doing the thinking while the workers yield the screwdrivers, you're convinced deep down that this is the right way to run a business. For you the essence of management is getting the ideas out of the heads of the bosses into the hands of labour. We are beyond your mindset. Business, we know, is now so complex and difficult, the survival of firms so hazardous in an environment increasingly unpredictable, competitive and fraught with danger, that their continued existence depends on the day-to-day mobilisation of every ounce of intelligence.

I do not believe the West is going to lose, although there will be losers. We must however heed Matsushita's words.

The opportunities presented to an organisation usually have a short shelf life. The ability and authority to act locally are essential if opportunities are to be grasped quickly. Opportunities do not present themselves only to senior managers, indeed they are probably the last people to see them. Opportunities happen in the market place. The people best placed to see and exploit them are those closest to the market – the front line. Neither are opportunities something that can be orchestrated. The key is to have the ability to see and grasp them. This requires an organisation where everyone has the right to propose, develop and implement new ideas, without reference, right up the hierarchy.

The freedom to do this is not without its responsibilities. New ideas may have a value in other places and therefore have to be shared early in their life. Sharing them before their shape is determined allows others to contribute their ideas, knowledge and experience, thus enriching the result. This process of contribution also builds support and commitment to the change inherent in any idea.

Not every idea works. I have certainly had a few that seemed right at the time, but were wrong. The job of a leader is to create an environment where trying and failing is preferable to not trying at all. This means allowing people to make mistakes but ensuring they and the rest of the organisation learn from those mistakes. This needs an open culture, where mistakes made for the first time are not a reason to beat someone with a big stick.

Bill Gore of GoreTex fame summed up the leader's problem in one of the company's four core values – the waterline. A hole above a ship's waterline won't cause it to sink, but one below it will. Certain decisions, say building a plant, demand consultation and agreement. Others, such as launching a new product, don't.[2] Gore used this value as a substitute for budgets in what he called his 'unmanaged' company. Helping people know where the waterline is, is the leader's job. It is not a fixed line. As people develop more skill in testing their ideas, the waterline can be lowered. Different people will see the waterline at different levels. The most common mistake of leaders is shifting the waterline arbitrarily. It is all too common (though perfectly understandable) for leaders to reign back power when things are going wrong. This not only destroys confidence and breeds cynicism, it prevents people from developing the real skills of developing ideas and exploiting opportunities. Real leaders will keep their nerve, knowing they have created an environment where self-discipline guides those with their finger poised on the drill.

ENCOURAGING SHARED VISIONS AND VALUES

I have already addressed this issue in Chapter 3, and will not repeat myself here. Suffice to say that if visions and values are to be useful, they have to guide the people in organisations. Indeed as many organisations are stripping out layers of management, visions and values will become more important. Control previously implemented through the bureaucracy will give way to self-control. What actions to take and what behaviours are acceptable will become inherent. People will make their own judgements using visions and values for guidance.

> 'Leaders succeed only when they embody or express, for better or worse, values rooted in the social character of group, class or nation.' (Michael Maccoby)

Creating these shared visions and values and imparting a knowledge of the whole is the work of leaders. They help people understand and contribute to visions and values and see the big picture. Describing how General Electric developed his values, Jack Welch said 'We went to the

organisation. We took two or three years to develop this thing on values
. . . reality, candour, integrity etc. It was brutal. We talked to five
thousand people at Crotonville [management development centre]. Now
we have the words, we're measuring people against these values and now
we're in the process of transforming' (Tichy and Charan, 1989). Welch
shows that large-scale, meaningful involvement is not impossible. It
requires a commitment to conversation and a willingness to act on the
feedback. It also requires leadership to kick off the process, and more
importantly, perseverance to see it through.

Actions speak louder than words, and top management actions scream.
Talking about visions and values is not enough. Leaders live them. They
never miss an opportunity to relate their decisions to the visions and
values. Decisions are then made consistent with those guiding ideals. The
Tylenol case is a perfect example of what can happen when values are
enacted. In 1982 Johnson and Johnson's Tylenol analgesic capsules were
maliciously laced with cyanide, resulting in seven deaths. The company's
market share plunged from 37 per cent to 7 per cent in one week. Without
hesitation the management ordered that Tylenol be taken off the shelf –
all 22 million capsules. Production was halted. The medical profession
and consumers were immediately alerted. The media was given full and
frank information. As the then chairman James Burke said, 'Later we
realised that no meeting had been called to make the first critical decision.
Everyone knew what we had to do. There was no need to meet. We had
the credo to guide us.' This credo, inspired by Robert Wood Johnson, son
of the company founder, starts off: 'Johnson and Johnson's first responsibility is to the doctors, nurses and patients, to mothers and fathers, and
all others who use our products and services. In meeting their needs
everything we do must be of the highest quality.'

Within five months the now tamper-resistant Tylenol had regained 70
per cent of its previous market share.

BUILDING COMMITMENT

Leadership of the future will succeed in creating an environment where
people want to come to work. This can only happen when people feel they
are a valued part of the organisation and are doing work that they feel is
worthwhile.

Real commitment comes when people have the opportunity to shape
what they do. Perceived wisdom suggests people resist change. This hides
the truth. People resist *being* changed. They are however more than

> 'The primary functions of any organisation, whether religious, political or industrial, should be to implement the needs of men to enjoy a meaningful existence.'   (Frederick Herzberg)
>
> 'If I had any insight, it would be that there is no substitute for getting people involved and excited.'   (David Kirk)

willing to embark on change that they decide upon. Leaders know this, and give people the opportunity to generate change themselves. This is not to advocate organisational anarchy, and it is only possible when the aspirations and values of the individuals and the organisation are consistent. People know what work is all about. They know success means being competitive, efficient and better than the competition. This does not mean that people cannot be involved or are unwilling to take difficult decisions. My experience is that when they are given the opportunity to make a meaningful contribution, people deliver amazing results. Too often managers decide everything and then wonder why people resist their logical, well thought out plans and decisions.

A cautionary word: not every situation lends itself to self-directed change. An organisation that is bleeding to death does not have time to engender widespread involvement. Such problems are often the result of the need for change being ignored, often because the organisation has chosen to ignore it. This type of organisation simply does not have the environment in which self-directed change can work. Strengthening central direction and imposing discipline are necessary for survival. I believe the key to enhancing and sustaining the return to success is to use this opportunity to rebuild the organisation's values and create an environment where self-directed change can work.

ENCOURAGING SELF-DISCIPLINE

As we move towards flatter organisations traditional control becomes more difficult. When fewer managers are responsible for a greater number of more knowledgeable staff a new approach is needed. If we are to give people more say in their work and more freedom to make things happen, this has to be balanced by greater self-control. Organisations that are true to their values ensure that the people who work for them are true to the same shared values. This requires more than lip service. As decisions are made, actions are taken and plans developed, values have to be at the forefront of the mind.

Leadership focuses on behaviour as much as performance, knowing that the values have been selected to enhance business performance rather than constrain it. Like other skills and behaviour, self-discipline can be coached. Knowing the values and being personally committed to them is only part of the picture. Frank, open and honest communication is needed to provide regular feedback. Feedback, often criticism, focuses too much on performance of the task and not enough on behaviour, the stuff that makes values come to life.

Jack Welch demonstrates the increasing focus on values when describing the four types of General Electric manager. The first type delivers on commitments and shares General Electric's values: 'His or her future is an easy call. Onward and upward'. The second type doesn't meet the commitments and doesn't share the values: 'Not as pleasant a call but equally easy.' The third type misses commitments but shares the values. Of these, Welch says 'He or she usually gets a second chance, preferably in a different environment.' It is the fourth type that presents the real difficulty, fulfilling commitments but fundamentally breaching General Electric's values: tyrannical behaviour, absence of teamwork and the like. Welch's conclusion is that:

> We cannot afford management styles which suppress and intimidate. Whether we can convince and help these managers to change, recognising how difficult this can be, or part company with them if they cannot, will be the ultimate test of our commitment to the transformation of this company and will determine the mutual trust and respect we are building. (Slater, 1993)

FOSTERING TEAMWORK

In an era when the knowledge content of work is increasing, teamwork is taking on greater importance. Real work happens in teams; rarely do individuals do everything. The skills involved in forming and developing teams are essential to leadership; indeed it is in teams where leadership skills are really practised. Teams are also the basic unit for developing and sharing knowledge.

Studies of high-performing teams show a number of common characteristics. All have a very clear and shared sense of purpose. The collective belief in their role is strong. Whilst this purpose is developed within and owned by the team, it is developed with the needs of people outside the group to the fore. In this way the team aligns its needs with the needs of those outside, be they customers, bosses, peers, the government or shareholders.

Strength of commitment comes from the emotional and intellectual investment each person makes in establishing that common purpose. Forceful presentation of views is coupled with a willingness to consider other views. This is a period of agreement but not of compromise.

This spirit of open and frank communication is not restricted to the formation stage. Regular feedback on performance and behaviour is needed to maintain the spirit of the team and keep performance high. This is only possible if people have the courage of their own convictions and, paradoxically, the willingness to admit when they are wrong. Increasingly people will work in several teams consecutively, each with a different purpose. They will have different roles in each team, sometimes.

The form of team leadership depends on the specific situation. Formal leadership, as determined by the organisational chart, may well give way to 'situational leadership' – where the person best qualified to address the issue takes the leadership role. Situational leadership is not new. Mary Parker Follet first expounded the theory many years ago. Simple in essence, it has failed to be widely adopted because of the power structures in organisations.

Situational leadership should not be viewed as abdication. As Peter Wickens of Nissan makes clear, whilst the supervisor's role is to enable, encourage and motivate members of the team to plan their own activities, this does not mean abdication of responsibility: 'The man in charge is the man in charge,'[3] Increasingly, however, leadership will be about gaining more responsibility and power by delegating more responsibility and power.

The ability of people to work in teams is only part of the picture. The leader's job is to create an environment where teams can easily form. This is not just a question of team skills but also of organisational design. Values are one aspect, but they are not enough. Too many of today's organisations are designed to inhibit teamwork. Structures are rigid, responsibilities tightly job related, rewards focused on individual performance. There is simply no room for teams that are not part of the formal scheme of things. Unfortunately the formal organisation is not renowned for its speed and agility. The competency approach described in Chapter 3 is one mechanism for reducing the need for structure, thereby fostering teamwork.

FOSTERING A NEW APPROACH TO CHANGE

Breaking the mechanistic approach to change will require strong leaders who recognise that successful change has a clear focus, but at the same time has to address many different factors. Systemic change recognises the complex interrelationship between the many factors involved in any significant change. Leaders of systemic change always start with the big picture, understanding how the technical, social and political aspects of change influence each other. They involve as many people as practical in the change, both to enrich the understanding and quality of the solution, and to build commitment through involvement.

Systemic change also recognises that planning is an imperfect science. It is ludicrous to believe that a single, up-front analysis stage can identify all the variables and allow plans to be developed to address them. This analytical approach also leaves little room for intuition, wisdom and opportunism, which defy analysis. Detailed plans need to be replaced by clear, shared visions that illustrate a future state without cluttering the picture with the details of implementation.

Implementation, the how to aspect, is an important next stage. Here too a change in how we manage change is needed. The world is littered with grand designs that have failed. The type of leader described above is far more involved in making change happen, starting at the point at which decisions are made about how things are to be done. This has to be delegated to those who know best – those who are to do it. The building of commitment through involvement begins here.

Discussions about change prompt the evolution versus revolution debate. Revolutionary change is often the inevitable outcome of the lack of continuous change. Continuous improvement on the other hand implies many small changes and it is certainly the case that most *kaizen* (continuous improvement) changes are localised and small. But to dismiss continuous improvement as insignificant misses the point. A radical vision implemented through multiple teams bringing about improvements is a powerful way of making change happen. This approach – the taking of many small steps where everybody has the right, the desire and the self-discipline to initiate change towards the vision – strengthens the power of involvement, an essential element of commitment to change.

'Just as every conviction begins with a whimper, so does every emancipator begin as a crank.'   (Heywood Brau)

Bill O'Brien, former president of Hannover Insurance, described his tenure of office as 'the orderly dispersal of power'. Spreading power around does not dissipate it, it enlarges it as each person adds their own personal power to that released from the top. In this context, power is less about the ability to wield the axe, and more about fulfilling the aspirations of people in their organisations – the power to fulfil the needs of both individuals and organisations.

Key to building the seven disciplines discussed above is the art of conversation. It is through conversations that leaders express their visions and share their values. And it is these conversations that give people the opportunity to test their leader's real commitment to them. Leaders do not shun these opportunities, indeed they welcome the chance to test their vision and values with any constituency. The challenge enables them to enrol more people and to improve them. It also allows people to test and understand what the words and intent mean for them. How will they work? What will be different? It is impossible to underestimate the importance and impact of these contacts. Seeing the whites of someone's eyes and feeling the passion they exude is an important element of communication.

Leaders considering this road should also recognise the dangers. For sure, we won't find out the real potential of the ideas or know the details of their implementation until we try them. There is a danger of throwing the baby out with the bath water – of throwing away all controls in the mistaken pursuit of ultimate empowerment. The new leader will recognise this challenge and grasp it with great glee, and with trepidation. The world we create (and it is in our hands) will be different. The approaches described here are becoming better understood, and whilst their application is in its infancy, the success of Avis Europe, Cigna UK, the National and Provincial Building Society, the RAC, General Electric and others provide pointers to what is possible.

THE NEW ROLE OF MIDDLE MANAGERS

The dynamic organisation needs to ensure that middle managers are actively involved. Whilst there are a diminishing breed in organisations that are flattening their structures, middle managers have three important contributions to make:

- They must convert company-wide visions, values and intentions into detailed operational activities, fine tuning the overall direction to suit the real world where supplies arrive late, machines break down and people come to work with a headache.

- They are the role models for the front-line staff. Middle managers' daily behaviour must epitomise the customer-driven, people-centred culture of the new organisation.

- They have learnt the hard way what works and what doesn't work. This rich source of operational wisdom, unteachable at business schools, must be captured and harnessed to the new direction.

But far from being valued for the contribution they can make, middle managers are held in contempt by many of their bosses. A former chairman of General Motors referred to his middle managers as 'the frozen middle', not unlike the 'concrete layer' described by another chief executive officer. When turning airline company SAS around, Jan Carlzon bypassed middle managers and went direct to the front line to endow new responsibilities and authority. He later admitted that this had been a serious misjudgement. Attempting to circumvent middle managers leaves a disenfranchised and often obstructive group of people. Successful change requires organisations to redefine their role and channel their experience into the change process. This is not an easy task, and not all middle managers be up to the task. Investment in the development of skills is therefore an important early step in any change.

Chief executives' concerns are certainly reflected in their actions. As companies flatten their structures and search for cost reductions through down-sizing, middle managers have often felt the axe. One estimate suggests a loss of one in three European middle management jobs.

Finally, middle managers are scorned by the MBA executives who are so popular with many multinationals, believing that qualifications gained in the classroom have more value than on-the-job experience. As Henry Mintzberg (1988) points out, wisdom based on substantial and intimate experience seems to have lost out to rationale and numerical analysis. According to him, 'The problem with all this aggregated rationality is that it drives out judgement and intuition. How can you feel if you cannot see for yourself? How can you sense if you cannot experience first hand?' It is middle managers who are in the best position to feel these things. Whatever happens, organisations will always have middle managers, however their role will change.

The traditional command and control style of management and organisation that is typical of most modern organisations was designed to deal with unskilled, unmotivated workers. As more work is becoming knowledge-based and requires higher skilled workers, and as we begin to

'A company which has a philosophy to motivate employees and which employs good managers who can convey this philosophy to their employees and which allows all employees to share common information under an equal human relationship, is a strong company.'   (Ryuzaburo Kaku)

understand that poor motivation is due to lack of skilled leadership, not a lack of desire among people, the command and control approach is becoming obsolete. In the dynamic organisation, middle managers are enablers, trainers and coaches – true leaders. They use their experience and skills to bring out the best in others.

Mr Tadashi of Honda described this new role:

I continually create dreams, but people run in different directions unless they are able to directly interact with reality. Top management doesn't know what bottom management is doing. The opposite is also true. For example, John at Honda Ohio is not able to see the company's overall direction. We at corporate headquarters think differently, and face a different environment. It is middle management that is charged with integrating the two viewpoints emanating from top and bottom management. There can be no progress without this integration. (Jackson and Humble, 1994)

There are a number of factors influencing the change of the middle manager's role.

The IT Revolution

Information technology is increasingly making information easier to access and share, replacing the middle manager's traditional role as a key link in the communication chain. To date, however, information technology has focused on the data surrounding the transactions of an organisation. Information technology is now providing ways of sharing information across organisational, time and geographic boundaries that are far superior than the methods formerly used by its human counterparts. Embellished by too many middle managers, information gathering and disseminating has been the source of much of the bureaucracy that has crippled organisations.

Rosabeth Moss-Kanter (1989) explains this vividly:

The traditional manager was a link in a reporting chain – a gatekeeper to ensure that things stayed within bounds; an interpreter to the troops below of the sentiments of those above and a message carrier to higher levels. Did middle managers add value? In too many cases, as administrators they subtracted value rather than added it, by taking extra time, by telling eager subordinates that the upper echelons would never approve their proposals, by dampening enthusiasm and direct access.

Information technology is also vital to the empowerment of front-line staff. Without the information to do the job, empowerment is a non-starter. IT is a key tool in providing the information needed and it is fundamental in flatter organisations – those where so many middle managers have been removed.

> 'I cannot hear your words for the actions that thunder above your head.' (Henry David Thoreau)

Information was (and still is) used as a personal power weapon by many middle managers. With modern computer and communication technology this weapon has been rendered increasingly ineffective. Using video recordings, bulletin boards and electronic mail, Anita Roddick of the Body Shop communicates directly with her workforce. There is no doubt about her wishes and concerns and there is little room for misleading interpretations to creep in. The front-line troops increasingly have as much knowledge of the boss's ideals and wishes as the middle managers they report to. Of course leaders such as Roddick support their communication with clear, visible action. Or perhaps I should say their words support and explain the actions they take.

New Career Paths

Lifelong, secure employment was never in the middle manager's contract. Many however took it for granted that good performance, long service and unquestioning loyalty to an organisation would provide security. That is no longer true, and there is a great deal of bitterness that this invisible contract has been broken by organisations restructuring to remain competitive. As steep hierarchies have flattened, opportunities for promotion have disappeared. Many remaining middle managers feel uncertain about their future, even after restructuring. A survey of over 300 000 US managers founded that one in three frequently worried about being laid off.[4]

Perceptive middle managers recognise they no longer have a job for life. What they do possess and can exploit are experience, skills and knowledge. Job security is being replaced by continuous employability, which is only possible if someone's skills, knowledge and experience are up to date. Coincidentally perceptive employers have recognised that the new role of middle managers is more demanding, technically and managerially, and are placing renewed emphasis on keeping up to date those middle managers they do need. Those that offer such development are more likely to retain these key managers, who are placing greater importance on continual development.

Jack Welch, chairman and chief executive officer of General Electric, explained the importance of continuous education during an interview with the *Harvard Business Review* (1989):

> As for middle managers, they can be the stronghold of the organisation but their jobs have to be redefined. They have to see their roles as a combination of teacher, cheer leader and liberator, not controller. But with that must come the intellectual tools, which will mean continuous education at every level of the company. At GE, we spend $500 million a year on training and education. We see that not as an expense but as an investment in continuous renewal, the key to productivity growth.

Creativity

Continuing to do things because they have worked in the past is a certain recipe for disaster. Middle managers, bounded by their old jobs, are often trapped in the mindset of yesterday's experiences. In a world of increasing uncertainty, where speed of thought and response are vital, managers have to learn how to unlearn. They have to reduce the self- and organisationally imposed constraints that are impeding their creativity and reducing their potential. Not only do they have to tackle this problem, for themselves they also have to foster the creativity of their subordinates.

Fortunately the creativity tool kit is growing. Edward de Bono's contribution through lateral thinking and Tony Buzan's 'mind mapping' have led the way. By helping both individuals and teams to think, these techniques can elicit different perspectives of problems and issues.

Values

Quite simply, values, what they truly and deeply believe to be important, govern the day-to-day behaviour of people, inculding middle managers. If, for example, a manager believes that customers are a darned nuisance, always asking for too much and complaining unreasonably, this will certainly govern the relationship he or she has with customers. Political survival may mean that strong beliefs will have to be masked by cosmetic lip service, but the reality will be unchanged.

Recent research has, in this respect, given some encouragement.[5] Most organisations have written values statements and some 89 per cent expect that corporate values will become more important for success in the next three years. This development is vital to the role of middle managers – in periods of rapid change, staff need the stability and guidance of clear corporate values.

The top corporate value identified by this research was 'PEOPLE – We believe our staff represent a crucial asset for our success'. When asked to identify the areas where most improvement was needed, the respondents suggest that the following were important: 'Ensuring that our employees understand and have a sense of ownership of the organisation's values' and 'Ensuring that our employees are committed to the organisation's objectives.'

Without the total commitment and support of middle managers the dynamic organisation is not possible. After all the front-line staff may watch the top management video once, they may read the values in the corporate magazine once, but it is the hour-by-hour, day-by-day inter-actions with their managers that most influence their behaviour. Middle managers must take the values statements, typically expressed in general statements, and translate them into effective operations and behaviour. Through their actions, values will be translated into daily behaviours in every part of the organisation. Without their active support and involve-ment, values become just another poster on the wall.

It is in periods of change and uncertainty that middle managers need something firm and enduring to hold on to. Understanding and sharing corporate values provides this foundation of strength and guidance.

BACK TO BASICS

It is obvious that the turbulent, competitive times we face will call for major changes in strategies, markets and structures. It is equally obvious that middle managers will have to change to respond to this different world. The five needs of any manager shown below were suggested by John Humble in 1967, but in principle they are just as fresh and relevant to managers in the 1990s. The basics have not really changed.

1. Agree the results you expect from me:
   - Job results and standards are clear and understood.
   - Expected results are equitable internally.
   - Results are challenging but achievable.
   - Results are discussed and agreed not imposed.
2. Give me an opportunity to perform:
   - Authority is clearly defined.
   - The organisation structure does not impede performance.
   - There is a reasonable amount of self-control in the job.
   - Innovation and experiment is encouraged.
3. Let me know how I am getting on:
   - Regular, timely ad comprehensible progress information.
   - Regular review and discussion on personal development and career prospects.
   - Recognition for outstanding progress.
4. Help, train and guide me:
   - On the job coaching and counselling.
   - Organised professional education and training opportunities.
   - Job rotation to expand experience.
5. Reward me according to my contribution:
   - Financial rewards which are equitable internally and externally.
   - Clearly defined career paths.
   - Job security.

What has changed is the way middle managers operate. If their needs have not changed, the way they treat their subordinates has to. The list above is as much a charter for managing front-line people in the new world as it is a statement of needs of middle managers. As front-line staff become knowledge workers the way they are treated must change. The model exists: it is the same way they want to be managed.

DEVELOPING TOMORROW'S MIDDLE MANAGERS

The inexorable influences of information technology, flatter organisations, outsourcing and the empowerment of front-line staff all mean fewer and fewer middle managers. The decline in numbers will undoubtedly continue. The dynamic organisation, however, recognises the important role played by this group of people.

Jack Welch has radically changed General Electric, and along with it the role of his middle managers. A substantial part of the investment in training has gone into General Electric's Crotonville management development centre, where thousands of middle managers are exposed to the General Electric way. Extensive learning activities, both on the job and off, must underpin the changing role of middle managers. Without this people will lack the confidence, and perhaps the skills, to carry out their new role. Even worse, they may drift back to the old ways they are comfortable with.

Poor performance above all results from poor placement. Failing to match the right person with the right job will have a great impact on corporate performance. Flat organisations do not carry fat. There is no place to hide, no body to cover up or correct mistakes. Accurate profiles of people and their roles (including the behavioural factors of both) will be essential. Selection methods will have to improve.

Rewards will also have to be revisited. The new middle manager will be more aware of his or her market value. The less tangible benefits of continuing training, broader opportunities and freedom to operate will form much of the incentive for people to join an organisation, and even more of an incentive to stay. Nonetheless pay will continue to be important. The late Sam Walton, founder of Wal-Mart, believed that superior rewards at all levels are vital to superior performance. In his autobiography, *Sam Walton – Made in America* (1982), he said 'The more you share profits with your associates – whether it's in salaries or bonuses or incentives or stock discounts – the more profit will accrue to the company'. (See also Chapter 5.) Share ownership will also play a greater part in retaining the key middle managers. Within his first thirty days in office, new IBM boss Lou Gerstner introduced stock options for over 2000 managers in an attempt to prevent the competition from poaching his best talent.

It is the interaction between all these factors that is important (Figure 4.1). Organisations will have to work on all of them, focusing special attention on those that a systematic analysis shows to be weak.

New Competencies

To develop the new breed of managers, we must consider the competencies we require of people in these positions. Many of the competencies

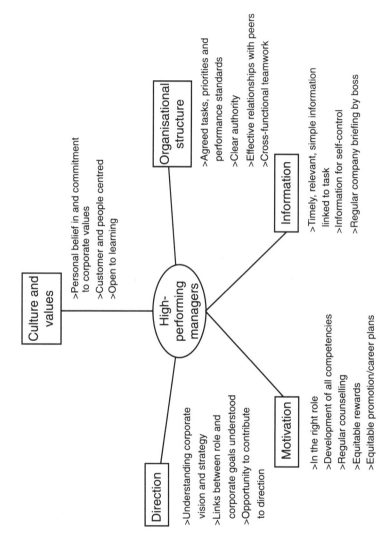

Figure 4.1 Developing middle managers

needed are known, although some might be more usually associated with counsellors, educators and consultants than with managers.

The competency profile will become key in expressing not just the skills required but also the behaviours expected of the person needed. Experience and life skills will form a significant part of the profiles, taking on a greater significance than the formal academic qualifications we currently rely on.

This focus on competencies may well signal a significant shift away from the view of management as a subject that can be taught in the classroom. Whilst techniques are important (although many are over-hyped), alone they do not make a successful manager. Much more attention has to be paid to developing people in the workplace, thus making learning and personal development a key part of everyday work. This will certainly be part of the new role of leaders, and something they will need to learn how to do. The difficulty, as Brian Wolffson, former chairman of Wembley Stadium, so aptly put it is 'How do you get managers to inculcate skills into their staff which they themselves never learned?'

Whilst fewer in number, middle managers will continue to play a vital role. Instead of being channels of communication and control, they will become conduits of change and challenge. They will remain because their new roles as coach, change agent and entrepreneur rather than bureaucrat are essential to the organisations they serve. They will translate directions into strategies and values into behaviours. They will be coach and motivator not controller and director. It is time for top managers to recognise, nurture and respect this untapped source of loyalty, experience and wisdom rather than write off middle managers as the fossilised layer of the organisation. Indeed one of the key roles of the top leaders of an organisation is to build an environment where leadership skills can be developed and honed. Attracting talented individuals is difficult enough. Failing to give them the opportunity to develop and apply that talent is criminal. As C. K. Prahalad commented, 'Some graduates of London Business School, for example, will go to top consultancies and some will go into companies, yet their corporate heads will eagerly listen to those with a McKinsey stripe, rather than the same people in their own organisations.'[6]

In Europe the pharmaceuticals company Eli Lilly assesses the potential of graduates as they join, and requires local country managers to make the best talent available to the company as a whole. This 'top talent' is then moved around the region to give them the breadth of experience needed to manage a multinational. This approach puts a particular strain on the branches in the larger countries, who do the majority of the recruiting, but encourages shared problem solving. The network that is built up through this approach helps both the individual and the company.

A new set of competencies are emerging, the most important of which are outlined below.[7] As you can see, most of the emerging competencies are behavioural, reflecting the increasing focus on softer skills.

- *Balancing stakeholder interests*. Right is rarely black and white. The needs of multiple, interested parties will have to be understood and weighed, and much greater effort put into finding solutions that satisfy all parties. At the macro level, successful organisations are those that balance the needs of three key stakeholder groups: shareholders, customers and employees. The same is true of many situations facing managers across the organisation.
- *Managing conflict*. Balancing the needs of different stakeholders will inevitably cause conflict. The ability to deal with this by bringing it to the fore and settling it will call for a degree of patience and diplomacy many managers pride themselves on not having. This competency has also been found to be vital to the development of self-managed teams. Cigna Healthcare include the management of conflict in its team-building curriculum (see Part II for more details).
- *Coaching*. As we rely more on the workforce to design and manage work, managers will have continually to coach them. In this context, coaching involves an intimate knowledge of people's skills and ability, monitoring performance and suggesting ways of improvement. This will include designing new challenges, spreading best practice, or more formal training. Coaching in the soft aspects will be part of the new leadership challenge. Conversations about what the organisation's vision and values means to an individual will become a part of the daily work of leaders.
- *Environmental scanning*. It is in the external world that real change occurs. A key competence of leadership will therefore be the ability to scan the environment and spot the first signs of change.
- *Pattern recognition*. A complementary competence to environmental scanning is pattern recognition – the ability to differentiate between a blip and an emerging trend. The blip requires minor corrective action, whereas an emerging trend represents a threat or an opportunity (or both) that requires much more careful consideration. The lack of this competence has cost companies dearly.

- *Managing complexity.* Growing recognition of the interconnectedness between the various aspects of organisations means we will have to face more complex problems. Dealing with this complexity – seeing both the wood and the trees – is something few people can do.
- *Building shared visions.* The ability to build visions has long been associated with leadership. The subtle shift however is to shared visions as opposed to visions shared. The latter is an individual vision well communicated, whereas the former is a collaborative thinking exercise, although it encompasses the ability to do individual visioning.
- *Story telling.* The need to communicate visions and values means we will have to find ways of communicating our intent. Our forefathers passed on their wisdom in the form of stories, we will have to rediscover some of these skills to make visions and values come to life.
- *Systems thinking.* The ability to see how a system as a whole operates is fundamental to the type of change I have described. Lack of this competence risks the introduction of solutions that only exacerbate the real problem. System archetypes[8] are a useful technique for developing systems thinking.

Development of these competencies needs to be built into leadership training programmes. I am a great believer in on-the-job training and the use of coaching to improve skills. Much of my real learning has come about by working with people whose values, skills and judgement I admire and I have actively sought out such opportunities. The learning came not so much from the work we did together, but from the many conversations (for which, sometimes, read arguments) we had. I would advise anyone entering any area of life to go out of their way to work with people who can contribute to their development.

5 People Do It All

It is people who design, distribute and deliver service. It is people who perform. Technologies do not perform. People perform. And it is performance which counts. People create the wealth. People throw away the wealth. People do it all.

(Tom Patterson)

Most organisations profess that 'in our business, the customer is king' and 'people are our greatest asset'. In most organisations, however, the propaganda does not stand up to scrutiny. The dynamic organisation derives its impetus from the outside world, notably its customers. Personal relationships are all-important. I may have transactions with an organisation, or even a machine, but I build relationships with people. Personal relationships are not an option in most businesses. One study of buying behaviour and drivers of customer satisfaction I was involved in elicited the following comment from a person who spent a six-figure sum annually with a particular supplier: 'The reason I buy from a supplier probably boils down to my perception of one or two people.'

Customers are people, not statistics in a market survey. We demand quality, we appreciate courtesy, we feel better when people are nice to us and we like to feel recognised, if not important. We are fed up with being treated like a number or just another body on the conveyor belt of business. We are also irrational. We will choose to buy elsewhere because people are nice to us; indeed we will often pay for the privilege. Even in the hard-nosed world of big business we will find reasons to buy from people we like. We might justify our decisions logically, but emotions guide the logic we apply. Try factoring that into a business model; you can't. However people who like people can. Their empathy, tact, intuition and patience can resolve most awkward situations – if they are allowed to. Of everything in this book, the importance of people rises above all else.

'One machine can do the work of 100 men, but no machine can do the work of one extra-ordinary man.'   (Anon)

Our ability to deliver the improved value customers demand from us and increase productivity to meet global competition cannot be done without the active support of our people. This will require us to ditch the Taylorist basis upon which people have been managed for most of this century. We have to start now to build organisations where satisfied people work together to satisfy customers. Fine words, but what do they really mean?

Ensuring customer satisfaction can only begin by understanding customers' needs and aspirations. The same is true of employees. Even the term 'employees' is no longer accurate. A significant proportion of the people who help an organisation to deliver its products and services are not directly employed by it – a trend that seems likely to continue. For this reason, and to remove the image of lesser beings that some people associate with the word employee, an increasing number of organisations are using alternative words. Mars and Gore-Tex call their people associates; the National and Provincial Building Society describes them as players; and we all know the Disney employs 'cast members'.

But whatever they are called, and I will use the words people or staff, what they want does not significantly differ. My own experience and a series of straw polls suggests that most people want the following things from work:

- A reasonable reward for their efforts.
- A feeling of belonging and involvement.
- A sense of pride in the organisation they work for.
- The opportunity to shape their work.
- The respect of and respect for their colleagues.
- Security of earnings.
- Development of their skills.

'One of the most important aspects to consider is the relationship of self-esteem to productive work.'   (Nathaniel L. Branden)

The management of people in organisations has focused on the first and last items on this list, but has done little to accommodate, let alone actively manage, the other factors. I recall the debate and hype when organisations changed the title 'personnel manager'to 'human resource manager'. The fact that the position was mostly held by the same people with the same beliefs seemed somehow unimportant. Perceiving people as a human resource to manage leaves me cold. I am not a resource. I am a living, feeling, worrying, creative individual with certain skills, knowledge and behaviours, moods and foibles. I give my effort in return for money, through which I can enjoy other things. I give my commitment because I enjoy my work and because I believe in something or somebody. And it is mine to give, not someone's to use as a right.

> 'The difference between a flower girl and a lady isn't what she is, it is the way she is treated.'   (George Bernard Shaw)

If people are to give willingly of their best we will have to change the environment of the organisations we work in. This is the job of leaders, but they cannot do it alone – they need the cooperation of their constituents. I am in no doubt, however, about who has to make the first move: it stats with leadership. It can be done. Bill O'Brien did it at Hannover Insurance, as did Arthur Large at RAC, George Simpson at the Rover Group, Mike Jackson at the Birmingham Midshires Building Society, David O'Brien at the National and Provincial Building Society and Doug Cowieson at Cigna Healthcare, to name but a few. The world is blessed with outstanding leaders, but by no means are there enough of them. Their role is covered in Chapter 4. In this chapter I want to focus on the importance and development of people.

REWARDS AND RECOGNITION

In January 1996 Adair Turner, chairman of the Confederation of British Industry, hit the headlines by claiming that economic growth was only sustainable if workers (his term, not mine) were given a fair reward for their efforts. That such an idea should be newsworthy in the first place says something about the political and economic environment of the UK in the last decade of the twentieth century. It certainly is not a new idea. Indeed there is much to suggest that leading companies have already put this idea into practice. Many organisations claim they cannot afford high pay, but fail to see the correlation between higher pay, satisfied customers and greater volumes of business. But whilst the evidence may point that way, few seem able to break the vicious circle that begins and ends with low pay. Low pay leads to discontent, which in turn increases staff turnover. This turnover depletes the skillbase of the organisation, which impacts on customer satisfaction and profitability. Low profits squeeze the cash available for pay increases, and the cycle begins again (Figure 5.1).

Turnover of people inflicts a much more infectious, gnawing damage on an organisation than simply the loss of skills. Regaining those skills incurs recruitment and training costs and the cost associated with the effect of the learning curve. But in many roles there is a more subtle cost: the cost of a lost customer relationship. I recall a conversation with a customer of a computer supplier. He was truly annoyed at yet another change of account manager, the result of the latest of a seemingly continuous cycle of reorganisation. He made two points. The first was the cost to him of a change of account manager. He believed it took at least four months for the new person to meet the key individuals in his organisation and to get up to date with their issues, culture and practices. Secondly, a truly productive relationship requires a degree of trust, something that is personal and cannot be built instantly. Customer focus means just that, and it starts with designing the organisation with the customer's perspective at the fore.

It is said, 'You cannot pay a man to go to war, but he will for a piece of ribbon and metal.' Recognition is a greatly underused tool in the armoury of motivation. Recognition is simply the act of publicly high-lighting, and therefore encouraging, the skills, knowledge and behaviours that make a difference. All organisations have their heroes and role models – the people others in the organisation look up to and seek to

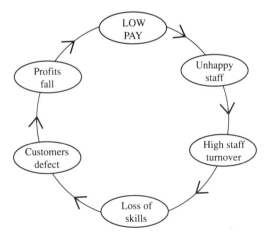

Figure 5.1   The vicious circle of low pay

emulate. Unfortunately many of these are operating according to the old paradigm. Managers have to determine the new behaviours they want to foster and, through public praise, sponsorship and promotion, build a new cadre of heroes. This does not have to be a high-powered, bureaucratic process, indeed that suggests a level of management involvement that is unhealthy.

To be effective, recognition has to be visible, quick, sincere and earned. Everyone in the organisation should have the opportunity, and power, to initiate a recognition award. You only have to look around most workplaces to see the power of recognition. Walls and desks are littered with mugs, certificates and similar memorabilia. It is vital that any recognition scheme is linked to those things the organisation values and is seeking to promote. One executive proudly described his company's recognition programme. Outstanding sales performance was rewarded with a colour TV set, outstanding service with a lapel badge. It was clear what was truly valued in that organisation. More importantly it was clear to the people in the organisation. They see those messages and act accordingly – sales at any cost.

Real success will come by going beyond recognition. Fostering self-fulfillment (which Maslow placed at the top of his hierarchy of needs) is the goal of managing people.[1] Self-fulfillment brings an openness to learning and an outward focus based on inner confidence – a personification of the organisation we all seek.

Customer input also has an important role to play in recognition. We are always ready to encourage, monitor and follow up complaints – and quite rightly too. But how many organisations do the same with compliments? As customers we all want good service and complain when we don't get it. But how often do we show that we are pleased with something. In the food and hospitality industry, tipping is a means of acknowledging good service. But in all too many cases, notably in restaurants, it has become institutionalised and depersonalised. It is an obligation, not a discretionary act. A kind word, a brief letter to the person (with a copy to the manager) or, for special cases, a small gift often has a wondrous effect on people's morale. We should all encourage our customers to praise as well as complain; a practice we can all start as customers ourselves.

EMPOWERMENT

Recognition is often more important in a world where the front-line people have greater responsibilities. The 'E' word – empowerment – is

'If you tell people where to go, but not how to get there, you will be amazed at the results.' (General George Patten)

increasingly popular in business circles, and for organisations seeking to improve customer satisfaction the rewards are significant. The bottom line of empowerment is just that – the bottom line. Lesley Colyer of Avis Europe explains that. 'customer satisfaction and retention is maximised when we do the job right first time and when we effectively resolve complaints. So the business case for implementing employee empowerment was very clear. It was one of the key processes to increasing customer satisfaction.' This of course is obvious. If you have a problem, you want it resolved there and then. At that point in time the focus is on getting the problem fixed – for your own convenience. The longer the problem remains unresolved the more it festers. An irritating delay becomes a major organisational failure. Problems grow with time and the threshold for a satisfactory solution also increases. It is not too long before all hope is lost. You vow never to be a customer of theirs again, and take any opportunity to tell others of your experience. Any process of handling complaints has a cost associated with it, and the longer the process goes on, the greater the cost.

Avis Europe found another reason for empowerment – management largesse. There seems to be an unwritten rule that the size of the gesture increases with hierarchical level. Avis Europe found that front-line staff offered compensation that was closely linked to the nature of the problem whereas senior managers seemed to express their own importance in the size of the gift they awarded. After all, if it had come to require their attention it must be serious.

Empowerment removes the need for much of the control exercised by middle managers. It minimises the need for costly and constraining procedured manuals and demands a simplification of the rules, which of itself removes swathes of costly bureaucracy. Image and loyalty also improve. An employee who has all the answers and the freedom to do what is needed to satisfy the customer is more likely to make a favourable impact than one who is constrained from doing anything but follow the rules.

Whilst empowerment may be financially sound, it is not easy to accomplish. It requires certain foundations. Empowerment can only be bestowed on people able to do the work – competent people. Access to information is also important. Empowerment without information is like sex on your own – it's possible, but lacks a vital ingredient. The third foundation stone of empowerment is a supportive culture. People will not take on responsibility if doing so leaves them open to criticism, or worse still, threat. It also requires a management that is willing to let go. Empowerment often fails in practice because executives pay too little attention to the important shifts of power and culture that are needed to make it happen. As Machiavelli noted, the best way to keep your reputation has always been to let someone do your dirty work for you. Empowerment and abdication are two different things.

> 'Implementation means dropping a solution into the laps of people informed enough to know it won't work but restricted from telling anyone with power what can.'   (Henry Minzberg)

Empowerment cannot be given, although it can be withheld and people can be authorised to do things. Empowerment is enjoyed by people who are confident in their abilities and have the support of those around them. A culture where mistakes are allowed but people work together to avoid mistakes is needed. Discipline too is needed. The freedom to act has to be balanced with a recognition of the needs of the rest of the organisation and a sense of purpose. A strong sense of purpose – an understanding of 'why I am here' – guides what has to be done. Clear values guide the behaviours that are acceptable in fulfilling the purpose.

Here again, leaders have to take the lead. Suddenly declaring that empowerment is in play is meaningless. Don Petrie describes how Robert Townsend (former chairman and chief executive officer of Avis, respectively) set about encouraging empowerment:

> After a week in the job, Townsend called every vice president of every department to his office, one by one. He asked them to make a list of what they wanted to achieve with their departments and come back the day after and show it. Then he would look at the list, maybe make a few changes and say: 'Okay, go and do it. If you run into trouble or need money, come back to me.'[2]

Empowerment is not a difficult process. It calls for clear goals, which the people themselves have a major hand in setting, full responsibility and authority, the space to get on with it (that is, no meddling) and shovel-fulls of encouragement. I never cease to be amazed at what people are capable of when they are given the opportunity to express themselves and use their creativity and skills.

Teams and Teaming

Nobody's perfect, but a team can be. No one in an organisation can fulfil all the needs of a customer. Teamwork is the only way. Cross-functional teams have always been promoted as the vehicle for change, but this overlooks their importance in carrying out day-to-day work. Satisfying a customer is the core work of an organisation – and the entire organisation has to be involved.

Shifting to a team-based organisation is made difficult by a world that still focuses on jobs. The world is full of job definitions and job descriptions, but what gets done is work. The role of work and processes in the dynamic organisation will be discussed in Chapter 6, so for now we will stick to teams.

Exploiting the opportunities presented by customers' changing needs requires teams. Indeed in this rapidly changing world people are increasingly spending their working days in a variety of teams: new product development teams, customer project teams, improvement teams. They might go under a different title – working party, steering group or task force – but they're all teams.

An increasing number of organisations will find that forming, operating and dissolving teams is a core competence. Traditional organisational models of hierarchy and matrix constrain the development of a flexible, team-based organisation. They confuse ownership of task with ownership of resources. We need a new paradigm of organisation, such as the one I liken to clouds. A cloud forms, performs it work and then evaporates. It's resources are not lost, they eventually become clouds again, but in a different place and at a different time. Whilst they seem to operate independently, clouds are governed by the laws of nature. Visions and values are an organisation's equivalent of the laws of nature.

The overall vision of the organisation should spawn a number of purpose statements, each a succinct description of the role a team must play in helping the organisation to achieve its goal. A good purpose statement must get to the core of why a particular group or function exists. One customer administration group, after looking very carefully at its role declared that its purpose was to turn orders into payable invoices. Others were responsible for winning the orders and for collecting the cash; this team did the work in between. This simple but very accurate description of their *raison d'être* provided the focus for them radically to change the way they worked and bring about remarkable improvements. The words themselves are less important (if at all) than the discussions that form them. It is here that a team forms a common purpose. Indeed focusing on the formation of a phrase, which is usually done at the outset, can lead to rigid adherence to a set of words that represent a shallow understanding of the task in hand. Initial thinking about purpose is important, but it is an ongoing process – something to be revisited throughout the life of the team abd contributing to the strengthening of the team. The Cigna case study in Part II shows the real power of teams.

COMPETENCY

When describing Avis's quest for customer satisfaction chief executive officer Alun Cathcart, said 'In Avis, marketing wins the customer, but training keeps them.' Customers expect people to be capable of answering their questions and solving their problems. People in the front line have to have to be trained in both the skills of the product/service and the technical skills of handling customers – communication, empathy, courtesy. Leadership equally has its skills.

But technical training – the development of skills – is only part of the picture. Competency has three elements: skills, knowledge and behaviours. Only if all three dimensions are managed can an organisation manage its people effectively. Remove any one of the triumvirate and the picture of a person's ability to contribute is incomplete. We have all met someone who clearly has the skills and knowledge to do the job, but just does not have the right behaviours. Unfortunately many of these people are in front-line jobs, where behaviours really count. Equally frustrating is being dealt with by someone who has the right behaviours but lacks the skills and knowledge to do the job properly. We shall briefly examine the competence triumvirate.

Skills

Skills are the technical and personal capabilities needed to complete the task. Technical skills are task-specific skills, including the use of specific tools and techniques. Arc welding is a technical skill, as is COBOL programming and statistical analysis. It is in the technical skills area that much work has been done in the development of competency profiles both within organisations and generically. Many common technical competencies are recognised in formal and vocational qualifications. These skills can be tested.

Personal skills are generic people and management skills such as teamwork, managing people and communication. A number of generic frameworks have been developed for this, for example McBer and MCI. Some competency frameworks describe these as behavioural skills. McBer for example lists both personal skills and behaviours as behavioural competencies. I feel this only confuses. Personal skills are important to organisational development. The shift to dynamic teamwork requires the development of team leadership, working with others and similar competencies. Recent discussions suggest there is substantial concern about the level of personal competencies in many organisations. As the focus of organisational development is shifting to the role and contribution of people, these personal competencies are becoming more critical. This is reflected in the lack of leadership skills, as evidenced by the growth in demand for leadership training.

Knowledge

Knowledge is simply those things one needs to know, the intellectual underpinning of the skills needed to do the job. For example a skill might be object modelling, which requires knowledge of the structures and properties of objects. It is not uncommon to find people who have the knowledge but lack the skills to apply it. As the saying goes: 'Those that can, do. Those that can't consult, and those that can't consult, teach'. Again, knowledge can be easily tested. Indeed most of our academic system is based on the testing of knowledge. One important aspect of knowledge is knowledge about the organisation. Knowing the organisation's way of doing things – both its culture and its formal rules – is important. In times of change leaders must rewrite, through their actions as well as their words, the organisation's knowledge book; ripping out old chapters and adding new ones. Some of this is done through formal statements, but much is done through the conversations I have continually referred to.

It is not uncommon to find competence schemes that combine skills and knowledge in one dimension. Whilst this simplifies measurement and administration, it removes a degree of flexibility from the management and development of the people involved. For example someone who has studied object orientation, but has no practical skills will probably be easier to develop into an object modeller than someone who has neither the skills nor the knowledge. The management of this has been made easier by the availability of competence management software.

Behaviour

Behaviour is perhaps the most difficult aspect of competence to define and manage – sometimes we have all probably experienced. And because of this, many organisations do not try. But behaviour is very evident and separate from skills and knowledge. Without the right behaviour, all the skills and knowledge in the world may be of little help.

> 'It's your attitude and not your aptitude that determines your altitude.'
>
> (Anon)

Of course measuring behaviours can only be done against some agreed view of what those behaviours should be. To date little work has been done on generic behavioural profiles, but many organisations are using organisational values to capture the core behaviours required in the organisation. Avis Europe's statement of beliefs and values (see the case study in Part II) is an excellent example. The cultural profiling tool DOCSA[3] is one way of developing and assessing the behavioural competencies of an organisation and individuals. Indeed this tool is used by one recruitment company to assess cultural fit between a potential senior executive and the client organisation. In many cases they are looking for someone who is countercultural – someone to stir-up the organisation.

By providing people with a clear statement of their competencies, an organisation makes it easier for them to match their existing abilities to development opportunities and other work opportunities. I believe this will become more prominent as organisations adopt competency as a tool. Such an approach also makes it easier to get people to take more responsibility for their own development. As schemes such as the CBI's 'Skills Passport' develop, the possibility of transportable competency profiles is growing.[4] Such schemes are vital if we are to enhance the mobility and flexibility of people. To date these schemes have focused on the skills aspect of the competence triumvirate. As our ability to measure knowledge and behaviours grows, they too must be added.

ISSUES OF EMPLOYMENT

Many organisations are operating an employment model that is increasingly untenable. In the past people gave their loyalty in return for long-term job security, often a job for life. This provided employers with a loyal workforce and people with the personal and financial security they needed. Career paths in steep hierarchies were easy to manage and provided recognition and status, further increasing loyalty.

Many of the structures and mechanisms that underpinned this model of employment are disappearing. As companies strip out layers of management the hierarchy can no longer support regular promotions – deserved or otherwise. The greater use of supply arrangements to replace in-house provision, of which outsourcing is a significant example, is shifting employment even if the work has changed little. This has been further exacerbated in the last few years by cycles of downsizing as organisations catch up with the commercial realities of greater competition and increasing customer choice. We are in danger of building a cadre of managers who only know how to balance the books by cutting costs.

Some commentators, notably Charles Handy (1989), have drawn up an alternative model of employment. The 'shamrock' organisation suggests a core workforce supported by an increasing number of part-time workers. Handy argues that by adopting this approach an organisation can achieve the flexibility required in the modern world.

In all of this it is often the individual that bears the brunt of the problems. Organisations that have implemented the shamrock model, have done so with little thought for the people involved. They have reaped the benefits of a lower-cost, more flexible workforce, but have done little to invest in support for those people. They may have made short-term gains, but thery risk long-term problems. When staff were in-house they typically had access to training and development. Temporary workers have to take om much of the responsibility for this themselves, as publicly accessible infrastructure has not yet been developed to support them. The real danger is that we will erode the skills upon which the future depends.

Even when organisations do not fully adopt the concepts of the shamrock organisation, problems still exist. As the half-life of ideas shrinks, the continuity of work that underpinned the traditional organisation is increasingly disappearing.

The great challenge for organisations is how to build the flexibility that is essential while maintaining support for the people who are key to making it happen. The teaming of competency mechanism described in

Chapter 3 is vital. Competency is the link between the work, the individual and the need for development. This is one of the key processes of management used by the dynamic organisation. It underpins the ability to form teams, both within the organisation and with customers and partners.

Competency is underpinned by a commitment to the ongoing development of staff, both full-time and contracted. In an organisation where the bonds of loyalty are being weakened, new links will have to be formed. One of these will be to demonstrate a commitment to the on going development of staff. Organisations seeking to retain the best staff members will have to deal with a paradox. Loyalty can be generated by offering people development opportunities that are difficult to find elsewhere. This commitment must be to their personal development, and might only partly relate to current or immediate-future job requirements. However in doing this organisations make these people more useful to other organisations, and without this commitment organisations have little that is tangible to offer the people they want to retain. The best people in any group recognise the need for ongoing development and are likely to seek out the organisations that, other things being equal, offer them the best potential for their development.

It is in this area that organisations can visibly demonstrate actions that people will recognise and value. This is particularly important in the early stages of a shift of this type when cynicism and concern is at its highest. It is at this time that leadership commitment will be most tested. Subjecting development to cuts in the early phases will be interpreted as a sign of pulling back from an important commitment. Leadership here will be about finding moneis for the budget when cash is tight.

If an organisation wants a flexible workforce it will have to reexamine employment contracts and move away from a single, standard form of employing people and introduce a variety of employment contracts to match the different ways the organisation contract, people. This has problems, not least because of the attitude of the Inland Revenue and the Department of Social Security. Both these governmental organisations tend to view the shift to flexible employment as an attempt by employers to dump their responsibilities for issues such as National Insurance and pensions. A serious move down the path outline above will have to involve these bodies in early discussions and plans.

Flexibility should also apply to benefits. In the new world, staff might want to build a basket of benefits that is different from those typical offered by large organisations. As employment becomes less permanent it will become increasingly important for individuals to have a benefits package where they 'own' the relationship, enabling them to maintain their benefits as they move between a portfolio of opportunities and clients. They will, however, want the scale of advantages that a company scheme brings. Negotiating a 'preferred contractor' scheme with providers might replace an employee scheme for things such as health care, pensions, car leasing, sickness benefit and so on.

The above paragraphs cover some of the infrastructural elements required, but these alone are not enough. An organisation will still have to make a case for being the preferred employer, but in the context of a preferred supplier of work opportunities. This will require greater clarity of vision and values than most organisations possess today. Whilst flexible employment gives employers more flexibility with regard to their workforce, it also allows people to be more flexible about who they work for.

Shell's recent experiences in connection with the Brent Spar oil rig, described eariler, clearly show the importance of public image to business. The same image will increasingly impact on an organisation's ability to attract the best contractors. Organisations that have and can project an attractive image will be most successful. I believe the best way of promoting this is through word of mouth. Nothing sells better than a satisfied customer, and the same applies here. As the shift to flexible working takes place, the organisations taking the lead in making it happen will have a unique opportunity to take the high ground, and in so doing become attractive to the very people who are best equipped to move away – the very people most organisations want to hang on to.

All of this will require leadership. It will require the management team to think through what it wants to be and how it wants to work. It will require intense communication. The management team as a whole and individually will have to be able to present a compelling case for the change, which will need to be flexibile in its implementation. Different groups of people will have different needs (a segmentation-based approach might be appropriate). Differences can be accommodated provided they are based on the equitable application of a set of common principles. Leadership also means taking the lead. This is an area of change where management must move first and not expect an immediate reciprocal step from the people affected by the change. Building trust takes time and demands constancy of purpose.

A number of actions are essential for success:

- Be crystal clear about the organisation's purpose and the core competencies needed to deliver that. Be able to explain these to a cynical workforce. Be clear about the reasons for the chance, the benefits for the affected groups and the possible pitfalls. Above all be honest.

- Establish, with representatives of the groups involved in the change, the principles upon which a flexible approach to employment is to be built.
- Start with a pilot. Choose a group where there is some support for such a shift. Do everything possible to make it work and use the supporters that develop from it as evangelists.
- Communicate, communicate, communicate, and in the spirit of two ears to each mouth.
- Work cooperatively with government agencies, unions and other companies following a similar path, but above all with the people who will take advantage of the scheme.
- Expect setbacks. Balance urgency with a recognition that Rome was not built in a day.
- Be flexible about how the concept is implemented, but rigorous in applying the principles equitably.

The process of creating an organisation staffed by people with the right skills, knowledge and behaviours begins with recruitment. Whether it is for full-time or part-time people, dynamic organisations such as Avis Europe and Disney put enormous effort into attracting the right people. Indeed it is during the recruitment process that the customer culture is first emphasised. The recruitment process stresses the importance of service excellence, and the interviews are designed to test customer empathy. In her book *The Complete Guide to Customer Service*, Linda Lash (1989), then of Avis, says 'The foremost question in the interviewer's mind should be, What will customers think of this person as a representative of the company?' Harvard Professor James Heskett suggests that the skills needed by customer-facing staff include flexibility, tolerance for ambiguity, the ability to monitor and change during the service encounter and empathy with customers. In one study the last of these attributes was found to be more important than age, education, sales-related knowledge, sales training and intelligence.

6 Building a Well-Oiled Machine

> Our daily objectives should include an honest effort to improve on yesterday.
>
> (Anon)

The focus on people so far reflects the important role they play in the dynamic organisation. But organisations are also collections of processes. The effectiveness with which organisations turn their understanding of customers into new products, and improvements in the way they conduct their business is vital to be dynamic. As already pointed out, having the right products is the foundation stone of quality, and being easy to do business with is a significant factor in a customer's perception of satisfaction. Both factors are underpinned by quality processes and systems.

This chapter will examine an approach to building the processes needed to sustain continued improvement, and the important role that information technology plays in the dynamic organisation.

Continuously adapting to the changing needs of customers is essential for the dynamic organisation. But customers do not always know what they want because they do not know what is possible. Improvement, be it of products or processes, is therefore a constant balancing of innovation and customer understanding. There is of course a connection between the two. The more the available data, the better one is able to spot patterns. There is a biological equivalent to this. A neurone in the brain can receive inputs from between 10 000 and 100 000 other neurones, building a complex pattern of activity. Alzheimer's disease restricts this interaction with devastating effects. What is key to organisations therefore is tapping into the rich vein of information and fostering the interaction of ideas that is so essential for innovation.

Research in Germany has thrown an interesting light on this phenomenon,[1] as Figure 6.1 shows.

Clearly organisations cannot rely on senior managers to generate the innovations needed to keep the organisation ahead. Finding ways of

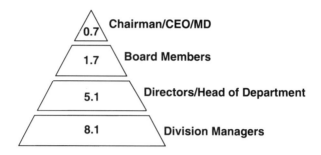

Source: Kienbaum Forum.

Figure 6.1   The ideas hierarchy – ideas generated each day

involving all an organisation's people in the improvement process is therefore essential.

The need continually to improve processes has been overlooked by many organisations in recent years as a result of the adoption of business process reengineering which according to Michael Hammer (1990), the founding father of reengineering, is 'The fundamental rethinking and radical redesign of business processes to achieve dramatic improvements in vital measures of performance (cost, quality, capital, service and speed). In his influential article,[2] Hammer criticises companies for using technology 'to mechanize old ways of doing business'. He advises them to 'obliterate them [the processes] and start over'. As it has been implemented by most organisations, reengineering has at best been a short-term fix.

The reengineering revolution has it roots in years and years of management complacency. If continuous improvement had been practised, many organisations would not have had the need radically to redesign their operations.

More importantly reengineering has fostered an approach to change that is discontinuous. This is partly due to the American psyche and its relative lack of interest in step-by-step improvements. In a study of worker attitudes in America, psychologist G. Clotaire Rapaille[3] found that Americans are not interested in step-by-step improvement; they want to achieve breakthroughs, to create the impossible dream. Compare that with the Japanese passion for continuous improvement founded in the philosophy of Zen Buddhism. Certainly if you read the business press it is difficult to overlook the disproportionate success of Japanese companies. BPR on the other hand does not have a good track record. CSC Index, the consultants who are recognised as leaders in reengineering, admit that only one third of such projects are really successful.[4]

There is in some places a fanatical belief in business process reengineering as *the* answer to an organisation's ills. This is dangerous. I disagree with Hammer, who said that whilst other facets of change are vital to a company, they are subordinate to the reengineering of its business processes.[5] Interestingly his partner in much of the development work on business process reengineering also seems to hold a different view. In an excellent article in the *Financial Times* the late Christopher Lorenz referred to comments made by James Champy at a conference. He argued that the reengineering revolution could never be more than half successful until management itself was reengineered; that is, until the attitude of managers at every level of the organisation, and the nature of their work, shifted from the traditional model of constant command and control to one of setting the broad direction and then mobilising others to manage themselves to a very considerable extent.[6]

Just as man cannot live by bread alone, organisations need more than processes to thrive. Organisations are collections of people. They are more organic than mechanistic. They are a complex interrelationship of emotions, politics, judgements, ambitions, intent, power, opportunity and, of course, processes. Of all these things, processes are the most tangible. They can be seen, measured and mapped with relative ease. It is their tangible nature that makes them so seductive as a focus for study. A *singular* focus on process, on structured problems, ignores the unstructured problems, the really difficult ones facing most organisations. Problems such as how to build organisations where people are happy to work, and where everyone works towards their own, individual vision whilst contributing to the common benefit of the organisation; organisations where change is welcomed because it is everybody's job every day, where the true potential and creativity of every individual is encouraged and tapped. The danger is in implementing a quick fix.

Simply changing processes will not solve these problems. They are problems of values and beliefs, of management philosophy and style. Peter Drucker put his finger on it when he said 'these companies now promise a turnaround through 'reengineering' operations. The reengineered operations do indeed improve, often greatly. Yet the company's overall performance improves little, if at all. Why is this so? . . . A company beset by malaise and steady deterioration suffers from something far more serious than inefficiencies. Its 'business theory' has become obsolete.'[7]

From some of my comments thus far you might think that I do not believe in process improvement, but I do – passionately. We all need to operate processes that focus on serving customers. We all need levels of productivity that match or better those of our competitors. We need to be innovative in how we conceive, sell, deliver and account for the products and services we offer. I strongly advocate efforts to simplify, speed up, remove and most of all humanise the processes we work with. Bureaucracy is any activity that does not add value to the customer or is not required by law. Included in the first element are essential support activities, notably leading and developing people and partners. Too few organisations actively consider what they can cease to do. This is particularly important as we change the nature of managing organisations. What we have done in the past is not always an accurate pointer to what we should do now. Much of what we do is rooted in custom and practice and old rule books, rather than in the needs of customers.

Process improvement should be a continuous, not a discontinuous activity. An activity carried out by everybody, every day; not a special programme. Reengineering therefore must be a tool kit that is available to everyone, a fundamental and everyday tool of performance improvement, not an expensive, consultant-led exercise. This is the approach adopted by Avis Europe. Their profit improvement programmes are embedded into the organisation. Everyone participates, anyone can initiate a programme, and the lessons they generate are shared across the organisation. Using such simple mechanisms, Avis Europe has experienced 13 years of productivity growth that far exceeds the results of any reengineering project. Like the Japanese, Avis has learned that cost reduction is not about dieting, it is about healthy eating. It is something that is done all the time.

> 'Whom God wants to destroy, first he delivers 40 years of success.'
>
> (Anon)

The need to improve processes has always existed. For many organisations the need is more urgent now as they are trying to operate in a modern, competitive environment using processes, tools and beliefs designed for the 1930s. This is as much a reflection of the lost opportunity of continuous improvement as it is a case for the discontinuous business process reengineering that some advocate. If organisations had not rested on their laurels, few would need such revolutionary change.

The need for radical change faced by many organisations is rarely the result of rapid changes. Oil crises do happen, as do large currency shifts, but they are rarely the cause of major organisational failures. These are usually caused by slow, gradual shifts in markets and evolutionary developments in societies and technologies. IBM's problems have not stemmed from an overnight shift to open systems and smaller, lower-cost hardware. That happened over many years and was predicted very early in the cycle. General Motors and Ford did not wake up one morning to find the Japanese camped in their markets with a new way of making cars. Taiichi Ohno of Toyota conceived the concept of just-in-time manufacturing on a visit to America in the 1930s. It was developed over a number of years, indeed it is still evolving. We are all too often the victims of our own lack of ability or willingness to recognise and internalise these changes. As a result we now have to make the major changes that are so painful. Surely it would have been better to change with the market – a continuous activity.

Processes are a vital part of business; our organisations cannot function without them. The danger however is that we will focus on them to the exclusion of the other aspects of business. Processes are a second-order problem. People and purpose come first. Processes are about how things get done. Purpose is about what is done. Too often organisations jump into answering the 'how' question (process) before giving adequate thought and reflection to what and why. This is not an analytical process, it is essentially intuitive. It is about questioning the assumptions that underpin the business theory, about daring to slaughter the sacred cows. It is also about seeking and respecting the different views of everybody involved. A common purpose is an individual and collective belief, not simply a statement that is handed down and to which everyone agrees.

Fundamental change is more likely to come from reframing 'what' rather than 'how'. Let me give you a simple example. I was recently asked to address a conference of logistics and purchasing managers. The conference title (its purpose) was 'To achieve the strategic awareness needed to improve business performance.' The search for strategic awareness (top management attention) takes priority over the real work, which is surely to improve business performance. I suggested that by improving performance, the awareness sought would come naturally. A semantic point? I would suggest not. The processes needed to achieve strategic awareness are very different from the processes needed to improve business performance. That is why purpose, the 'what', must precede process.

My second observation is that too often organisations delve too quickly into the detail. The issue is rarely how a single process works but how different processes interact with each other, with the organisation and with people. These interrelationships cannot be seen in the machinations of a single process, however broad the view. Organisations are complex organic systems, with thousands of interrelated effects, often without obvious cause. The narrower the perspective, the more difficult it is to see these interrelationships. This is why an holistic view is necessary.

Let me give you an example of the type of process improvement we need more of. The example is from Digital UK.[8] A few years ago Digital's customers were unhappy with the way it handled administration in the UK. So were the people who did the work. Digital's management held back from the normal 'we think and decide, you do' approach to change. Instead they gave responsibility for improvement to the people themselves.

The people started the task of changing their work by looking at why they existed. They talked to customers, to the sales people, to finance; indeed to anyone who had an interest in what they did. From the understanding they gained from this they developed a simple statement of purpose for the administration team: 'To turn orders into payable invoices'. If this is done well customer administration contributes to customer satisfaction, reduces arrears and makes other people's jobs easier. Now that may seem very simple, but try the exercise for yourself. Think of a short, simple statement that sums up why you and your group do the work you do. Now try to get a common agreement to it.

The group's simple statement of purpose was more than a slogan, it became the focal point of everything that was done. Around that single statement the staff identified the work that was essential to fulfilling that purpose. This was where the key process changes happened. As a result five disparate administrative groups combined into one, with each administrator responsible for all activities of a customer or group of customers. The changes delivered the sought-for improvement in customer satisfaction. In addition the number of staffing reduced from 86 to 53, managers from 12 to four and office space reduced by $600\,m^2$. The key thing to remember is that the people themselves did all the designing. Managers gave them their head and they delivered.

They succeeded not only because of the newly found freedom to express their creativity and intelligence, but because they were able to design the process they needed. With a common goal and the motivation that comes from trust and responsibility, people usually exceed your expectations of them. People really do it all.

Training people in the techniques and tools of improvement is therefore essential. If people do not have the skills to carry out the research, analysis and design and to implement the solutions, continuous improvement just will not happen. Basic quality tools, plus process mapping and competence mapping, form the core of the curriculum. As important, however, is coaching people in how to deal with the dynamics and conflict that team working inevitably brings.

Having the entire organisation working on improvements brings its own difficulties. There is a real danger that improvements in one area might be detrimental to other activities in the organisation. Being able to see the whole picture is therefore invaluable. Equally, sharing improvements saves time and effort. Improvements in a process designed for budgeting purchase spending might be equally valid for budgeting in other aspects of the business. It is for these reasons that the National and Provincial Building Society developed the Organisation Design Facility (ODF).[9]

ODF is a computer-based system that holds in software a model of the organisation, and how the different parts interrelate. The model captures the relationship between work, in the form of process definitions, the competencies need to carry out that work, the people and their competence profiles and the computer systems needed to support the work. Through an easy-to-use Windows[TM] interface people in the organisation can explore the organisation's elements and how they interrelate. If customer feedback suggests a change is needed in the way the organisation does business, the people responsible for that work can see which other teams are involved with that process, which roles are affected and which systems might have to be changed. This ability is extended by providing access to the tools needed to effect a change, for example process design, competency management and systems design. People do not have to worry about integrating these different tools. The software does that for them. The ease with which people can access the information and tools means previously that it is a short and simple task to see whether a solution to the problem has previously been produced by others in the organisations. If appropriate, they can borrow elements of an existing solution as the basis for their solution. Once finalised, any changes are visible to anyone in the organisation. I will return to the use of such tools later in this chapter.

THE NEW ROLE OF IT

Commenting on the development of the first general purpose computer in 1955, Professor Jay Forrester of the Massachusetts Institute of Technology said:

This is a machine with a lot of possibilities, but it will be at least three generations before anyone starts using it for doing something really new. For at least three generations, people will use it to do something they have already done, just faster. It will take at least that long before we start to use it to do something that we have never done before.

'Every now and then, a technology or an idea comes along that is so profound, so powerful, so universal that its impact changes everything: the printing press, the incandescent light, the automobile, manned flight. I joined this industry, and IBM because I believe that information technology has that potential.'

(Lou Gerstner)

Creating an environment where change is a way of life and creating an organisation to support the people who do the work is not a challenge that can be addressed without the use of information technology. But most senior managers see IT as a necessary evil. The roots of this disdain go back to the origins of computing.

In the very early days, computers were huge, extremely complex machines. Operating them was a highly specialised task, requiring experts to both configure the problem in a form the machine could work with and to keep the machines operating. Applications were written to solve particular problems. At that point the die of IT organisations was cast, and they have changed relatively little since. IT in business is still the domain of experts who translate the needs of business into the language of machines.

'A robust fact: there is no correlation between investment in IS and productivity.'

(John Seeley-Brown)

Executive concern about IT has been heightened by its ability to soak up ever increasing budgets whilst delivering no significant increase in productivity. According to *Newsweek* 'American companies have spent nearly $1 trillion on computer systems in the last decade – with almost no gain in productivity.'[10] The maxim was summed up by a colleague, with tongue only partly in cheek, when he described the IT development process from the chief executive's perspective thus: 'Sign a large cheque, wait two years, sign another large cheque, wait longer, and get something which meets a need you no longer have'. The special language that IT has generated (an area where it has easily outperformed its sibling functions) has served only to exaggerate the image of an expensive, eccentric child.

Paul Strassmann has proved that there is no link between spending on information technology and the success of an organisation, as Figure 6.2 shows.

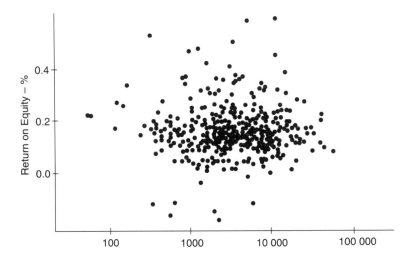

Source: Paul Strassmann.

Figure 6.2 The relationship between results and IT spend[11]

Strassmann concluded that it is not how much is spent on IT, but the quality of that spending. This, he decided, is a function of the quality of management. But for all its problem-child characteristics, IT is an essential element of business. Few businesses, particularly those of any size, could survive without it. But IT is much more than a tool for surviving. Used properly, IT has huge potential for improving a business. According to Alun Cathcart, chief executive officer of Avis Europe, 'High technology is the one thing – the biggest thing perhaps – which has changed how we respond to customers' service needs, be it in my industry, car rental, banking or in any other.'[12] There are numerous examples of IT playing a major part in the success of an organisation, the American Airlines SABRE reservation system being the granddaddy of them all.

IT has not just changed the work we do. It has also changed the way we build our organisations. There is a parallel between the style of computing that is predominant and popular thinking about, and forms of, organisations. When computers were first introduced into business they were large, expensive mainframes. The investment could only be justified by locating them centrally. People took their problems to the central mainframe – where the problems were input by a group of specialists – and waited for the answer. In the early 1950s organisations operated along similar lines. Power and intelligence was concentrated at the centre. Plans and suggestions were taken to the centre and input by a specialist planning function. The centre deliberated and produced an answer – what to do and how to do it – which was handed back to the business unit to implement.

In the 1960s, however, Ken Olsen[13] invented the minicomputer, a smaller version of the mainframe with the added advantage that the user could interact directly with the system via terminals. These machines were small enough to be affordable by individual departments such as manufacturing, purchasing and personnel to solve their own problems. They coexisted with the mainframe, with rudimentary exchange of information between the two. The growth of the minicomputer coincided with the advent of the functional organisation in the 1960s and 1970s. A corporate strategy was handed down to the individual functions, who 'translated' this into their functional strategy. Functions often placed their own agendas above the requirements of the corporate strategy, aided by control over their own information and systems.

The early 1980s saw the development of the personal computer – a machine for the individual. Now individuals could hold and manipulate their own data, using tools such as spreadsheets to improve understanding and manipulate figures to meet their own ends. It is at that time that the seeds of empowerment were sown. People acted more independently, although at that stage still around a centrally developed and handed down strategy. The PC also brought its own problems and hundreds of islands of information. Much time was spent arguing which view of the world was right, and again it was often might rather than right that took precedence. The PC was a useful tool for those rebels in the organisation who recognised the need to do things differently, but lacked the affordable computing power needed to help them in their quest for new business and new processes.

The late 1980s saw the growth of networks, spawned initially by the need to connect the islands of automation back to the organisation's mainstream. This era of communication also saw the beginning of groupware, with products such as Lotus Notes and the Internet. The language of organisations also shifted to the networked organisation, both within and across the boundaries of single organisations. Charles Handy (1989) signalled the shamrock organisations, heralding the advent of 'virtual organisation' and virtual teams.

In the 1990s we have seen the extension of the Internet, breaking the boundaries between work and play, office and home. The client server approach to computing is taking hold; paralleling the language of many corporations who are seeking to improve their focus on the customer. The client server concept of distributing computer power closer to the user whilst retaining some coherence reflects the organisational aspirations of many organisations today. However, the main development to gain mainstream attention in the 1990s and which underpins the future of that client server approach is object orientation. Object oriented techniques are used to build small software modules that combine functionality and data. An object requests another object to do something by sending it a message. What the object does varies according to the message. Because they are self-contained, the developer does not have about how it works, only what it does. Once an object has been developed it can be copied and reused – like cloning. The result is that once a library of objects exists, a system can be built by assembling existing and tested objects, much like snapping together children's building blocks. Unlike Lego, however, objects can be used many times concurrently. If an application needs an object that is being used, a duplicate can be instantly created. This will result in applications that can be built on a 'just-in-time' basis.

With developments in networks and the standards for manipulating data across them, it will be possible to build applications by collecting objects from around the ubiquitous Internet. Sun Microsystem's chief executive officer, Scott McNealy, is already working on this idea. He is seeking to enlist the support of leading universities to develop general purpose programmes using Sun's Java programming language. 'We are going to go to Berkley and Stanford and MIT and universities around the world and assign each of them the task of developing one programme; a word processor, or a spreadsheet or a spell-checker. These will then be available free to people to use as they wish.'[14] McNealy believes that rather than store programmes, users will discard them after each use, using the Internet to build applications on the fly as and when the need arises. This raises the possibility of developing applications to meet very particular needs, say the needs of an individual customer. It also threatens to turn the whole software industry on its head.

This technology, or at least the thinking behind it, opens up new ideas for organisational design. Organisations are made up of objects of competence, culture, processes, products, customers and systems. We can mix and match them to meet a particular need or pursue a new opportunity. We are not restricted to working within our own organisational boundaries. Just as we will be able to use the Internet to find new software objects, we can use our personal networks to identify required capabilities outside our own organisation. Object technology is certainly not completely here yet, but object thinking in the organisational context is lagging further behind.

My analysis of the relationship between computing and organisations is illustrative and certainly not perfect. It is important to note that the different phases evolve from each other and coexist. Mainframes have a place in the world of client server and object orientation. But it is also interesting to note that the leaders of one phase are rarely the leaders of subsequent phases. Success blinds people to threat and opportunity. I believe that organisations that are not open to thinking about their organisations in different ways will also get left behind. The big difference in this shift is that for the first time we are not just moving from one stage to another, we are moving from a static view to a dynamic view – a view that has change built into it.

ALIGNING BUSINESS AND IT STRATEGIES

The starting point for a discussion about the role of IT in business is typically about aligning business and IT strategies. The quest to align business and IT strategies has been a constant in the upper reaches of issues facing IT managers for several years. Is it not strange then, that something that obviously keeps IT managers awake at night, rarely figures in the list of issues that chief executive officers worry about? Issues such as building a customer-focused organisation, entering new markets, reducing costs and maintaining competitiveness. In fact, when it comes to IT senior managers seem more concerned about the drain on cash and return on investment than about gaining competitive advantage.

Let me state my beliefs quite clearly. The quest to align business and IT strategies is a worthless one. It is worthless because it is the wrong question.

Firstly, there is a fundamental mismatch between the nature of business strategies and their IT equivalents. The IT systems we have built are rigid and inflexible. Just witness how much most organisation spend on maintaining and updating the systems they have. For many this represents the bulk of their IT expenditure. Businesses, on the other hand, are extremely dynamic. They are constantly changing – often against their will, but changing nonetheless. There is such a fundamental difference between the nature of the two beasts that any attempt to align them along the lincs discussed in the IT community to date is akin to comparing chalk and cheese.

But just for a minute let's forget this basic problem (which should not be difficult given that that is precisely what we have managed to do for many years) and look at strategy. In Chapter 3 I discussed the problems many organisations are facing with the traditional thinking and approaches to strategy planning. Let me quickly recap. Strategy has become a much abused phrase in business circles. At its most basic, it is simply about how things are done, and as such always follows a decision about what should be done. Just as in architecture, form follows function, in organisations, strategy follows purpose. Purpose is about what the organisation is there for, what its *raison d'être* is. Answering the 'how' question before agreeing on 'what' results in aimless wandering. The first action when planning a route is to decide on the destination.

So aligning strategy is pointless unless first there is agreement on direction. But even this premise must recognise the recursive nature of strategy and action. The direction guides the choice of path. The action of progressing down that chosen path in turn creates new possibilities; new paths become apparent. Our approach to strategy has to accommodate this. So does our approach to building IT systems. Users cannot express their needs accurately because they can not predict all the business conditions they will face in the future. If they had such foresight they would have won the lottery by now.

Strategic planning has essentially failed and efforts to align business and IT strategies have failed with it. The world is littered with stories of major IT projects that have horribly failed to meet time and cost targets. Research into construction projects seems to suggest that the most successful projects have been subject to less planning than those that fail. The overall framework is clear, but much less effort is put into detailed planning of the elements of the project. In business too we can see parallels. Companies in Japan and Germany have relied much more on continuous improvement than the stop–start, big bang, megaplanned approach to change that is so popular with many US and UK organisations.

'What we delivered in the past is inadequate. Our response to the present is inadequate. Therefore, our performance in the future is probably going to be inadequate.'   (John Zachmann)

When we seek to align business and IT strategies, not only are we asking the wrong question, we go about finding the answer in the wrong way. No wonder we have problems. So let's acknowledge that the emperor has no clothes and stop this fruitless quest for alignment or developing business and systems architectures that are expensive, that nobody understands, and that add cost but no value. In one fell swoop we have saved money, helped reduce the likelihood of some managers getting ulcers and put a few charlatans out of work. Not bad for a day's work.

THE WAY FORWARD

So if we don't align business and IT strategies, and it is clearly a waste of time, what do we do?

I have already argued for an approach to strategy that focuses on visions and values, on creating the environment of the organisation. I believe there are parallels in IT. Vision creates a view of what the organisation is trying to become and values guide the behaviours that are acceptable in getting there. The president of one of Europe's leading packaging manufacturers described a vision that positioned the company as both a leading supplier of corrugated packaging and a positive contributor to the environment. Within this vision he established, in broad terms, a number of overlapping areas of importance. To drive manufacturing improvements he set the goal of exceeding Japanese levels of efficiency and quality. To improve the company's environmental capability the German market was set as the benchmark. And to improve customer focus he set the goal of becoming the industry's service leader. He did not describe in detail how these goals were to be achieved, although he had, and regularly shared, his views on this. He left the appropriate parts of the organisation to figure out what needed to be done.

Now let's apply these concepts to our problem of aligning business and IT strategies by looking at three key areas:

- Establishing purpose and principles – vision and values.
- Creating the infrastructure.
- Redefining roles and responsibilities.

Establishing Purpose and Principles

The starting point for IT is the same as for any business moving forward: ask the question, 'What is the purpose of the IT department:

why does it exist?' I strongly suspect that more chief executives than IT directors are asking that question, but not for the same reason, or with the same considered tone! This concern is partly behind the growth in outsourcing.

Purpose can only be, and should always be, drawn from the outside. What do customers, bosses and other stakeholders expect? Real breakthroughs come from rethinking purpose, not finding new efficiencies. This shift has certainly not filtered through to many IT departments, which are still internally and engineering focused and see the development of applications as their role in life. They are in for a shock.

Redefining purpose in terms of what is delivered to customers starts with understanding what customers value. This in itself is often an eye-opening experience. IT managers who previously thought that development times, operating costs and response times were key measures, find that customers place problem solving, support, and speed of response to change higher on their list of needs. The chief executive officer of NatWest Life, Lawrence Churchill, has given his IT director the task of building an IT infrastructure whose qualities he summed up in two words: flexible and responsive. This reflects the needs and aspirations of the business and quite clearly requires a change in the *modus operandi* of most IT departments.

IT departments should also develop their equivalent of an organisation's values statements: those principles that guide the way they support the business. Pharmaceuticals company Eli Lilly established six principle to describe the IT environment they are trying to create to support the business.

It is important to remember that whilst responsibility for defining purpose and principles rests with the leaders of IT, it is a task that must involve the entire business. But changing purpose and establishing guiding principles are useless unless they are reflected in changes in the work that is done, and in the measures of success. Without this nothing really changes. A purpose statement such as 'operate a low-cost, efficient IT environment' suggests different work than a purpose statement such as 'develop a flexible and responsive infrastructure'. The priorities are different, as are the measures of success, for example the time to profit of a new product rather than return on IT investment. Most importantly, those activities considered to be central to meeting that purpose also differ. IT departments, as they shift from internally to externally focused purposes, must change their core work to reflect more closely the needs and aspirations of the business they serve.

Establish an Infrastructure for Change

I believe the core work of IT departments will increasingly be about building an environment and an infrastructure to facilitate the need businesses have to respond rapidly to a changing environment. The business cycle is speeding up, but to date there has not been a commensurate change in the IT development cycle. An IT manager I know in one financial services company does not believe an IT project of less than two years' duration can have any real value for the business. That sort of thinking, if allowed to perpetuate, locks the business into a response cycle of two years, during which time the industry may move on significantly.

The infrastructure puts into place the capability alluded to in the earlier examination of the relationship between computing and organisations. At its core is the concept of object orientation. Object orientation provides the best way for IT to deliver the level of flexibility and responsiveness that is needed to thrive in a rapidly changing environment.

Infrastructure is always worthy of extensive consideration because it is something that everybody needs but no single part of the business can afford. Imagine having to pay for the exchange and the lines every time you made a phone call. Infrastructure is an essential investment for an organisation. Just as the transport infrastructure of a country in large part determines its competitiveness and quality of life, so does the IT infrastructure of an organisation.

Focusing on infrastructure also highlights the difference between 'what' and 'how'. For years business managers have involved themselves in decisions about the base technology. This is understandable, given the sums of money involved, but all too often it has led to amateurs becoming involved in things they don't understand. Here again many organisations have turned to outsourcing to acquire flexibility and expertise. There are however limits to what can be outsourced, an issue to which I will return later in the chapter.

The infrastructure of the dynamic organisation will provide the following facilities:

- *Organisational model*: a model of how the organisation functions will be at the heart of the infrastructure. This model will be the repository of the organisation's current design and a workspace for those looking to improve aspects of the organisation. Using the model, people will be able to explore the complex interrelationships between different aspects of the organisation. With this capability the task of organisational design can be spread more broadly, which is essential for supporting a culture of continuous improvement.

- *Tool integration*: access to and interoperability of business and systems development tools. This capability, together with the organisational model referred to above, will move responsibility for the design and construction of business processes and systems much more into the domain of business managers.
- *Network services.* The facility required to move information and functionality around the organisation and to its customers, suppliers and partners. Easy and rapid access to information and functionality is essential. The network must support transactions, interpersonal and group communications and information searching. The network must be able to reach outside the organisation, making use of public networks such as the Internet to provide access to customers, suppliers and partners and provide people with the ability to work wherever the work is or wherever people prefer.
- *Access services.* The amount of available information has grown immensely but our ability to know what information and functionality is needed and where it can be found has not grown at the same pace. Tools to help identify and locate information will be essential in the dynamic organisation. The systems equivalent to an address book is only the starting point. Software that monitors information sources against a list of keywords is already available. Context-sensitive monitoring services and others that consider your preferences will be widely available in the next few years.
- *Security services.* A facility to say who can use what will need to cater for external access in order to support the concept of virtual organisations and customers' and suppliers' requirements for electronic commerce. This should be based on inclusion rather than on the 'need to know' basis of most existing approaches to security. Whilst providing security presents technological problems, a bigger problem is the shift of culture that most organisations will have to make. The 'information is power' syndrome still dominates many organisations.
- *Translation services.* As information is moved around systems much more, the infrastructure will need to be able to convert the information into the format the user (system or person) can use. The shift to object orientation will ease this, but the history of computing to date suggests that innovation and vendors' desire to develop proprietary solutions will always make some translation necessary.

This infrastructure has one aim: to allow the business to change when it needs to, according to a timetable it sets. This means not being constrained by the speed at which IT has traditionally worked. The infrastructure is focused on rapidly integrating different elements of data and functionality as and when they are needed. It is an infrastructure that reaches outside the organisation, because that is where customers, suppliers and partners are. It is very different from that which I have observed in most organisations.

Redefining Roles and Responsibilities

Fifty years ago, if a manager wanted to change a business process he considered how the work was being done and what changes were needed. He designed the new process, the forms and procedural manuals, the reports and the files. In today's world IT people and the business work together to design a system to perform all this although many organisations seem to have a strange definition of 'working together' if you look at how such projects actually run. The introduction of IT has led to the fragmentation of what was once the responsibility of the business manager alone.

The approach to computing described above will help reconnect these two activities. Many have tried to describe some of the changes we are experiencing by describing new roles and responsibilities for functions. The problem is that we need to break the functional mindset. Respected MIT Professor Venkatraman says IT departments will have to cease acting as service centres and become centres of business knowledge that understand how to take the lead in promoting investments that will generate new streams of profitable revenues. But such business knowledge already exists. Rather than seeking to own this knowledge, IT should be focusing on developing the infrastructure and tools to capture, share and develop it. As IT focuses on the infrastructure, a new role will emerge for users: application assemblers.

The shift towards becoming a dynamic organisation will involve those in the line taking much greater responsibility for the applications they use. They have to accept the responsibility they have always claimed to want: that of defining the functionality needed to do the job, just as it was before the advent of IT. It is true that some overzealous IT departments have sought to emasculate business people who, in their pompous view, were not competent to specify IT systems. It is equally true that too many business managers have not accepted their responsibility to develop the skills needed in the field of IT. Both will have to change if their

organisations are to thrive. This represents a significant shift in responsibilities. Using an electricity analogy, it is users who decide which
appliance to use based on their perception of what is best. The people
behind the socket merely insist that any appliance should meet certain
minimum standards to ensure it will function properly and will not
destroy the rest of the grid.

The National and Provincial Building Society's use of the Organisation
Design Facility puts it ahead of the field. In time, these models will
become a vehicle for managing the business. As the underpinning models
improve and become closer to reality, managers will find them invaluable
as the organisational equivalent of a spreadsheet, enabling them to do the
'what-ifs' of organisational design, and then to look at the implications of
the change and develop plans accordingly. The holistic nature of the
model means that this can be done without losing sight of how the change
will impact on the big picture.

Let me say now that this should not lead to total automation of the
organisational design process. Leo Cherne once said 'The computer is
incredibly fast, accurate and stupid. People are slow, inaccurate and
brilliant. The marriage of the two is a force beyond calculation'. As in
most marriages, the two partners are not equals. I believe that the
marriage with IT works best when people wear the pants. For too long
we have made people subservient to the needs of the computer. Computers are most effective when they are supporting people.

This reconnection of process and systems minimises the problem of
resistance faced by many projects using traditional IT development
methods. But there is another advantage. Because the focus is always
on what is needed to *support the people who do the work*, the benefits tend
to flow more quickly. This, coupled with aggressive reuse of existing
components, adds up to better returns on the investment. Indeed some
systems developed this way claim a payback period of days, and in one
case just four hours!

J. P. Morgan the international banking group, uses an information
system called Kapital for derivatives trading in New York.[15] Using
Kapital, traders can interact with the system and create a new financial
instrument, simulate its performance in terms of risk and profitability,
and, if satisfied, price and trade with it immediately. The software does
this by making available to traders fine-grain elements of financial
instruments that the trader can combine and recombine. Business rules
ensure compliance with key design parameters. The software is essentially
a database of objects together with a tool for manipulating them. Using
Kapital, traders can build an instrument in hours to meet the specific

needs of a customer. Kapital is one small example of what will become the norm.

A shift of this type will of course need a fundamental rethink of the competencies we require in both computer professionals and business managers. Business managers who currently boast about their lack of knowledge of and inability to use computers are foolish dinosaurs. Information technology has always been a part of business, and it always will be. Understanding the capabilities of technology requires some knowledge of that technology. The best drivers understand the rudiments of car technology. They might not be able to strip and change a gearbox, but they know what it is and how it works. IT is no different. This shift will also place much more importance on knowing the market and being creative in conceiving tailor-made solutions for increasingly smaller niches. These skills will be even more necessary for organisations at the sharp end of the service chain. Whilst customers might recognise that a number of suppliers are involved in delivering the package, they expect the organisation they are dealing with to know it all. Vertical integration, the vogue strategy of the early 1980s, has given way information integration and partnerships and alliances operating across a complex web of organisations. The IT approach described here is fundamental to this.

THE FIRST STEPS

Whilst the new technologies and ideas about how we can reconfigure our organisations develop in tandem, they are not perfectly parallel. Object technology is still in its infancy and it will take several years for it to become commonplace. Object development tools are available, but the market envisaged for business objects is very embryonic. Nonetheless, it will emerge. IT vendors are investing heavily in developing libraries of objects that they can tailor and sell to clients. This does not, however, mean waiting to take the ideas on board. Thinking in object and client-server terms already provides great benefits, and goes hand-in-hand with the people-centred approach described throughout this book. Techniques already exist to enable an old system to be manipulated as a series of objects. This alone allows a degree of flexibility that those systems do not inherently display.

There is no overnight solution to the problems that the traditional approach to information technology has left us with. The practice is still relatively new, and we are learning more each day. But the promise is great, supported as it is by some very significant successes. Nor is the approach described here the only answer. There will continue to be a place for large-scale greenfield developments. And client-server does not mean the death knell of the mainframe computer. Adopting this approach will begin the process of building the type of infrastructure needed if organisations are going to win the challenges of business.

There are a number of key stages along the path. The first is to foster a common view of the new paradigm of systems development in both the business and IT communities. Do not expect to instantly convert everyone – even Jesus Christ started with a very modest community of 12 disciples before tackling the world. Find the business managers who have been frustrated in their efforts to introduce change by the inertia of slow systems development. You will also need one or two converts in the IT department. If they don't exist, or cannot be created, do not worry; plenty of help is available in the outside world.

Using these disciples, identify projects where the business case is overwhelming. Look for projects where the problem is to integrate existing information and systems. Prime candidates are:

- Building up a comprehensive view of the customer from data held on disparate systems.
- Developing a system to support a reengineered process.
- Building a management information system.
- Integrating new technologies (for example image processing) with existing systems.

The next step is to acquire the right tools to do the job. Remember that in addition to the tools you will need to train people in their use. Some organisations choose to buy in the capability as a service package rather than develop the capability internally. Use a consultant to help you with initial projects but look to transfer the skills in-house as the projects develop. These are essential skills when building a dynamic organisation.

The initial project can probably be completed with just a few items of the rich toolkit available. Whilst the business case is the primary reason for choosing subsequent projects, look for those that will also allow you to acquire additional tools and skills.

This approach to developing systems will not deliver benefits if you follow the rule book for systems development found in most IT departments. The traditional approach of plan, design, build, test and (eventually) operate, and only then reap the return has been ossified in arcane systems development methodologies that are logically perfect but do not reflect the business pressure of speed and flexibility. Throw them out.

Put the people who have the problem together with the developers and charge them to come up with an answer that will show a measurable return within one month. When they have done that, move on to the next problem and ask them to deliver in three weeks. Work hard at building this group of people into a team. Do not allow organisational structures and politics to get in their way.

Many say that anything that can be developed in four weeks cannot be of any value. Not true. Many cases of caused by significant customer dissatisfaction are small irritations, for example having to wait while someone consults two or three different systems for the information needed to answer a query; or having to repeat a story because the organisation has not stored and shared the information previously given. Jan Carlzon, when writing about the turnaround of the airline SAS, said it was the 'thousands of moments of truth' when the customer meets the organisation that constitute service. Information in the right hands is essential if such moments of truth are to be a positive experience. Many of these problems can be addressed quickly.

When the project is completed, do not forget to measure the results. The measurement should be of the number of new customers won, the additional revenues generated from a new product, the increase in customer retention, or reduced cycle times. Following this approach has been very successful. Use your success to attract more disciples and build up more pressure for change.

The approach to IT described here is more than a way of building systems. It is an essential element of a different way of enabling change; a way that is gaining an increasing number of followers. This is not about managing change through a series of proscriptive and discrete steps. Rather it is about creating a view of how the world will operate and kicking off many smaller projects to bring about that new world. This paradigm sees organisations as much more like coral than buildings; following organic rather than mechanistic patterns of growth.

Client-server computing and service to customers share much more than a common language. The principles upon which both are based have much in common. Both make the customer the focus of their activities. Both recognise the need to support people in the work they are doing. Both accept the need for flexibility to address the constant pressure for change. Both seek continuous improvement. Like the art of service to customers, client-server is still evolving. Experience is still outweighed by intention. But just as focus on the customer has proved to be the most effective strategy for an organisation, so will client-server become the dominant strategy for computing.

This approach cannot be adopted by all organisations. Organisations that have not adopted the flexible approach to strategy described in Chapter 3 are unlikely to be able to adopt the approach to IT described here. The language set will not match. The cultures will clash. Measurement systems will get in the way. That of course is natural. Organisations are holistic, and the different elements have to be forged from the same set of ideas.

The US secretary of labor, Robert Reich, once said 'In the high-value enterprise, profits derive not from scale and volume but from the continuous discovery of new linkages between solutions and needs.' Client-server is computing's equivalent to Reich's high-value enterprises.[16]

PARTNERING

The well-oiled machine does not stop at the organisation's boundaries. No organisation can do everything itself. The most expensive item for most manufacturing companies is the purchase of goods and services. There is growing recognition that meeting customers' rising expectations means being the best at many things. We also know that an organisation cannot be an expert at everything. The pace of change makes it difficult to stay up to date with everything. This is one of the main reasons behind the growth of outsourcing.

Outsourcing, or partnering, can be a valuable way of reducing costs, and it can be a way of releasing management time to focus on the capabilities that are central to the organisation's success. Partnerships with other organisations that can add an advantage in these non-key areas therefore have a very important to role to play in the dynamic organisation. In addition to cost reduction, outsourcing or partnering can bring other advantages. Resources, both people and capital, can be freed for other activities, and preferential access to limited resources secured.

The dynamic organisation goes beyond these supply and cost related issues, which is not to say it does not recognise and exploit the value of them. Partnering is likely to be driven as much by adding value to the customer as it is by reducing costs. It is therefore a coherent part of the organisational design.

The process of choosing which activities to move to partners begins with the company's direction and the activities it considers essential to achieving that direction. The National and Provincial Building Society, as part of its organisational design, has categorised capabilities as 'distinguishing' or 'enabling'. A distinguishing capability is something that enables the organisation to differentiate itself from its competitors. Excelling at distinguishing capabilities puts clear water between the organisation and its competitors. An enabling capability is something that is essential to the smooth running of the organisation, but where being better than the competition only generates a 'so what?' response from customers. The National and Provincial decided its distinguishing capabilities were in two main areas. The first was the way it interfaced with its customers: giving advice and guidance, understanding requirements and providing the service itself. This did not include back-office processing. The second area was how it dealt with its people, the design of teams, processes and the development of competency. Payroll, facilities and catering are common examples of an organisation's enabling capabilities. Through the use of partnering to provide the enabling capabilities, the National and Provincial is seeking to benefit from other organisation's distinguishing capabilities.

This is not to say that all the elements of the distinguishing capabilities are conducted in-house. It does, however, guide the type of relationship they seek with a partner. Here unique solutions are important: 'me too' does not distinguish. The intellectual property of any development will remain with the buyer. Partners are selected because of their ability to add real value in the thinking as well as in the doing.

Many organisations have jumped into partnering or outsourcing with a singular focus on reducing costs, and had not fully thought through the implications of their actions. Some organisations have recently taken to outsourcing customer service, though interestingly enough many of them do not wish to be named. I find it strange, if not downright schizophrenic, that an organisation can on the one hand purport that 'customers are our greatest asset', and then seek to move a key point of contact with them to another organisation. How will they build relationships? How can they ensure they are picking up on customers' concerns, let alone their nuances and foibles? I remain to be convinced that this is anything but harmful. Losing the opportunity to learn is one of the dangers of partnering.

7 Dynamic Organisations: The Greater Context

Certain changes have been going on in business practice which are destined, I believe, to alter our thinking fundamentally. I think this is the contribution which business is going to make to the world and not only the business world, but eventually to government and international relations. Men may be making useful products, but beyond this, by helping solve the problems of human relations they are perhaps destined to lead the world in the solution of those great problems.

(Mary Parker Follett, 1933)[1]

Throughout this book I have shared my prejudices about how an organisation should be run. The dynamic organisation is one that operates with principles and beliefs, has a sense of purpose, a clear understanding of its customers, simple but effective processes and, above all, respect and concern for people.

> 'Those companies prosper most and are more clearly aligned with the fundamental role of business, that choose to serve society rather than abuse it.' (Rinaldo S. Brutuco)

But an organisation does not exist in isolation. It is part of the society from which it draws its customers and its people, be that local or global. An organisation cannot divorce itself from these things, although that is precisely what many have tried to do. Many organisations seem to operate in ways that put them at odds with the greater world. This cannot be blamed on a small number of tyrannical individuals, except in a few extreme cases. Talk to most senior managers and they are equally concerned about the environment, the loss of job security and the increasing divide between the haves and the have nots. Like most problems, the difficulties lie in the system. In this chapter I want to examine some of these issues. I do not have a stock of answers for the problems of the world, but hope that stimulating the debate will bring to the fore ideas and solutions.

Such issues are important for business managers simply because business is now the dominant form of organisation. Large corporations operate with budgets that are larger than the gross domestic product of many countries. They can create and axe jobs around the world, and governments are powerless to do anything. But organisations also wield a more significant, pervasive influence. Work is a central part of many people's lives. How they are treated at work influences how people feel about the world they live in, as well as the opposite being true. Leaders in dynamic organisations recognise this responsibility and take it into account in their decisions. That is not to say they do things simply on the basis of altruism. They do, however, look to balance the needs of the different stakeholders. I hope such leadership can be an example not just to other business leaders, but to the politicians who should be the guardians of society.

The World Business Academy has explored the role of business in society. In one of its publications,[2] it argues that business will emerge 'as the leader of society, accepting responsibility for the whole'. To fulfil this greater role, people in organisations will consider issues that are not currently the accepted domain of business. Social accounting will be widely practised, helping organisations take into account the social impact of their actions on the health of the planet and its people, as well as economic gain. We have already seen the emergence of organisations that develop policies to address environmental concerns. The damage a poor environmental policy can inflict has started the ball rolling, in the first stages, often to avoid a negative public reaction. The Body Shop has done far more than most in this area, and not as a defensive move. The entire organisation is founded on social responsibility. When it opened a new soap production plant in Glasgow it gave 25 per cent of the profits to the local community to improve the local area. The moral stance of the organisation has certainly not prevented it from growing, although it is not always the darling of the city. A headline in the magazine *Inc.* once said, 'This Woman is Changing Business Forever.' And the Body Shop is not alone. London Underground assesses projects to develop the underground rail network according to an approach known as social cost-benefit, which takes account of the broader social costs and benefits of the development when making investment decisions.

The dynamic organisation has moved from a command and control mentality to one that embraces the needs of its people. It is a meritocracy where people are valued for their ability to contribute and are encouraged to maximise their potential. The top management team spends a considerable amount of time developing the shared values and purpose of the organisation – developing a sense of community. Dynamic organisations actively canvass the views of non-customers to identify needs they are not addressing. In this group lies a rich vein of opportunity. Politicians have much to learn from the dynamic organisation.

> 'It is clear that the business community grasped the need to systematise its code of ethics much more quickly than the public sector in Britain.'   (Lord Nolan)

To succeed the dynamic organisation needs a thriving society. It is an active player in developing this, but it cannot do it alone. We need to change some of the policies of government. I cannot address these changes without first commenting on the role of culture and values – the centrepiece of the dynamic organisation. Our politicians seem to have lost this sense of value. This is not a party political point. I do not sense deep values in any party, here or abroad. There are examples of politicians extolling one set of values while practising others. To quote Henry David Thoreau again, 'I cannot hear your words for the actions which thunder above your head.' It is fascinating that the very people who should be guiding the country's principles have to wait for a crisis of confidence among their constituents before recognising the need for a shared set of values to guide their own behaviour. Unfortunately Lord Nolan's seven principles of public life,[3] innocuous though they seem, have simply served to highlight the lack of shared values among British political leader at the moment. This is not only a British disease. Italy, for example, has suffered far more turmoil than most in this respect. Lord Nolan's seven principles are reproduced below because they are also worthy of the consideration of leaders in private sector organisations:

- *Selflessness*: Holders of public office should take decisions solely in terms of the public interest. They should not do so in order to gain financial or other material benefit for themselves, their family or their friends.
- *Integrity*: Holders of public office should not place themselves under any financial or other obligation to outside individuals or organisations that might influence them in the performance of their official duties.

- *Objectivity*: In carrying out public business, including making public appointments, awarding contracts or recommending individuals for rewards and benefits, holders of public office should make choices on merit.
- *Accountability*: Holders of public office are accountable for their decisions and actions to the public and must submit themselves to whatever scrutiny is appropriate to their office.
- *Openness*: Holders of public office should be as open as possible about all the decisions and actions they take. They should give reasons for their decisions and restrict information only where public interest clearly demands.
- *Honesty*: Holders of public office have a duty to declare any private interests relating to their public duties and to take steps to resolve any conflicts arising in a way that protects the public interest.
- *Leadership*: Holders of public office should promote and support these principles by leadership and example.

There should be more debate in the country about the values of the society we are all a part of. The UK lacks a shared framework of values. We cannot even point to a poster on the wall, as the Americans can with their constitution. A discussion about the core values of the UK did begin to emerge recently, but it got lost in petty, party political sniping. Until we have that debate, generate those conversations, we will struggle to move forward. An organisation without vision and values is doomed to bump along from day to day. We certainly do not need to get 'back to basics'. We need to be creative, to look forward and do what is best for our children and grandchildren, not what worked for our grandparents.

Let us turn to more specific changes the dynamic organisation needs from government.

CHANGING EMPLOYMENT

As organisations seek greater flexibility and competitiveness, the structure of employment is changing. New work is being created, but much of this is part-time, and goes nowhere near replacing the jobs lost. One estimate suggests that Europe will have to create new jobs at the rate of 60 000 per hour between now and 2005 to keep track with those lost. Whilst some of this job loss is due to the misplaced focus on efficiency without growth, and to overseas competitors, many more have gone for ever as technology and innovation increase productivity.

We are shifting to an economy with a growing proportion of self-employed. To borrow a phrase from Star Trek, 'It's life Jim, but not as we know it.' Organisations are shifting towards Handy's shamrock organisation, discussed earlier, but unfortunately the mechanisms of state are not moving with it. Our taxation and welfare systems were designed to suit an economy where full employment meant that all those available for work could be found full-time, permanent jobs. That situation is never likely to return. We need to reexamine our definitions of employment and unemployment to suit the new world of work – a world that supports rather than penalises people who move in and out of work, and encourages lifetime learning (see below). Like any significant change, this will take boldness and courage. Organisations will have to participate in this change. Our employment packages are biased towards full-timers. Indeed some organisations constrain themselves from adopting flexible work patterns.

We need to develop a new form of national insurance to cater for people who are constantly in and out of work. If dynamic organisations truly want flexibility, then they must work in partnership with the state to develop new approaches for pensions, sickness and child care. This will require us to consider measures of performance that go beyond (for which do *not* read exclude) the economic factors. The dynamic organisation profits from being responsive and agile. It cannot do that if it is constrained by employment policies. On the one hand politicians expound the need for such flexibility, but the next day their officers harangue companies for reemploying workers on temporary contracts. When this is done by organisations just to avoid paying the state its rightful dues, such haranguing justifiable. But a number of organisations that have, with the agreement of their people, attempted to make a change to flexible working have been constrained from reemploying them in any way by Social Security regulations. As a result, both the organisations and the people who want to make this important shift are being prevented from doing so. This cannot continue.

LEARNING AND DEVELOPMENT

The dynamic organisation lives or dies by the skills, knowledge and behaviour of its people. The economic power of a country lies in its people. Economic growth and the development of people are inextricably linked. It is worrying therefore, that the UK is ranked twenty-fourth in the world league table for the contribution its people make to competitiveness.[4] Much of what we learn is experiential. Our skills, knowledge and behaviours go beyond formal qualifications, be they academic or vocational. When assessing candidates for an appointment, just consider how much time is spent trying to get to the person behind the CV. As workforce mobility increases, the workload will increase for both people and organisations. We have to be sure we are taking on people who can do what they say. There are a number of schemes around to address this. The development of National Vocational Qualifications is a plus. Interested parties are also active. The Confederation of British Industry has recently launched its Skills Passport; a mechanism for recording the ongoing development of people through formal and informal training. Campaign for Learning is a scheme launched by the Royal Society of the Arts to encourage learning throughout life. Success cannot be based on these initiatives alone, they must become part of our infrastructural fabric.

As mentioned in Chapter 5, the organisations that take the lead in providing for the ongoing development of the people they employ and help people to prove their learning to other organisations, are paradoxically most likely to create preferential access to the people they are equipping to be mobile. When security of employment no longer exists, loyalty will go to those organisations which can prove a clear commitment to the wider development of people.

DEVELOPING THE INFRASTRUCTURE

A change in the fundamental nature of the world, as the shift from the industrial to the knowledge era implies, brings changes to society. Many of these we are unable to perceive at this stage of events. One however is very clear. Full membership of society will depend on access to information. Ten years ago research for English or geography homework meant a trip to the school library, and occasionally the local library. My fourteen-year-old son's first port of call is a CD-ROM encyclopaedia, and then the Internet. However, the technology for this is only readily available to the better-offs. A recent study[5] examined the use of technologies to tap into the information superhighway (Table 7.1).

It is interesting to note that in all categories but computer games, use falls off lower down the social spectrum. This may be an educational issue, or it could be that consumer goods companies are better than computer vendors at reaching the broader audience. It will be interesting to see how this trend changes over time, change it must. While people are

Table 7.1   Regular use of IT by social group

| | Social Group | | | |
	AB	C1	C2	DE
Personal computers	59	40	37	19
Modem	26	13	15	3
Internet	14	11	3	4
Home computer games	24	20	22	24

denied access to something as fundamental as this important technology, we can never hope to develop the full potential of all those who want to participate in and contribute to society. And in my opinion that is the vast majority.

> 'I feel that mankind is entering a new age, and that the world is beginning to obey new laws and logic to which we have yet to adjust ourselves.'   (Mikhail Gorbachev)

The roots of the turnaround of many organisations that are now looked upon as leaders, lay in abject failure. These organisations have fundamentally changed the way they operate and have redesigned themselves from top to bottom. I believe the changes we are facing are of such a magnitude that nothing less than a fundamental reevaluation of the purpose, values and process of government is needed. Tinkering with what we already have would be akin to putting sticking plaster on top of a rotten bandage. The complexity of legislation is burdensome, both to the participants in society and the policy makers themselves. I am not arguing that the necessary protection of the disadvantaged members of society should be thrown away. We have to rise above the detail and ask fundamental questions, that is, what are the core values and beliefs that drive our country and what processes of management do we need to enact them? After that, let's leave it to people to get on with the job of building the country. Evidence from organisations suggests that is the route to success.

8 Change: Seven Sins, Seven Virtues

Success is never final, and failure is never fatal; it's courage that counts.

(Anon)

Let me begin this final chapter by quoting a definition of change drawn from my *Yorkshireman's Dictionary of Business Terms*:

Change, *chanj, v.t.* to alter or make different: to pass from one state to another. *V.i.* to suffer change. – *noun* the act of changing. Change management: the process of creating confusion and disillusion amongst an organisation's people: the latest money spinning venture of expensive consultants.
See also: pain, anguish, opportunity, redundancy, common-sense, life.

This book is about change in organisations, and as Macchiavelli pointed out, that is no easy task. But that does not mean it is a task we cannot perform. Part II will briefly describe a number of organisations that have succeeded. They are our beacons of light through the fog.

In this final chapter I want to summarise the do's and don'ts of change. They are the checklist to guide the actions needed to achieve change. They are the seven sins and seven virtues of change.

CIA SYNDROME

The first sin, the CIA syndrome, I have already described. Be under no illusion, it is our mindsets and attitudes to the outside world that are vital to the survival of our organisations. No matter how great your organisation, the world does not owe it or you a living. If you don't believe me, find an executive of PanAm and ask him or her.

SECRECY

Number two is about secrecy. People don't like surprises. They need time to assimilate ideas – particularly those that have an impact on them – directly or indirectly. Too many managers are afraid to leak any details of the change until all the 'i's have been dotted and 't's crossed. There are three problems with this.

The first is about who is keeping the secret. Typically it is senior managers – the people who staff the change team. The problem is that they often have an incomplete, sometimes downright inaccurate picture of the real world. They are making decisions about how the nitty gritty of the organisation should work but are not always best qualified to make those decisions.

The second problem is that secrecy, and the detailed planning that goes with it, does not leave space in the plans for people to contribute, and this is key to ownership and successful change – more on this later.

The third problem is that one system in the organisation always works very well: the grapevine. Most secrets leak out, or parts of them do. Then the grapevine takes over circulating and embellishing rumour and gossip. This often forces managers to make silly statements that they later regret.

I do recognise the need for secrecy in some circumstances. Often you cannot tell people about plans for acquisitions and mergers until they are consummated, otherwise the price goes up. The same is true of divestments. But the majority of organisational changes do not require secrecy. The fact that it exists is a function of the culture of most organisations, or more specifically of their management.

LOGIC RULES

> 'It seems that I have spent my entire time trying to make life more rational and that it was all wasted.' (A. J. Ayer)

My next two sins are very closely connected. The first is that of the rational manager. This is the person who *can* prove that logic is better than sex! Many managers are natural planners, they love charts and diagrams that show what happens next. They are enraptured by methodologies that cover every step of the way.

They make some fundamental mistakes. Plans shape actions, which shape outcomes, which shape plans. The world is not linear, it is recursive. Cause and effect is often cause and cause, and effect is nowhere to be seen, except over a distant horizon. The main elements of any change – people – are not logical. We are emotional, irrational, inspirational, condescending, cynical. And these characteristics shape our thoughts and actions. We have preconceived views of people, we know that what they are going to say is rubbish before they say it – we just know it.

How does logic cater for that? It can't. And that brings me to my next sin.

THE ULTIMATE PLAN

This is the sin of the zealot planner, and there are plenty about. They are the high priests of our traditional approaches to planning. If you look at many approaches to planning they follow a similar 'plan, design, implement and manage' cycle. This is true of traditional strategic planning and software development methodologies, and is true of many of the change management processes being touted by consultants. It is based on the fallacious belief that you can plan a change in detail at the beginning, and then expect everything to run to plan.

A very successful director in a company I worked for had a simple rule: no action should be taken if it cannot produce some results in 90 days. This leads people away from interminably long planning cycles into action, and it is action that produces change.

Plans don't leave space for people to make their own unique contribution, that act which allows someone to say, even if just to themselves, 'See that; I did that'. The problem with the planning zealots is that they have not woken up to the fact that the reason for their plans – change – is no respecter of plans. Change is a malicious beast. As soon as you set a plan, along he comes and throws a spanner in the works. Of course, many believe that once they have been signed off with commitments, deliverables and resource allocations plans can't change. So a system to control the change management plan is needed. And before you know it, the planning task is greater than the doing task. But of course the planners love that, it makes them more important. Today the plan, tomorrow the world!

PARALLEL ORGANISATIONS

Some organisations seeking change set up a special full-time change team. They provide the resources and send the team away to come up with the change plan. The problem with this approach is that it divorces change from the real powerbase of the organisation: line management.

As I have already argued, change is a deeply political activity. Separate groups foster secrecy, often only perceived, but nonetheless real. These parallel organisations, divorced from the powerbase, do their blue sky thinking while the rest of the organisation gets on with real work. The groups are treated with suspicion, people are wary of the information they supply to them. They distrust their motives, no matter how well-intentioned. Communication is often obscured by a search for the hidden agenda, even though it often does not exist.

We see this phenomenon played out in the news. The European Commission, a parallel organisation if ever there was one, holds itself up as the agent of change in Europe. Yet we all know that the real change is brought about in meetings between Chancellor Kohl and President Chirac, and between President Chirac and Prime Minister Major. But they still act out the play. They have to – as the people who helped form the institutions, they cannot be seen to be undermining them.

THE EASY OPTION

Change is not a comfort zone, as anyone who has been involved knows. Yet too many managers fail to face up to their responsibilities. They know that something has to be done, but fail to step up to the mark. There is a saying 'Don't worry, things can't get worse. So I stopped worrying and things did get worse.' Many sinners know that to their cost.

Change demands realism, and that starts with numbers. A company I worked for, Digital, underwent huge change because it had to. It shed 70 000 workers during several years of cuts, a classic case of corporate anorexia. It was clear to anyone who could do a couple of simple calculations on the back of a cigarette packet that the organisation was either grossly overstaffed or under selling, simple sales per person pointed that out. The company got into a mess because it failed to face up to reality. It ignored the PC market because that did not fit its paradigm of computing. It ignored Unix because that threatened its revenue base from proprietary systems. Both these markets were growing rapidly, and customers were demanding the products. But addressing them would have meant taking difficult decisions. It would have meant killing the existing money spinners and relegating the existing heroes. It would have required change. Instead Digital pooh-poohed the PC and called Unix 'snake oil'. Instead of controlling its change, it stepped away from difficult decisions and led itself into a major crisis, from which it has still not fully recovered.

IGNORE PEOPLE

I have saved until last the biggest and most deadly of the seven deadly sins. Change is about people, but so often the individual needs of people are ignored. Many think change is about shuffling boxes on an organisational chart. This is an age-old problem. 'We trained hard but every time we were beginning to form up into teams, we would be reorganised. I was to learn later in life that we tend to meet any new situation by reorganising and a wonderful method it is for creating the illusion of progress while producing inefficiency and demoralisation.' Those words were spoken by Gaius Petronius, a Roman centurion in 200 BC. How little has changed; how little we have learned.

People are the real challenge of change, not boxes on a chart. They are also the real opportunity. Just look at what they do in their own time. They are school governors, sports coaches, amateur actors or producers. They have hobbies that demand great skill and creativity. They manage money, they manage their careers and their lives, taking decisions that are complex and far reaching. Their talents are endless, so how come we treat them as children? Change badly managed ignores people as people.

So there are my seven deadly sins. You can doubtless think of another seven – probably from bitter experience. It would be unfair to leave you with just the bad news, so here are my seven virtues – my pointers to success. Again it is my personal list, based on my experience of helping a number of organisations with significant change activities and having lived through a number of major changes.

APPROACHES TO CHANGE

The first rule is to recognise that, like the truth, change is a multifaceted thing. There is no one way to manage change, because there is no single change. I have found a little threesome, given to me by Peter Moyes, a former colleague, to be very helpful: change to, change with and change by.

Change to is to be used in those situations where a serious crisis is in train and fast action is needed. If the ship is sinking, the last thing to do is call a meeting to discuss the situation. You need someone who will quickly take stock of the situation, and then issue instructions about what is to be done, by whom, and when. This is the fastest form of change and, given the power, the easiest to implement. It is also the most predominant form of change, whether the situation calls for it or not. The problem with this approach is that people quickly tire of it. They become demoralised and obstructive because it does not provide them with the opportunity to make a meaningful contribution. It will remain the preferred form of change management for incompetent, autocratic managing dinosaurs.

Change with is again management led, but this time it fosters greater involvement. Managers set the goals but leave more opportunity for others to determine how the change will be implemented. Managers operating in this mode are actively involved in the change. They chair regular progress meetings and retain control of key decisions.

Change by is, for many, the holy grail of change. This is where people take the initiative and institute change for themselves. They decide what is to be done and how it is to be implemented. It is 'change by' that underpins organisations that are building continuous improvement cultures. How far this approach to change can be allowed to go is a subject of much debate. Perhaps the best analysis was provided by Bill Gore when he talked about his staff initiating changes to the organisation, which he likened to a ship. He commented that he did not mind about the changes they made to the superstructure, 'but when they start drilling below the waterline, they sure as hell had better take good advice'. He did not prohibit drilling below the waterline, but sought to encourage self-discipline, a sense of shared responsibility to go with it.

Dynamic organisations will continue to use all three approaches to change. What differentiates them, however, is mix. The dynamic organisation has more 'change by' and 'change with', recognising the confidence and trust it has in its people, and knowing that the organisation's vision and values and the coaching skills of leaders will see it through most situations.

VISION AND VALUES

The second lesson is to work hard at creating a vision of the change. Vision is about creating direction. It is about building a clear and shared picture of what the world will be like in the future. People who are good at managing change spend time with people, with all the constituencies affected, not just the managers, in describing what the new world will be like. They paint a realistic picture, but focus on the good things. They encourage people to see themselves in the new world, and to add their own detail, to build their own vision.

Values guide the behaviours people should use to achieve the change, indeed the behaviours they should use in work generally. Real organisational values are not abstract concepts on a wall. They are interpreted by people throughout the organisation and manifest themselves in the everyday behaviours and measures people adopt and the processes they use. Values are what make an organisation customer-focused, people-friendly, results-oriented. Organisations that excel at change work hard at the values level.

As organisations are flattened and change becomes less and less of a special event, new mechanisms are needed to guide. Visions and values are being adopted by progressive organisations as the mechanism to replace detailed planning for change.

FOCUS AND CLARITY

Here is a paradox. To be successful, change has to address a broad range of factors in the organisation: work, values, rewards, processes, technology, measurement. But despite this, if people are unclear about the change that is required, it will fail. For this reason successful change has a clear focus. Some use the latest fad, such as business process reengineering or total quality management and wrap everything in that. The more successful choose to focus on a more noble cause: increasing customer focus or building an organisation where people enjoy their work. The value of a focus of this kind is that it isnaturally holistic; it cannot be answered by a single approach.

Such seemingly altruistic foci for change are also dynamic: the goal-posts constantly change, setting new challenges for the organisation. There is no natural end point to them. But despite the constant change, the focus – the reason for the change – remains constant. In this way change is not change, it is a continuation of a theme. It is the next step on a known journey. Providing some continuity is important, people get nervous and uneasy if they have nothing to hang on to. Providing a dynamic focus is a powerful mechanism for change and continuous improvement.

To be effective the focus must be crystal clear. If change cannot be simply expressed, it is less likely to succeed. It is a true skill to be able to distill a complex situation into a simple idea. By this, do not confuse simple with simplistic. Let me give you an example. When Arthur Large took over the RAC Motoring Services, he set the context of change in a phrase expressed from the viewpoint of a stranded motorist – their key customer. It was simply 'Getting through, getting there, getting moving.' That short, simple phrase embodied a change of huge proportions, but throughout it all it acted as a guiding light. Distilling the essence of the change requires depth of thinking. (See the RAC case study in Part II.) Too many organisations fail to think rigorously through their intent and end up with woolly-minded phrases that have no real meaning.

INVOLVEMENT

Change is about people and people only change if they want to. Everyone resists change – or so the saying goes. But we all accept change, indeed we all have changed. We don't resist change – we resist being changed. Change we initiate is welcomed.

That being so, we have to find ways of involving people in change that give them the opportunity to shape their own worlds. This is not about handing over the asylum to the inmates, as some people put it. Most people are responsible and simply want to play a valued and challenging role at work.

For me, this is what empowerment is about, – the freedom to act based on the knowledge that doing so has the support of the organisation. In turn this requires individuals to exercise a greater degree of self-discipline. This can be done by managers leaving space for people to play their part. David Kirk, captain of the All Blacks and adviser to the New Zealand prime minister, once said 'The leader's job is to set the direction and get out of the way.' He added that most managers fail to get out of the way. Peter Wickens provides excellent advice[1] for people who want to foster involvement: 'JUST DO IT.'

LEADERSHIP

Leadership lies at the heart of change and is very different from management. By leadership I mean the skills of building shared visions, generating commitment, managing conflict. Whoever heard of a world manager or a religious manager? World leader, yes.

Most of us can remember the pleasure of working for someone we really liked and respected. We can also recall the pain of working for a prat. The difference is immense; the difference is leadership. Good leaders have certain characteristics. They communicate much more, and by communicate I mean listen much more than speak. They are confident of their ideas, their vision of the world, but not so confident that they cannot spot someone else's good idea. Indeed they build shared visions through dialogue, not through presentations. These people understand that part of their work, an important part, is conversation. They converse with a broad caucus. They seek out alternative and even conflicting viewpoints, so that they can improve both the content and the presentation of their vision.

Above all, leaders act. So many so-called leaders confuse their audiences because their actions thunder loudly above their words. Real leaders have these two in sync. Leaders also recognise that leadership of change can be a lonely task. Leaders do not plan to be liked, although they are often highly respected.

The final thing about leaders is that they do not have to be at the top of organisations. Indeed the organisations that win tomorrow will be those that develop leaders across the organisation. You can be a leader.

COMPASSION

Whilst it is not always the case, many changes involve some people getting hurt. Change can involve loss of status, uncertainty or loss of jobs. Dealing with this with compassion is important, not just for those who are directly affected by it, but also for those who survive or benefit. It is well documented that those who survive redundancy often feel demoralised and guilty that they have survived when others have suffered.

By compassion I do not mean being a soft touch. Compassion is about not putting off what everyone knows needs to be done – grasping the nettle. Too often people put off difficult decisions. Sometimes this is in the misplaced belief that the problem will go away, but often it is a fear of acting. A compassionate manager is open, honest and frank, holding the best interests of the future of the organisation to the fore, but fighting for fair play for those who loose out as a result of the change. A good change manager (leader) is like a skilled surgeon. When performing an operation the skilled surgeon is not tentative. The cut is deep and true. But once the operation is complete, the surgeon turns physician. He or she counsels, motivating the patient to become well. Healing becomes the order of the day.

Compassion is also about considering the individual and adapting the standard process to suit his or her needs. Equally, it ensures fair play.

FOCUS ON RESULTS

Change comes when people do different things differently. The sooner that starts, the sooner change can be seen to be working. Good leaders focus people on providing results. Whilst communicating widely, they avoid all-in, 'sheep dip' communication. They help different parts of the organisation to focus on specific, challenging and measurable results, and then help them achieve those results. These results give confidence, make the sceptic's life more difficult and deliver the returns needed to fund the next round of changes.

Change managers have access to a rich toolkit, though many are ignorant of its contents. There are tools to help leadership teams create visions, tools to profile organisational culture, action learning sets to foster involvement in the change process, measurement techniques that link change goals to day-to-day operations. The list is a long one.

AND FINALLY

Some people talk of mastering change: I am not sure that is ever the case. We can all improve our ability to manage change. Leading change is perhaps what we should strive to excel at.

I have a saying: 'If you can keep your head when all about you are losing theirs . . . you haven't grasped the reality of the mess you're in.' Steve Rothmeir, former chief executive officer of Northwest Airlines, said of change:

> I thought it beat any Indiana Jones movie. The change effort starts out with a real nice beginning, and then suddenly you get one disaster after another. The boulder just misses you and you get a snake in the cockpit of the airplane. That's what it's all about. You've got to be down in the blood and the mud and the beer.

Don't despair. Life is messy. Any attempt to change that basic fact is doomed to failure. It is better to direct your energy towards improving your ability to deal with it when it inevitably comes. That is perhaps what separates the winners from the also-rans.

> 'Our greatest glory is not in never falling, but in rising every time we fall.' (Confucius)

Part II

Dynamic Organisations in Action

Introduction to Part II

In my studies and work, I have come across a number of organisations that display the characteristics of what I call a dynamic organisation. A number of these have already been documented. Hannover Insurance in the US is referred to constantly in Peter Senge's *The Fifth Discipline* (1990). The outstanding story of how Jack Welch has led General Electric is told in *Control your destiny or someone else will* by Noel Tichy and Stratford Sherman (1993).

I have selected the following organisations because they are exemplars of the dynamic organisation. Not all the organisations display all the characteristics I have described in the book. Nonetheless they are all doing excellent things. Some of the cases are the result of recent turn-arounds. Others have been successful for a long time.

In presenting these exemplars I gratefully acknowledge the help and support people have given me. Despite their busy schedules they have found time to talk to me, to let me visit them and to review the drafts of my material. I have learned much from them. My very sincere thanks go to the following: Lesley Colyer and Alun Cathcart of Avis Europe Ltd; John Hughes, John Rodgers and Tony McGarahan of the Birmingham Midshires Building Society; Douglas Cowieson of Cigna Healthcare; Denis Klecha and John Patrick of Disneyland Paris; Frank Schaper of KLM; Paul Chapman, Graham Russell and Dick Powell of the National and Provincial Building Society; and Frank Richardson and Ron Hewitt of RAC Motoring Services Ltd, both of whom have subsequently moved on.

I am sure these people would also want me to acknowledge the excellent work done by all their colleagues. In winning organisations such as these, it is refreshing to see the depth of quality of the people working for them. I might add that most organisations are equally blessed. Their managers just haven't realised it yet.

Because of the outstanding things these organisations have done, they regularly appear at conferences and seminars. If you get the chance to listen to them, take it. They have much to share. But consider the words of a Japanese manager I met when visiting Japan. When asked why the Japanese are so willing to share secrets of success, he replied 'We are already years ahead of you, and we are continuing our efforts to improve.

And anyway, we are not convinced you will do anything about it'. But remember, whilst there is much to learn, copying is not the thing to do. There is no real learning in copying. Listen and learn and then build that learning into a culture and system that suits your organisation. Every organisation is different and there is no single model of success. Only in this way will you build an organisation that is both dynamic and sustainable.

9　Avis Europe

When looking for organisations to illustrate the points raised in the book, my first choice was Avis Europe. I have followed events at Avis for almost ten years now, and everytime I meet an Avis representative, there is more to learn. The organisations in this section are listed alphabetically, but it is appropriate that Avis comes first. In my opinion it can claim to be one of the best managed companies in the world.

Avis Europe Ltd is the leader in the rent-a-car business in Europe whether measured by market share, profitability, customer satisfaction or outlet locations. Formed in 1965, it separated from its former owner, Avis Inc., in 1986. Avis Inc. was started in 1946 by Warren Avis with three cars at Willow Run Airport, Detroit. The two companies still cooperate very closely. A common reservation system, a single, global image and coordination of marketing activities ensures that the customer sees a single public face. This is backed up by extensive joint working, from cross-membership of the two companies boards (Avis Inc. holds just over 8.7 per cent of Avis Europe's holding company), shared problem-solving teams and regular, on-going contact between staff.

Avis Europe is represented in 96 countries in Europe, the Middle East and Africa through a combination of wholly owned subsidiaries, licensees and joint ventures, delivering a consistent and recognisable service from over 2700 locations.

The story of Avis's success can be summed up in three very famous words: 'We try harder.' This phrase lies at the heart of what is one of the most powerful organisational cultures I have seen.

Avis's current success can be traced back to 1962 when, following 15 years of unbroken losses, Robert Townsend took over the company, three years before Avis established a presence in Europe. Townsend asked an advertising agency, Doyle Dane Bernbach, to create advertisements that would have the same impact as those of Avis's larger competitor (Hertz), but at a fifth of the price. The agency spent 90 days looking for a positive difference between Avis and its competitors. It could find nothing, other than its employees: they seemed to try harder. That comment became the centrepiece of a long-term advertising campaign and 'We try harder' is now one of the ten most famous advertising slogans of all times. It recognised, honestly, that Avis was 'number two', not the biggest, but it was striving to be the best. The advertisements focused on the essentials of car rental service: clean, new, reliable cars, full fuel tanks, heaters that work and so on. But the advertisements also stressed that being number two meant Avis could not take customers for granted, and would try harder to make sure they returned.

Townsend put a copy of each advertisement into every pay packet before it was launched to the public, letting its people know in advance what the company was promising its customers. The standard was set. In 1963 Avis produced an advertisement that asked customers to complain if they found something wrong, saying 'It's for our own good', adding 'Our people will understand. They've been briefed.'

Setting standards in such a public way and generating enthusiasm has been done by many companies in the short term. But Avis has kept this going for over 30 years and has maintained market leadership since 1973. How? Avis Europe has built continuous improvement into its culture. It is so deeply embedded, that it is sometimes difficult to see. There is no explicit process for much of what Avis does – it has succeeded in making the continuous change process implicit. It does it naturally, anything else is alien – 'How could you run a company any other way?' is its natural reaction. This is the deep seam of the Avis culture coming to the fore. It is the bedrock of its success. If culture is the bedrock, training, measurement, information systems and recognition are the building blocks of Avis's excellence.

VISION, VALUES AND LEADERSHIP

But what of direction? Avis is an excellent example of the concept of visions as conversations. Avis entered Europe with the vision of building the best and fastest-growing car rental business. That vision has not changed for over 30 years. It is not surprising then that each and every employee is clear about what the company is trying to achieve. This vision has driven what Avis does with its people, its network of outlets and its technology. This vision, and its very strong culture, has resulted in a consistency of approach, irrespective of changing political and economic circumstances. The company did not pull out of South Africa, indeed, it expanded its operations while ensuring that its culture of equality and fair play was reflected in the employment practices of the South African operation.

The company has a business planning process that matches its empowering culture. The group sets out guidelines for achievement, covering people, customer satisfaction, revenue growth and financing. These guidelines are used by local management teams to construct their annual plans. The group has yet to reject a plan submitted by a country management team. Annual planning is supplemented by *ad hoc* profit improvement plans (PIPs). A rolling list of PIPs is maintained, some of which are group-wide projects, others local. Staff from any part of the organisation can suggest areas for a PIP to address. The PIP approach cascades to all levels of the organisation, and is one mechanism by which the company ensures continuous improvement.

Of paramount importance to the people in Avis is the way they do business – their values (see below). I have yet to see an organisation where the values and culture are so clearly understood and lived. Any conversation you have with someone at Avis will at some time turn to their culture. Below is the statement of beliefs and values that is issued to every member of the Avis staff and to many customers and suppliers.

Compared with many statements of values and beliefs, this is comprehensive. It was not, however, the result of a series of workshops and meetings. The initial draft was based on material that was 'around the company'. The culture existed long before it was written down. When the existing material was collected, it seemed perfect for the business Avis has now and wants to continue to have. When I asked about how the values are tested to ensure they remain appropriate, I was told that the values are 'so fundamental, we believe them to be timeless.' I do not disagree.

The focus of the culture is people – customers, staff, business partners and the public at large. 'We try harder' is no longer a recognition that Avis is number two, but the essence of the need to out-innovate the competition and retain that hard-won leadership position. Avis's devolved culture, recognises that this can only be done by tapping into the creativity and enthusiasm of everyone, but also that innovation, at the point where the company meets the customer, is perhaps the most important form of innovation for a company whose strategy is customer retention.

The company's values are visible in a number of ways, as the rest of this case study will show.

PROCESS OF MANAGEMENT

A key part of the organisational culture of Avis Europe is the trust managers place in their people. This can only be realised in an organisation that is decentralised and has a high degree of local autonomy. This

AVIS Europe

The following statements encapsulate our beliefs and values and our approach to doing business throughout our operating territories

Business ethics

We believe it is in the interest of our shareholders, our customers and our employees that we maintain a highly acceptable public image supporting a progressively profitable company. Honesty, integrity and fairness in dealings must and will be absolute and an integral basis of our total philosophy.

Customers

We believe in providing consistently high standards of integrity, service, quality and value in satisfying customer needs. This operating ethos maintains our industry leadership and retains the loyalty and respect of our customers.

Employees

We aim to stimulate duty, mutual loyalty and a sense of pride in working for Avis through employee involvement at all levels, continuous updating of knowledge and skills and attractive and competitive recognition and reward systems. We believe that employees should be actively encouraged to grow and develop their careers with Avis and we always seek first to appoint candidates from within the Company to fill positions at every level - both nationally and internationally. To this end, we will provide the environment to help employees improve and develop themselves.

Management and Leadership

We believe in local autonomy, working within broad guidelines and underpinned by strong support services at the centre. We are committed to professionalism in leadership; clear direction, clear team work development, clear communication, clear and sensibly quick and consistent decisions based on 'what' is right rather than 'who' is right. We recognise that excellence and professionalism amongst Avis management and employees is a key marketing tool. It gives customers confidence and competitors an inferiority complex.

'We try harder.' Ethos

We believe that sustainable competitive advantage comes from our ability to continuously innovate ahead of the competition. In achieving this we look for continuous improvement, no matter how small, in every thing we do and at the same time quantum improvement in the way we do business. We will never hesitate to adapt to new and more profitable ways of working provided that the integrity and honesty we apply to our business is not compromised. We actively encourage a 'try harder' and 'can do' mentality and operate a climate of TRUST at all levels. The only mistake is not to try something.

Community

We operate as responsible members of the community and within the laws of the countries within which we do business. We recognise and respect the attitudes, characteristics and customs of local populations.

Environment

We recognise our corporate responsibility to the community at large for public health and safety and environmental protection. We fully comply with all legislation in this respect and actively pursue environmental and safety initiatives on a local, industry wide and global basis.

Suppliers

We ensure integrity and professionalism in all dealings with suppliers and expect the same in return. We seek economic quality and efficiency of service in all supplier relationships and, where possible, 'added value' to the mutual benefit of both. We continuously foster strategic alliances and partnerships with major travel industry organisations who share a mutual respect of the customer, a commitment to quality and a desire to maximise and enhance the reputation and value of the brand.

Costs

We regard efficiency as central to our whole business philosophy and we continuously search for means to reduce the cost of delivering a better product for the customer.

Avis Europe corporate beliefs and values

local autonomy of course has to be balanced with the need to provide a consistent brand and level of service across all operating locations. Again culture counts, as Alun Cathcart, Avis Europe's chief executive officer, explained: 'We do not do this by policy manuals and rule books but through a system bound together by a common vision of Avis's beliefs and values and a simple charter of operating principles in each of the markets in which we operate.'

The local operating units are supported by services provided centrally. Avis Management Services (AMS), the headquarters of the Avis Europe Group, combines corporate leadership with specialist support functions: marketing and sales, operations, personnel, finance and IT. AMS provides policy determination and strategic direction; setting objectives and priorities. The group managers spend much of their time coordinating the constituent parts of the group, a metaphor for encouraging shared learning and cooperation. Indeed the group acts much more like a consultancy operation than a typical group organisation. Strength of leadership comes from the ability of the management team to coordinate, encourage and guide rather than direct. AMS takes the lead on negotiations and relationships that cross national boundaries, with customers, suppliers and other partners.

Avis works through six key organisational and management processes that are aligned to its strategy of customer retention and empowerment of staff (Figure 9.1). The six paired processes are:

- Goals and practices: providing direction.
- Rewards and expectations: providing motivation.
- Feedback and modelling: providing guidance.

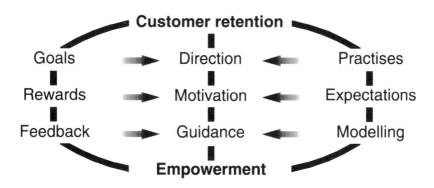

Figure 9.1 Avis organisational processes[1]

The model reflects the Avis value of simplicity and the link, through the actions of management, between customer retention and empowerment.

Goals and Practices

Management sets direction by what it measures and what it pays attention to. One of the most important ways of reinforcing behaviours and encouraging certain actions is through measurement. At Avis, measurement starts with the customer, integrating the results into the management of the organisation. Data on customer satisfaction (see below) are sent to each location, not just as a set of numbers but as individual customer scores and comments, together with the rental agreement number. By enabling the team to compare actual feedback with their records of the transaction, they can identify the actions and circumstances that were responsible for the specific customer feedback. Where appropriate, corrective action follows.

Rewards and Expectations

Expectation setting begins with recruitment. Avis focuses on hiring people who are entrepreneurial by nature – responsible risk takers who thrive in an environment of minimal constraint within the broad framework of the Avis culture. Above all, Avis hires people who like people. Recruitment is the first process in inculcating the Avis culture, as the advertisement opposite shows.

The service and 'We try harder' ethic is the focus of an induction programme that is competency based, with a strong emphasis on organisational understanding: the Avis culture. Clarity is a key competence in Avis; clarity not only of the employees' own role, but also of how that interrelates with others and with achieving the company's vision. It is what Avis calls 'cathedral vision'. Cathedral vision is based on a story of two stonecutters told by Jan Carlzon, a former chief executive officer of the airline SAS and author of *Moments of Truth*. Both were doing exactly the same job, chipping way at a block of stone. The first was unhappy, and when asked why he replied 'So would you, sitting here day in, day out chipping away at a block of stone.' The second was very happy and explained 'Because this stone I am chipping is part of that cathedral over there.' Cathedral vision is the key to sustainable empowerment. It provides a greater context for daily work. This is one of the reasons why the Avis Rental Sales Agent Development Programme, the front-line induction programme, takes 18 months to complete. It encompasses a

broad-based understanding of the dynamics of the car rental business and the implications of the participants' performance and behaviour to the overall success of the business.

Avis operates a range of mechanisms for achievement, emphasising customer satisfaction and retention, both on an individual and a team basis. 'Spirit of Avis' is a recognition programme that can be initiated by colleagues, suppliers and of course customers. An award is given to those who do something that demonstrates the values in action. Each nomination is a recognition in itself, but to encourage continuing performance, the nominations are cumulative, leading to bronze, silver and finally a gold award that is issued personally by the chairman. Team recognition programmes include awards for those locations scoring the highest in customer satisfaction and for the most improved location in a given period. These schemes are designed by the people themselves, not handed down from on high.

The importance of keeping pressure on costs is fostered through an award scheme called PIPS: Positive Ideas – Profitable Solutions. This award is given for employee suggestions that simplify procedures, reduce errors, improve quality, reduce costs or increase safety. The information on these improvements is shared across the group, thus promoting learning and generating further improvements in performance.

Feedback and Modelling

The final set of organisational processes relates to feedback and modelling – management gives guidance through feedback and the way the managers behave. Whilst the ultimate feedback is from the customer, managers can encourage and guide through the things they do and say.

Feedback in Avis is a two-way process. Employee satisfaction is monitored as rigorously as customer satisfaction. An annual survey embracing all employees measures satisfaction against 28 attributes that Avis believes are essential to the delivery of excellent customer service. Naturally, a commitment to satisfying external customers is included. Other areas explored include: 'friendliness of fellow employees', 'effectiveness of your team', 'management behaviour', 'the company's commitment to its employees', 'quality of relationship with your manager' and, of course, 'job satisfaction'. Like customer satisfaction, data from the surveys is fed to countries, functional teams and directly to employees, and is used to drive continuous improvement initiatives. Internal and external benchmarking fosters more learning and improvement.

One of the key processes at Avis Europe is 'visible management', part of Avis's operations for 25 years. Every manager, including the chairman, spends at least three days a year serving customers and working with employees at the grass roots of the business. In addition, senior managers spend the vast majority of their time away from their offices: at the rental stations, with customers and key suppliers. In all these activities they use every opportunity to reinforce the company's values.

Business measurement at Avis is based on a scorecard that reflects the operational as well the financial aspects of the business. Two key review forums are the 'key issues and strategy' meetings and the 'business review team'. The key issues and strategy meeting (KISM) is a fortnightly meeting of the group's senior managers. The title tells it all, except to make clear that in Avis the key issues are people, suppliers and customers as well as financial performance. The KISM team members are also members of the business review team, which includes the regional managers. This monthly forum focuses on what is happening in the environment and what action is needed. It is also the group's main forum for generating policy and monitors the profit improvement plans. Through this broad involvement in strategy, the group ensures that the strategy is relevant to the business as well as generating the level of personal commitment and ownership that is essential to the success of any change.

UNDERSTANDING CUSTOMERS

As indicated above, the basis of Avis's success is an in-depth understanding of the needs and aspirations of its customers and how the company is doing in meeting those needs. The company uses three mechanisms for understanding its customers: surveys, enquiries, and complaints, and meetings with staff and management.

Avis Europe has one of the most extensive systems for measuring customers' reactions to the service they have received. Each month over 12 000 customers are selected at random from among those who have rented a car in the previous month. These customers are sent a questionnaire and asked to record the level of satisfaction they received from Avis's people, quality of the vehicle and administration. They are also asked to express their overall satisfaction and how likely they are to use the service again. The questionnaire is linked to a specific rental agreement. Questions are therefore about service on a particular occasion, rather than general questions about service. This ability to link feedback to a specific event makes root cause analysis and improvement easier to effect.

The analysis produces a series of reports that start at board level and are used throughout the organisation. Each location receives regular feedback, including the specific comments of customers. Using the Wizard system (see below) the local teams can see the rental details and compare the individual customer scores and comments. This provides a strong learning opportunity by identifying what likely actions, circumstances or behaviours were responsible for the specific customer feedback. Learning across the organisation is encouraged by comparing performance between countries, districts and rental stations.

Customer feedback is not just used by the operations function. Marketing personnel are able to monitor satisfaction by product, day of the week, location and nationality, enabling improvements in product development. The fleet function is able to monitor satisfaction by make and model, data which is used to guide fleet purchasing decisions and is also made available to vehicle manufacturers to improve design and model acceptability. The training and customer service functions use the data to identify where changes are needed to procedures and what new skills and knowledge are needed by staff.

Major customers also receive reports on customer satisfaction for the activities covered by their contracts. This is a powerful way of demonstrating the standards of service being achieved, and is used jointly to agree new targets. This process forms a key part of contract negotiation and acts as a powerful tool both to demonstrate that service standards are being achieved and to agree service guarantees, with penalties for non-performance. This visibility of service quality standards is a major source of advantage and enhances the relationship between Avis and its major customers, thus aiding retention. To date no customer has invoked the penalty.

Any contact between Avis and the customer is logged into a comprehensive contact management system, available to all Avis locations across Europe. The contact is coded to identify the type of contact – for example complaint and enquiry – and is followed through to resolution. This information is disseminated to the local level together with, when appropriate, the rental details. The local team can then take appropriate action. This is another example of a process that reflects the decentralised nature of the organisation as well as a recognition that local contact and relationships count. A sample of customer contact events are surveyed monthly, measuring professionalism, responsiveness, overall satisfaction and repurchase intention.

It is this constant flow of information that fuels the continuous improvement activity.

OPERATIONAL EXCELLENCE

The intense focus on the customer is not done at any cost. Avis has always maintained a tight control on costs, reflected in a record of 13 successive years of productivity improvements. Its programme of profit improvement plans is an important contributor to this. The drive to improve service is constantly matched by the quest for lower costs.

This form of continuous improvement would not be possible without the Wizard system. The core of Wizard is a real-time, on-line reservation and rental administration system, handling 2.5 million transactions per day. The Wizard network, operated by a separate company, Wizcom, for both Avis Inc. and Avis Europe, consists of more than 16 000 terminals in 1177 rental locations world-wide. Wizard also allows Avis to offer its services through the world's major reservations systems operated by airlines and travel agencies. These include Sabre, Amadeus, Gallileo, Apollo, Worldspan, System One and SITA.

Wizard underpins the quality of service Avis can offer and enables new service innovations to be introduced. The Wizard card is a loyalty card; holders present their card and all standing details are automatically entered on the rental agreement. Data is also held about corporate rates, discounts and insurance preferences. A Wizard card holder can complete the rental agreement in less than two minutes, which is vital when speed of service and accuracy are important aspects of customer satisfaction. Access to special services such as Roving Rapid Return, Avis Express and Express Preferred are also provided by Wizard.

In addition to providing the mechanism to run the business, Wizard provides vital data for sales and marketing. Again data is shared with major customers, enabling them to plan and control their travel costs. This data is also used to set performance standards for customers, which Avis measures. This enables Avis's corporate customers to reduce their travel expenses.

ENGAGING PEOPLE

The company believes very strongly that the quality of its business performance reflects the quality of its people. Indeed people are the heart of the company.

As mentioned above, inculcating the company's culture starts with recruitment. By bringing in people in who have an empathy with the culture the company avoids problems later on. It is important to note that the company rarely recruits senior people, indeed one of its stated values is 'We believe that employees should be actively encouraged to grow and develop their careers with Avis and we always seek to first appoint candidates from within the Company to fill positions at every level – both nationally and internationally.' Over 90 per cent of the top 200 managers in Europe reached their positions by progressing careers through the company. This ensures that the all-important culture is not diluted. One result of this policy is the degree to which people know how things are done. There is no need for extensive manuals and records. People know what to do, they know their colleagues and they just get on with it. This is not to say that Avis is insular. A number of strategic external appointments are made both to fill certain skills gaps and to inject new energy into management teams that might be in danger of becoming complacent. A strong team of non-executive directors also provides an outside-in perspective, as does regular attendance at conferences and industry events. This is all on top of a culture that places relationships between Avis staff and customers and suppliers at the heart of the business to begin with.

Such a policy demands significant investment in training and development. As the chief executive officer, Alun Cathcart, once said: 'Marketing might win the customers, but it's training that keeps them.'

Avis Europe has an extensive training programme for its front-line staff. The programme is designed to develop the knowledge, skills and behaviour to serve customers in a way that will provide them with a unique level of value that is not available from any other service provider in any industry. A team of employees and managers was charged with developing a training proposal, the result of which was the Avis Rental Sales Agent Development Programme. The same team subsequently developed the programme. The programme is based on developing 144 competencies with independent assessment throughout, and takes 18 months to complete. Completion of the programme requires the agent to undertake a major project linked to quality improvement, revenue growth or cost reduction. A project board of company managers has to be satisfied with the overall standard before the final certificate is awarded. The programme carries external recognition.

Development does not stop at the rental counter, which in Avis is where, leadership development begins. In addition to technical and professional competence, Avis looks for the qualities of people-consciousness and affinity at recruitment and seeks to develop these throughout the person's career with Avis. These competencies are not only developed through formal courses but through a living, breathing example of success – Avis itself. Avis seeks to encourage an open organisation with an air of respectful informality and openness at all levels, up, down and across the organisation. This is facilitated by a number of group activities at the local, national and international levels.

All this stimulates people not only to communicate, share experiences and cooperate, but also to appreciate each other's contribution to the whole. Above all it provides an opportunity to influence the organisation and be influenced by it. True empowerment.

10 The Birmingham Midshires Building Society

Care more than others think is wise. Risk more than others think is safe. Dream more than others think is practical. Expect more than others think is possible.

This case study examines a company that has recently undergone significant change in order to stay in business. The case shows a successful approach to creating a dynamic organisation. The key elements are all evident: customer focus, leadership that focuses on establishing the organisational environment (vision, values and the management process) and engaging people. Note that the turnaround was only effected after a new leadership team had moved in.

The Birmingham Midshires Building Society (BMBS) is currently the tenth largest mutual building society[1] in the UK, with some 2200 people managing £7.7 billion worth of assets across 120 branches. It is head-quartered in Wolverhampton, where it has based its recently opened, state-of-the-art customer service centre. Other customer service centres are based in Bracknell and Plymouth.

In the 1980s, the society was languishing. Now it is flourishing, with stockbrokers UBS exclaiming: '3 years ago, they were on the danger list. They are now on the prize winners list'. This is taken from material provided to me by BMBS.

The BMBS is the result of 50 mergers since 1849. The mutual society (a status it retains to date) only really began to grow in the 1980s, its assets growing from £150 million to £3 billion by the end of that decade. This in itself was not spectacular: the entire building society sector grew con-siderably, fuelled by an explosive demand for mortgages and significant merger activity. However, the company also took advantage of the 1986 Finance Act, which allowed building societies to expand into real estate and insurance broking activities, among other things. This freedom fuelled a further round of acquisitions across the market.

The poorly directed and uncontrolled growth that was typical of the sector crashed with the deepening recession of the late 1980s and early 1990s and particularly with the collapse of the UK housing market – the society's traditional market. The society went rapidly downhill. Not only was direction lacking, but mergers, which had resulted in the acquisition of numerous other building societies and mortgage books, had brought their own problems. There was no sense of corporate culture as people from the different companies had brought their own values into a cultural vacuum. As the 1990s began the BMBS was among the worst-performing players in the sector. The choice facing the board was to change or to be taken over. The board chose the former.

Change management all too often begins with changing management. The BMBS was no different.[2] In September 1990 the board of the BMBS appointed Mike Jackson as chief executive officer. Jackson came from Citibank, where he was a senior vice-president. He was given the goal of building the BMBS into a world-class business whose primary focus was on providing excellent customer service.

Jackson began by changing the executive team. Of the ten former executives, only one remains. The first task of the new management team was to get to grips with the organisation. Through a series of team workshops the executive built up a picture of the malaise of the society, examined the options open to them and faced up to a number of tough decisions. The first priority was to divest some of the acquisitions of the past and close down unprofitable products and services. Attention then turned to what was left.

VISION AND VALUES

Towards the end of 1990 the executive team concentrated on formulating a vision for the future. This was a participative exercise, involving all senior managers and people drawn from all levels of the society (some 100 in total). This was essential to get a true picture, tap into people's creativity and generate commitment to, and ownership of, to the changes that would follow. As an input to the exercise, extensive customer research was undertaken to obtain the views of existing and prospective customers. The bottom line was that an opportunity existed to capture the high ground in the financial services market by motivating the society's people to meet the goal of exceeding customer expectations.

The workshops involved novel techniques for getting the groups to think about the needs of customers and their perceptions of the BMBS. One technique involved cutting out pictures and words to build up a montage of the society's future. The words that appeared most were 'first' and 'choice'; hence the workshops developed the theme 'First Choice' as the centrepiece of the new culture. This spawned further customer research to identify the most valued. The slogan 'First Choice' and the results of the research formed the basis of the BMBS vision statement: 'By being First Choice for our customers, our people and our business partners we will grow, profitably'.

To support the First Choice vision, the BMBS developed a new set of values, called the 'pillars of excellence'. These values are the foundation upon which the BMBS's First Choice organisation is built:

- A belief in being the best at what the society does.
- A belief that people in the organisation should be innovators and should take calculated and communicated risks without feeling that they will be punished if they fail.
- A belief in the importance of attending to details in doing a job.
- A belief in the importance of people as individuals.
- A belief in superior quality and service.
- A belief in the importance of informality to improve the flow of communication through the organisation.
- A belief in the importance of economic growth and profits.
- A belief in the importance of 'hands on' management, the notion that team leaders should be 'doers', not just planners and administrators.
- A belief in the importance of a recognised organisational philosophy, developed and supported by those at the top.
- A belief in the importance of having fun at work.

The pillars of excellence clearly set out the style of organisation the BMBS wants and guide people in deciding what to do, without constraining creativity in any way.

First Choice has developed into a customer-focused, continuous improvement process designed to attract, retain and build lifetime relationships. FIRST is a mnemonic of the buyer values BMBS identified as vital and upon which the company has focused it's turnaround: Friendly, Informed, Responsive, Service-oriented and Trustworthy. Everything at the BMBS is FIRST oriented. The measurement of customer and people satisfaction is centred on FIRST.

The prioritised goals for delivering the vision are:

First Choice Service
>*through*

First Choice People
>*with*

Expert Risk Management
>*achieving*

Best of Breed Performance
>*and*

Superior Growth

These goals spawned a number of teams to address the task of turning the BMBS in to the first choice society in each of the areas. This has subsequently become embedded as the continuous improvement process depicted in Figure 10.1. As you can see, this process links teams, individuals, appraisal and development in a cycle driven by and feeding into the society's stated direction.

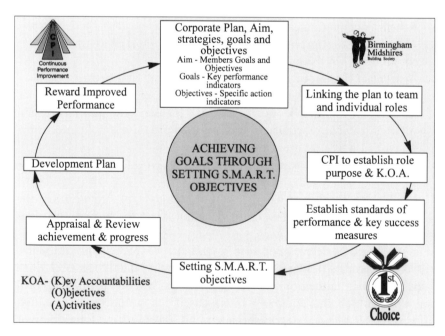

Source: © Birmingham Midshires Building Society, 1996.

Figure 10.1 Continuous performance improvement cycle

At the start of 1991 the vision and values, together with details of the quality-based strategy, new organisation structure and divestments were communicated to all those concerned. Every member of staff received a copy of the 'Rocket Document', a 26-page description of the future of the BMBS. This was supported by 17 top-management roadshows, which were attended by all but a few of the people. Any change creates uncertainty and doubt, and First Choice was no different.

The communication exercise was quickly followed up with the establishment of nine change teams charged with fleshing out the strategy. Membership of the teams was cross-functional and involved people with experience of making change a reality. The nine teams balanced the top-down direction with the bottom-up involvement so vital to building up the commitment required for a successful and dynamic organisation.

The work of fleshing out the details took much of 1991, although action was taken throughout the year as the need arose. The new approach was packaged into three booklets.

'Our Strategy and Goals' is a 19-page booklet explaining the vision, strategy, positioning, goals and targets for the next five years. The booklet outlines financial, product volume and customer satisfaction targets together with an explanation of how these will be measured. Signed by each leader of the business and support teams, the booklet closes with the plea 'Let's work together to turn our full attention on customers, turn the heat on the competition, deliver First Choice service, and have some fun on the way.'

'Our Behaviours' explains the pillars of excellence and includes charters covering the behaviours required of the society's people. Also included is a profile of a First Choice person and explanations of the society's attitude towards the environment and business partners. The role and form of communications is outlined. The booklet shows how the pillars of excellence will be measured, and the current scores. The booklet ends 'You'll always have a job as long as you're changing, adapting and growing and as long as there is meaningful work for you and you accept locational and role flexibility.'

'Our Structure' lists the roles, responsibilities and key leaders of the different parts of the organisation. It includes a description of the roles of the main board (including a target for the chief executive officer's allocation of time) and the business and support team leaders. The role and composition of the change teams are also described, highlighting how the rest of the organisation can work with them. The BMBS has moved to a team-based organisational structure centred around three business teams, which are responsible for the major elements of serving the society's customers and four support teams: people support, corporate relations and quality, finance and compliance, and servicing.

THE KEYS TO SUCCESS

The keys to the successful change at the BMBS, in no particular order, are as follows:

Building the Right Top Team

In 1991 a significant change was made to the top team. Having the right leadership skills was critical both to the management of the change itself and to modelling the culture the BMBS wanted. Of the original team, only one remains, the majority of the new top team having been recruited from outside on the basis of their success in implementing radical change. This experience of change was critical in effecting the transformation in such a short time.

Developing Leadership Behaviour

Leadership is not the sole responsibility of the top team. The BMBS has heavily invested management time and money in developing the leadership skills of business and support team leaders. Most of their time is now spent communicating with and motivating people throughout the organisation to achieve the vision and uphold the values. This is done through both conversations and coaching. To reinforce the one-team feeling, titles, departments and offices have been eliminated in favour of team working, open plan and equal status. Not even the chief executive officer has a walled office and no one has their own parking space.

A change of this magnitude naturally engenders resistance. Team leaders are regularly assessed and given feedback on their performance and adaptability to the changes. The top team categorised senior managers as 'adventurers', 'adopters' and 'abstainers'. Adventurers were encouraged to lead the change effort, while abstainers were encouraged to follow. Succesful adopters were given more responsibilities and turned into champions to help coach others and provide an example to those who were having difficulties. These people were counselled and given as much support as possible. Those who continued to fail to adapt (about one in four) were encouraged to leave.

Much of the resistance to change was overcome through BMBS's focus on encouragement and support.

Communication

From the outset the leadership made a great effort to communicate the changes and the rationale behind them. A variety of techniques were used:

- An annual attitude survey, 'Listening to you First', generated a whole series of actions that were refined by focus groups. In 1992, 165 actionable items were agreed. For each action a nominated person has been made responsible for its implementation. The annual attitude survey is supplemented by a monthly climate survey to provide rapid feedback on emerging or recurring issues.
- First ascent meetings: each month the teams meet to report to each other on how the change programmes are progressing and discuss the results and performance of the business. The notes of this meeting are shared across the organisation.
- Face to face: each top team member has a target to visit branches and teams in the centre. The agenda for these meetings is set by the group being visited. At these meetings the top team get a first-hand view of the issues in the organisation. About 200 actionable items are generated annually from this programme.
- Celebrating wins: when the BMBS won a recent award for customer service, all members of staff received an individual letter of thanks and a certificate personally signed by each member of the top team. They also received business cards printed with the award logo and presented in a silver personal card holder with the BMBS's vision statement engraved on the back.
- Performance information: in addition to the regular performance updates, people receive an annual concertina card containing the society's vision statement and supporting goals, with measures of progress for each goal as well as broader financial progress.
- Quality forum: every three months, a large open quality day is run for about 200 people (15 per cent of the society's population). Speakers are drawn from the BMBS itself, as well as members of other companies and individuals recognised for their knowledge of best practices. The focus of these events is on exceeding expectations. The event is also open to business partners.

The key point of the communications is that they are two-way; it is as much about listening as telling, pulling rather than pushing. Embedding communication in this way is critical to the ongoing success of a dynamic organisation.

Use of Symbols and Recognition

Research into corporate cultures (see Chapter 3) has identified symbols and rituals as key dimensions of culture. The BMBS has themed the whole change and the ongoing development of the organisation around First Choice. Winners of First Choice awards are nominated by customers and recipients are presented with a First Choice lapel badge and cash rewards. Each year a First Choice person of the year is selected, based on contribution to service excellence and nominations from colleagues and customers. The selection is made by a cross-functional BMBS panel and the recipient is rewarded by the chief executive officer. Business and support team leaders, the organisation's middle managers, have a budget for awards. This fund is used to recognise people for efforts above and beyond the call of duty. In all, 129 performance awards were issued in 1993. This was followed by 144 awards in 1994 and 173 in 1995.

Objective Setting and Appraisal

The continuous process improvement (CPI, outlined above) operates from the board and throughout the organisation. A key part of this is the definition of a person's job purpose, key accountabilities and objectives that are measurable and relate to corporate goals. The CPI appraisal process enables each member of staff to identify, set and agree objectives with team leaders. Personal development plans then document the training and learning experiences to be gained in the following year. The formal system is backed up by an informal system. For example teams often meet for a self-appraisal and personal feedback session, providing a more continuous source of feedback and therefore improvement.

Recruiting, Developing and Keeping People

Getting the right people begins with recruitment. The BMBS has a formal hiring policy linked to quality. Full use is made of assessment centres and psychometric testing. Each new member of staff attends a three-day induction programme, which is followed by on-the-job coaching. In addition to the leadership development mentioned above, the BMBS emphasises the importance of training and development. On average, people receive six days training per year. As part of the change, everyone went through a programme entitled 'First Choice Leadership.' The programme combined outward-bound, adventure-based training with experiential learning and review sessions. Each member of the course assessed themselves and their peers, and frank but constructive feedback was given. The course also focused on the values and purpose of the BMBS, and was key to building a shared sense of purpose and values and a common vocabulary. The society invests in 8500 days of training per year, covering 50 different types of course, 76 per cent of which focus on values and behaviours, the remainder being skill oriented. The last two years have seen a focus on professional selling skills, with a resultant increase in income and major improvements in customer satisfaction.

People satisfaction is high, especially considering the significant change the organisation has experienced, as Table 10.1 shows.

Table 10.1   Measure of employee satisfaction

	Per Cent
I am satisfied in my job	63[*]
I believe that the organisation is close to realising its vision	67
I understand the organisation's key goals and objectives	90
I would recommend Birmingham Midshires as a place to work	64

[*] This compares with an average of 57 per cent for the financial services industry as a whole, according to figures compiled by MORI.

A retention rate of 92 per cent underlines the degree of satisfaction, and 83 per cent of people say they are satisfied with internal communications – the highest in the UK, according to MORI's normative data.

As First Choice is at the core of the organisation, it is only natural that it is reflected in the reward scheme. Annual bonuses are determined by the attainment of both profit and customer satisfaction targets.

MEASURING SUCCESS

Detailed measurement processes support the leadership of the organisation, the most important aspects of which are customer and people satisfaction. The measurements are linked to the society's First Choice goals as follows:

- First Choice service: customer satisfaction; competitive benchmark comparisons.
- First Choice people: annual people attitude survey; monthly people climate survey; people retention rates; applicant levels.
- Expert risk management: repossessions and arrears; charges for the year/pre-provisions; fines, frauds or censure costs.
- Superior growth: profit comparison; cost/income and expense to asset ratio comparison; retention of customers.
- Best of breed performance: return on capital.

The measurement of customer satisfaction centres around the customer values summed up in First Choice. This has been translated into a number of views the customer holds about the society, as shown in Table 10.2.

Table 10.2   Interpreting First Choice

	Intermediate View	*Ultimate View*
Friendly	The process we use is business like and friendly	Memorable
Informed	We give customers the information they need	Expert
Responsive	Available and dependable when needed	Always there
Service-orientated	Easy to do business with	Easy to do business with
Trustworthy	Honest, responsible and ethical	Confidant

In support of customer satisfaction measurement, over 700 000 questionnaires have been issued to date. Each returned questionnaire prompts a reply from the branch: a thank-you to those who express satisfaction and an apology to those expressing dissatisfaction with some element. The latter are also promised a commitment to solving the problem, with the appropriate business or support team people taking responsibility for problem solving. If the problem has no natural team to solve the problem, then a special team is formed. This was the case when customers expressed dissatisfaction with how the society managed MIRAS – the tax relief associated with mortgages. A team was set up to deal specifically with the issue and improve customer satisfaction. This link between measurement and improvement is a key feature of any dynamic organisation.

RESULTS TO DATE

The results to date are impressive. Customer satisfaction scores have reached 97 per cent, up from 88 per cent four years ago, with 16.8 per cent of these saying that the society's service exceeds their expectations. Nine out of ten customers now say they recommend the BMBS to friends, colleagues and associates. This level of customer satisfaction is 10 per cent ahead of the average of other building societies and 35 per cent ahead of banks in the UK. The focus is now shifting to increase the percentage of customers that are highly satisfied. In the first half of 1995 the BMBS achieved a 'highly satisfied' rating of 75 per cent, an increase from a base of 50 per cent in 1990.

Competitive benchmarks confirm the leadership position of the BMBS, as research by NOP found in response to the following question: How would you rate the service of your bank/building society (with respect to savings accounts) over the past six months? (Table 10.3.)

Table 10.3 Comparison of retail financial service providers (per cent)

	Five Major Banks	*Five Major Building Societies*	*Birmingham Midshires*
Excellent	21	22	29
Highly satisfactory	26	30	43
Exceeding expectations	47	52	72
Satisfactory	48	46	27
Meeting expectations	95	98	99

All figures for customer satisfaction are reviewed monthly by the board and communicated widely throughout the organisation.

The BMBS change is a recent story, and in many respects the BMBS is still in its infancy as a dynamic organisation. It does however prove that much can be achieved in a relatively short period of time. The figures for customer and employee satisfaction show that an excellent foundation for further development exists.

The improvements in people and customer satisfaction have not been achieved at the cost of productivity and financial performance. Productivity rose over 100 per cent in five years; the cost-to-income ratio improved from 71 per cent in 1990 to 51 per cent in 1994; after 1990 the expense-to-asset ratio fell for five consecutive years from 1.8 per cent to 1.3 per cent. This is all reflected in the bottom line, where profits rose from £6.3 million in 1990 to £44 million in 1996, despite an adjustment for closed accounts reducing profit by £13 million per annum.

The senior managers at the BMBS display the right mix of self-confidence and self-doubt; they are justifiably proud of their achievements, whilst recognising that much remains to be done. An extensive IT systems development will support front-line people in dealing with each customer contact as a unique service encounter, designed to increase both customer satisfaction and revenue generation. Further process changes will be made to improve customer satisfaction and efficiency. It is a testament to the depth of cultural change that one in five of the society's people volunteered to serve on the new change teams for this project. Changes to the grading structure will eliminate the current 16 levels. The new system will be based on identifying the key success factors for every role in the society, and the competencies required to deliver the role. The next phase of the corporate plan will focus on making the BMBS the first choice for target families (as against individual customers) by the year 2001.

Whilst much has been done to change the BMBS, and more is planned, it is clearly accepted that the work will never be finished. With a goal of constantly exceeding customer expectations, all that lies ahead is more change. But until customers stop wanting more, that is the only way to win. This desire to win by focusing on the customer was rewarded recently when the BMBS won the 1996 Management Today/Unisys Service Excellence Award.

11 Cigna UK

Cigna UK, based in Greenock, Scotland, is part of the giant $35 billion Cigna Corporation. Cigna UK offers company health, travel and other insurance products to organisations such as Rover, Glaxo and Motorola. The company is now levering its reputation and expertise into the insurance-based personal benefits market. This case study examines how Cigna UK managed a radical change involving changes of location, staff, culture, processes and even the business they were in. The study focuses on how Cigna UK uses a powerful team-based culture to meet the needs of its customers.

Cigna UK was formed when the US-based Cigna Corporation bought Crusader Insurance, based in Redhill and Livingstone. In 1988 the business had a number of problems that were causing the company's profits to decline. These included high levels of customer dissatisfaction, a broad product range (none of which were market leaders), excessive operating costs and a hierarchical and bureaucratic structure. The corporate culture of the US parent was to fix it or fold it. A radical solution was needed. The company closed its Redhill and Livingstone offices and looked around for a new location. The original plan, driven by the US parent, was to create a European service centre for Cigna. It chose Greenock because of the high level of linguistic skills available there. The plan to develop a pan-European service centre was killed off, but the move to Greenock was still to go ahead, although at the time the shape of the company had still not been determined. As an interim measure Cigna moved into a warehouse and kept the pensions and life assurance business ticking over.

From May to September 1991 the company carried out a detailed review of the business to decide its future. It was clear that Cigna UK could not be a significant competitor in the life assurance and pensions business. It did not have the size to compete in a commodity-based market, where market share brings considerable advantages. The life and pensions business was sold to Britannia Life Assurance in 1991.

The company's research showed that there was an opportunity to succeed in the corporate health and employee benefits market, but most of all there was an opportunity for a company that placed service at the top of its agenda. Hence the goal of Cigna UK to be recognisably as the best in customer service was set. This was supported by economic modelling of the various options for change. It must be pointed out that many would say there are few organisations who have the opportunity (some might say the luxury) of taking 'time out' to rethink the business. Many organisations have suffered, or even gone out of business, because they have assumed that life will continue as normal. One of the lessons of the Cigna UK case is that it can be dangerous *not* to take this time out.

With the decision made about what the business was to be, attention turned to converting the existing business into a new company.

The health insurance business is different from many other forms of insurance. It is known and expected that 80–90 per cent of what is taken in premiums is paid out again. One in three people will claim. Customer satisfaction is considerably driven by the quality of the service provided throughout the administration of the policy, notably during claims, a period of great stress for customers. Any delay in payment places clients in an awkward position as they are often being pressed for payment from their healthcare providers. Many insurers believe that controlling claims and delaying payment improves profit and cash flow. Research by Cigna UK showed that this approach involves significant additional cost. Customers who have not received their payments constantly telephone to find out why the payment has not been forthcoming. After seven days overdue, the volume of calls increases by 75 per cent, imposing a significant additional cost for service.

Cigna UK started with a blank piece of paper and then posed the question 'If we could create our own world, what would it be like?' Customers were involved in the process and it became clear that they wanted an organisation that was flexible, understanding and caring as well as products that met their needs.

To launch the new business many changes were made, but in this case study I want to focus on the use of self-managed teams, for it is in this area that much of the change in Cigna was, and still is, effected.

An important part of a dynamic organisation is the effort it makes to ensure that all its people understand the totality of the business. This does not mean that everyone has to know the intricacies of every aspect of work. It does mean that everyone knows what business the company is in, and the fundamentals of how the business works. Without this people will do things that cause problems, not because they are malicious, but because they do not understand the knock-on effect of their actions. Cigna's efforts in this direction have clearly worked. When I visited the company I was struck by how knowledgeable the team members were about the business. They fielded questions that many senior managers in other, similar companies have struggled to answer.

The organisation was flattened to four levels between the most junior level and the managing director. The staff were then grouped into teams, at the heart of which are the customer service teams. Before the introduction of these teams Cigna UK was functionally organised, just like most insurance companies. Eight delivery functions (post, new business, renewal, credit control, claims, files, membership and billing) were combined into a number of customer-aligned customer service teams. This dramatically reduced the number of hand-offs in the process and enabled Cigna UK to reduce claims turnaround from 14 days to three. This had a dramatic impact on customer satisfaction. When introducing the teams the organisation was guided by the maxim 'Try it. Test it. Fix it'. There was a clear view of where the organisation was going, but many of the ideas were worked out as the changes progressed.

Cigna UK has gone beyond simple teams and has now moved towards self-directed teams for both business as usual in the form of customer service teams, and *ad hoc* project teams.

The customer service teams are responsible for a customer or group of customers and all the interactions with them. This starts with the preparation of the proposal, indeed it is commonplace for the team to present the proposal to the customer themselves. Each new client is assigned to a team, which then deals with every aspect of its business. The client's employees are given a named individual within the team, who will deal with any interactions with them.

The allocation of work is done by the team on a daily basis. Each morning the team members sit down and share with their colleagues what targets they are setting for the day and their results from the previous day. Throughput statistics and any quality of service issues are discussed at meetings held by the team and with team facilitators, again daily. Here teams volunteer to help other teams that are having difficulties because of increased workload or sickness. This forum is also an important way of teams staying in touch with the rest of the organisation. Afterwards the facilitators share this information with their own teams.

In addition to the customer service and support teams (finance, human resources, systems and management), the company operates a number of virtual teams. These are used to solve particular problems, or introduce organisation-wide changes. A virtual team may exist for just a few weeks or several months, depending on the nature of the issue they are addressing. In most cases the members of the virtual teams also continue with their normal team duties.

Developing a team of teams like this is not an overnight exercise, and it took at least a year at Cigna UK. Moving to self-directed teams meant problems for the people, the managers and the teams themselves. People who have lived in a blame culture, where management was responsible for problem solving, and where direction came from above, cannot switch track overnight. Blind faith suddenly meets the reality of day-to-day problems and issues.

One of the major problems within the teams at Cigna UK was communication. One of the reason teams fail to reach high levels of performance is the unwillingness of members to be open and honest with each other. This prevents certain problems from being recognised and solved. Cigna UK placed great emphasis on training people in techniques to expose and manage conflict.

A core component of the training was a programme in facilitation and facilitative leadership which developed leadership and team skills in four main areas, as shown in Figure 11.1.

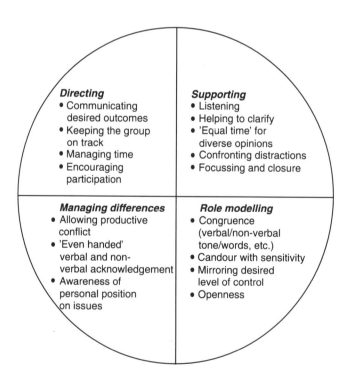

Directing
- Communicating desired outcomes
- Keeping the group on track
- Managing time
- Encouraging participation

Supporting
- Listening
- Helping to clarify
- 'Equal time' for diverse opinions
- Confronting distractions
- Focussing and closure

Managing differences
- Allowing productive conflict
- 'Even handed' verbal and non-verbal acknowledgement
- Awareness of personal position on issues

Role modelling
- Congruence (verbal/non-verbal tone/words, etc.)
- Candour with sensitivity
- Mirroring desired level of control
- Openness

Figure 11.1   Cigna UK facilitator skills model

- *Directing*: these skills help the team accomplish specific tasks in order to reach their goals. Key here is deciding the degree to which the team leader should exercise direction.
- *Supporting*: these skills encourage the support of other people's ideas and opinions. Without this, people will not risk putting forward their views and ideas.
- *Managing differences*: these are the skills the facilitator uses to expose and manage constructive conflict. Dealing with inevitable disagreements is a key role of the facilitator.
- *Role modelling*: if facilitators are to encourage listening, they must demonstrate listening in their actions. The same is true of candour and honesty. It is nothing more than 'walking the talk'.

Team members were selected and put through a series of exercises to improve their skills of teamplay and leadership. Training for team dynamics, conflict management, decision making, communication and providing constructive feedback was provided throughout the development of the teams. Team members were encouraged to practice these new skills within their teams. This was reinforced by the management through their participation in all the training sessions, and their role in coaching and encouragement. As their skills developed the teams themselves took on the responsibility for cross-training team members through on-the-job coaching and training.

In addition to team-based activities, a periodic climate survey gives everyone the opportunity to express their thoughts and concerns. The teams and the interplay between teams and managers have now reached a level of maturity where issues do not become significant. They are aired early on in their life and dealt with. This maturity was not of course achieved overnight. The initial customer service teams were unfocused and lacked confidence, often looking to management for help and guidance. Support was provided from the change team of internal managers and consultants.

Problems were not restricted to teams and their members. Managers also faced difficulties in moving from a command and control to a coaching approach. The existence of self-managed teams does not totally remove the need for managers. They remain responsible and still have to manage, but in a very different sense. One of the major issues was the setting and use of performance measures. Under the old regime this was the domain of the manager. He or she set the measures and carried out the reviews. With self-managed teams, however, that responsibility has shifted to the team itself.

These problems and how they changed as the team-based organisation matured are illustrated in a little cameo related by Doug Cowieson, a director of Cigna UK much involved in the changes.

> When teams were first introduced, a member of staff had a problem and was half-way along the corridor before she realised I wasn't going to solve it for her. I was going to say 'Well, what would you do?' She said that for the first few weeks of being in these teams she wasted more of her time walking down the corridor, only to get half-way there and think, he is not going to solve this one for me. Her approach was then to come up with a solution and then come through and say 'Douglas, how would it work if I did this?' Now she is into the mode where she doesn't come to my office. I have to go round to the teams and sit in them and find out how things are going.

Cigna UK went through four phases in its progress towards high-performing, self-managed teamwork. The first was chaos, not in a negative sense, but simply reflecting the lack of clarity of purpose and roles. Here the facilitator provided order, structure and guidance to get the team moving. The second phase has been described as a 'false team'. This looked like a real team, but lacked the level of commitment and depth of thought needed to get the job done properly. Here the facilitator had to probe and test and bring to the surface issues and opinions that were being repressed. The conflict phase brought out the significant issues and opinions and the team members began to understand their colleagues and appreciate their views and skills. The final phase was the 'true team': where the high levels of focus and productivity were able to withstand temporary chaos such as the addition of a new member.

Cigna UK has developed team facilitation to a high degree, a process that took several years to master fully. The culture at Cigna UK reflects the team ethic, which is expressed as a number of commandments:

- *Help people do and learn.* This commandment is aimed at encouraging people to teach others how to do their work. The role of the facilitator shifts from doing things in the way a supervisor of old would have done, to helping others learn to do it for themselves. This is essential to self-managed teams who take on many of the responsibilities previously carried out by the supervisor. This increases responsibility and accountability and generates enthusiasm.
- *Let people own the results.* Making the shift from supervisors owning results, and the associated praise and blame, to the team owning those

results is a big one. If true empowerment is to be achieved, the actions and their outcomes must go hand in hand. Supervisors and managers typically have more difficulty letting go of the ownership of results than do the staff in taking them on.

- *Know when to use and lose your power.* Many assume that the move from supervisor to facilitator involves a loss of power. Cigna UK has found the opposite to be true. As they exercised their newly found skills in coaching and facilitation, the facilitators began to exert significantly more influence on the actions of their colleagues. This is a different form of power; one that is much less direct but much more enjoyable. The trick is knowing when to act in a directive role and when not to. The natural urge to tell the team what to do and how to do it in every case closes off opportunities for others to develop their skills. But there will still be cases when the facilitator will need to be directive.
- *Provide no more or no less than what is needed.* The facilitator has to develop a feel for, an understanding of, what the team members want from him or her. This unwritten agreement allows the facilitator to assist without treading on the team's toes.
- *Become transparent.* Facilitators at Cigna UK have discovered that they are most effective when they are transparent, when the team functions well without them. This is the true measure of a facilitator. Excellent facilitation is the art of nudging; a gentle, perhaps imperceptible intervention that has a significant impact on the team's efforts and results.

The teams have devised a new scorecard of key measures. These cover productivity, quality, service and premium arrears. The measures are monitored by the teams themselves, who decide what corrective action, if any, is needed. The targets for each measure is set by the teams themselves, and differ according to the business mix.

As part of the change a new compensation plan was developed. Part of the plan is based on team performance, which further reinforces the team culture. Quarterly team results are evaluated against the set tragets at five levels; 70 per cent of the incentive is paid as a team element and 30 per cent as an individual element. This individual element was initially allocated equally to team members, but now the teams have reached a level of maturity and trust the teams themselves allocate the money to individuals based on their assessment of contribution.

Throughout any process of change, people will resist. Cigna UK's Doug Cowieson imaginatively classifies the people associated with them.

Status Quo people are happy with the way things are. However, they quickly adapt, and a few weeks into the change they are happy with the new culture and go along with it. *Zealots* are reluctant to take the change on board, but once converted they are like former smokers and become evangelists. The final group are what Cowieson calls the 'Indiana Jones tribe'. These people are insidious blockers. They do not openly express their resistance, rather they use their influence to undermine the change. There is a point in the film *Raiders of the Lost Ark* where Indiana is faced with a rebel brandishing a huge sword, which he waves around menacingly. Indiana pulls out his gun and shoots him. Recognising the stages and forms of resistance and having strategies to deal with them is important.

In describing Cigna's effort to build a team-based organisation, Doug Cowieson has revealed a number of valuable lessons which are worth sharing and extending.

The first is that senior managers need to be evangelical about the change. If they are not enthusiastic, it will not work. It is not enough for the chief executive officer to support this, she or he has to be 101 per cent behind it. Recognise also that the person introducing the change might not be the right person to keep it going once it is established. In general the person taking on such a change acts as a 'benevolent dictator', breaking the old culture and bringing in the new. However, this is probably not the person to take the organisation further, as she or he will want to break something that no longer needs breaking. What is needed is someone who can keep the organisation focused on the external world and foster the continuous improvement culture.

Situational leadership is not a new idea. Few organisations and even fewer top managers think about the point when the leader has served a useful life and should move on. This is obviously an easier issue to address in an organisation the size of Cigna, where there are many more opportunities to meet new challenges. It is however something that is worthy of thought at the beginning of the change. At that stage, success is a remote and distant dream, and there are more pressing things to worry about, so the issue is rarely addressed.

Focusing on being effective rather than efficient is the second lesson. When Cigna UK was being audited by a US-based Cigna group it was asked why it did not put in place a process for auditing the number of claims going from person to person. 'What happens if they go missing?' asked the auditors. The simple answer was that nothing had gone missing. There was no evidence of a claim being lost, no complaint from a customer. Nonetheless the auditors insisted on the need for a tracking process. It transpired that in the US the staff were given fifty claims a day to process, and received full pay only if all fifty claims were dealt with. Claims were going astray, typically the difficult ones to deal with, which of course required a process to track them as they passed through the numerous hand-offs. When the team is responsible for the entire process, in a culture where teams help each other and reward is based on customer satisfaction and profitable growth, lost claims are not a problem.

Another important lesson is that even with self-directed teams, managers still need to manage. Empowerment and abdication are different things. But in the process of developing the teams, the team becomes more able to take on its own management, as Figure 11.2 shows.

As this happens the manager's role shifts from responsibility for the day-to-day actions of the team to responsibility for the development of the team and its members. Coaching shifts from development of the task to development of leadership and team skills and from the work processes to the organisational processes. This is why managers themselves need coaching. They have typically been promoted because of their technical skills but now find that aspect of their work disappearing.

So what have the changes at Cigna UK achieved? In addition to being recognised as the centre of excellence for change within Cigna's worldwide organisation, a view supported by the representatives of many other

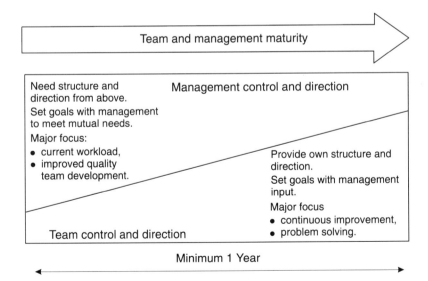

Figure 10.2 Maturing teams

organisations who have made the trip to Greenock to see what has been done, the company has won awards for excellence in customer focus. More importantly it has achieved success on the bottom line. The company calculates that changing to a team-based structure generated savings of approaching £1 million in two years. This in the same period as its volume of business increased. Cigna UK is justifiably proud that it has not not lost a single corporate customer since making the change. Employee retention and satisfaction are also remarkably high. Between 1991 and 1994 the company turned a £9 million loss into a £5 million profit and increased productivity by 30 per cent

I never cease to be amazed at the results seemingly 'ordinary' people can achieve when they are allowed to take on responsibilities that traditional management practices deem beyond them. Cigna UK provides an excellent demonstration of the capability of people when they are freed of unnecessary constraints by courageous leadership.

12 Disneyland Paris

This case study examines how a large, centralised service organisation transformed itself into a network of small customer focused businesses.

Disneyland Paris is the European resort of the Walt Disney Corporation. Whilst the link to Disney is clear, the Walt Disney Corporation owns only 39 per cent of Disneyland Paris. Prince Al Waleed owns 24 per cent, with the remainder openly traded on the Paris Bourse.

The park, located south-east of Paris, has 40 attractions, 60 shops and 29 restaurants and has its own motorway and rail links. Six themed hotels and one ranch offer 5200 hotel rooms, from luxury to economy together with a vacation village. A staff of 8000 people, rising to 15000 in high season served the 36 million people who have visited the park in the first 3 ½ years.

Walt Disney established the first theme park in California in 1955 to provide an experience to visitors, whom he insisted were to be called and treated as 'guests'. Disney wanted the parks to be different: 'I don't want guests to see the world in which they live while they are inside the park. I want them to feel they are in another world.' Following the success of the California-based Disneyland, the company opened further parks in Florida (1971) and Tokyo (1983).

In building the resort in Paris, the Disney Corporation came with a strong track record of the success of the US parks. Tokyo Disneyland, built by Disney, is owned and operated by the Oriental Land Company, a wholly Japanese company. The Japanese are a homogeneous, US-orientated culture, a factor important in the success of Tokyo Disneyland.

Quality is an inherent part of the culture of Disney, stemming back to Walt Disney's own personal beliefs: 'Well I think that by this time, my staff, my young group of executives and everyone else, are convinced that Walt is right. That quality will win out. And I think they're going to stay with that policy because it has proved it's a good business policy. Give people everything you can give them. Keep the place as clean as you can keep it. Keep friendly, you know, make it a fun place to be.'

The culture and the language the company uses reflect each other. Visitors are called *guests*, inferring a more friendly, ongoing relationship. Staff are known as *cast members*, who, like actors, are constantly performing for the public. Cast members are therefore very much actors in the creation of the experience. The engineers who design the attractions are called *imagineers*, emphasising the importance of creativity and innovation. Indeed the concept of the resorts is closely related to the Disney film heritage, and not only in sharing the wonderful characters. Producing a film and operating a park share other characteristics. Both are in the business of show business. In films, the creativity, individual talent and direction of the acting staff has to be backed up by excellence in the techniques of set design and construction, photography, costume, sound and marketing. Disneyland Paris have matched this balance of talented people and process excellence in creating and operating the resort. In both films and resorts it is the marriage of the two elements that creates the magical experience both want their customers to experience.

The resort opened in April 1992, as EuroDisney, after seven years of planning and construction. The first year was very much about learning on the job. Eight out of ten guests expressed satisfaction but identified a number of problems. They required more table-based service at the restaurants, particularly the European guests used to wine with a meal. Other areas of dissatisfaction included too few attractions and too much queuing for both attractions and meals. Prices were too high, for the park, hotel and food. Many of the points of dissatisfaction were due to the adoption of the American view of service, reinforced by the success of the other parks. European customers are a less homogeneous group, with different cultural characteristics. Failure to understand this was a fundamental mistake.

In the first two years the park made an operating loss, exacerbated by huge debt costs. This required a restructuring in 1994, part of which involved the loss of 1000 jobs. Whilst the changes helped, they did not directly solve the more fundamental problem; that the product was successful, but the business was not working.

The first step was to act on the information gathered from customers. New attractions were added, two new white-knuckle rides, *Indiana Jones' Temple of Doom* and *Space Mountain,* and for younger children, *Casey Junior* and *Story Book* rides. Restaurant capacity was doubled to address concerns about meal queues and attractions were redesigned to reduce waiting times by 40 per cent. The price of hotels was reduced by 13 per cent and park entry by 22 per cent, whilst the cost of counter service (fast) food was brought into line with other outlets in France. These measures all helped to address the concerns expressed by customers.

Cast members had also expressed their concerns. They wanted the organisation to consult and listen to them more. They claimed that the corporation's structure and mission were unclear. People did not feel that their talents were being used effectively and expressed concern about the lack of teamwork and their inability to respond to the individual needs of guests. At this time, large units looking after the major parts of the business, the park and the hotels, formed the basis of the organisation. This organisational structure had been inherited from the American operation where it was already considered to be unsuitable and was in the process of being changed. Each business unit had its own functions: human resources, finance, training, marketing, and so on. The staff in these groups rarely met their peers in the other business units. Duplication and fragmentation of effort were commonplace.

The problems and the desire for growth demanded a more fundamental change. This was started by bringing together the company's 60 senior managers to develop a new vision of the organisation. It was the first time many of them had worked together in this way, indeed for some, it was the first time they had met each other.

Through a series of workshops, the senior managers developed a new vision – the *raison d'être* of the company. This was expressed visually and is shown in the diagram in Figure 12.1 below. The vision 'Together, let's win the hearts of Europe' reflects the emotional nature of the product, and places an emphasis on teamwork and success. The three pillars represent the fundamentals of success and build on the foundation of the organisation's core values.

This vision of the organisation demanded a new, and fundamentally different approach to organisation. One of the attractions at Disneyland Paris, *Small Worlds*, is a boat ride for young children through animated models of different parts of the world. *Small Worlds* was chosen as the theme for the new organisation, which sought to make a shift from an organisation employing 10 000 people to 250 businesses each employing 40 people. In this way, Disneyland Paris sought to bring the people responsible for running the business much closer to the guests, and thereby seek the improvements in quality, service and the management of people that were, literally, the pillars of successful profitable growth. Breaking the organisation down in this way reduced the levels of hierarchy from between six and eight, to three.

Disneyland Paris created a management development programme of 18 days for the new *Small World* managers. The programme comprised a series of seminars, workshops and action learning activities, each derived from the *raison d'être* and structured into four modules: service, leadership, finance and organisational management. The programme was

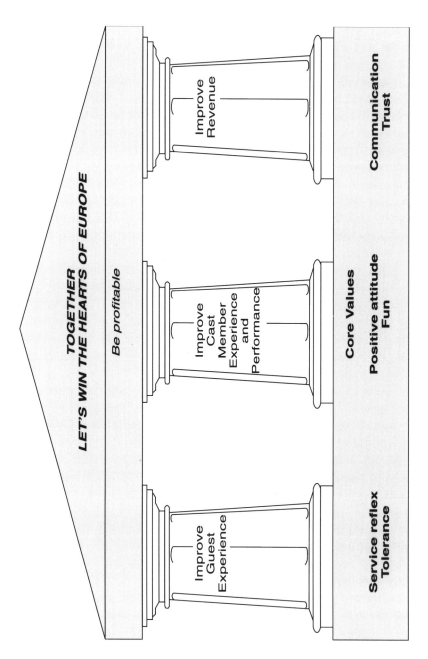

Figure 12.1 Disneyland Paris 'raison d'être'

delivered intensively between January and March 1995 to give the new organisation a powerful start. The programme represented an investment of 32 000 training hours and, in addition to developing the key skills *Small World* managers needed, created a network of people who they knew and could turn to for help.

To ensure everyone in the organisation knew and understood the *raison d'être* and the *Small Worlds* concept, an organisation wide communication programme was put in place. Through newsletters and a cascaded programme of briefings, the message was communicated to all cast members. In addition, the *raison d'être* became a cornerstone of development, with aspects of it built into training programmes at all levels.

Small Worlds is the business face of the organisation. However, delivering service comprises a series of similar activities. Disneyland Paris have identified seven families of skills, knowledge and behaviours that are common across all the *Small Worlds*.

- Receiving guests (be welcomed)
- Selling (supply)
- Maintenance (be in a world where everything works)
- Administration (be in a world where everything is simple)
- Catering (savour)
- Show and entertainment (be enchanted)
- Cleaning (be in a clean and beautiful world)

It is around these seven families – the professions – that the central human resources function organised their support for the business. Development programmes sharpen these skills and, again, provide a valuable opportunity for people to meet colleagues from other parts of the business and form informal networks. The power of these self-built learning networks should not be underestimated.

The loose matrix of *Small World* businesses and families of professions strengthens the feeling of belonging to a single organisation. The values and culture on which this is founded, notably service, are at the core of any training and development activities. New starters undergo a two-day induction programme. The core of the programme covers trends in service, the profiles and expectations of guests, the basics of quality, the use of quality tools, delighting the guest and service recovery. Particular emphasis on the term 'Service Reflex' reflects the importance of treating guests in an individual way, avoiding the robotic response experienced in many service organisations. As the resort celebrates its fifth year, people hired at the start are going through a revision of the induction programme to refresh their understanding of the values.

To support the new organisation, Disneyland Paris replaced the grade based pay structure with an appraisal and reward system based on recognising performance within the role. Appraisals are an annual event where managers assess performance against the three pillars of excellence, or those appropriate to the role. Excellence in performance is rewarded financially and through a broadening of the role. For example, someone who is good at their role and shows an aptitude for developing others will take on responsibilities for training. In this way, the job is enriched and the person rewarded without having to promote someone vertically, an important point as the flattened structure provides far fewer opportunities for this. People are moved to new roles at least every 13 months. This minimises the risk of boredom with a role, which if allowed, leads to a drop in the high standards of responsiveness to customers

Disneyland Paris also accepts that turnover of front-line staff will occur. Young people coming in to work for the first time are, however, given excellent training and, in return, give excellent service to customers. Management at Disneyland Paris sees the development of these young people as a contribution to the greater community, and therefore a source of pride. The majority of staff who have worked at the resort have few problems in finding jobs elsewhere.

Small Worlds and the seven professions would be impotent organisational structures if there was no information on which to base the continuing development of the businesses. Disneyland Paris expend great effort in understanding customers' needs and improving to meet them. Guest satisfaction surveys, issued in the customer's local language shortly after their visit generate significant feedback. Disneyland Paris issue 50 000 surveys annually, the sample reflecting the characteristics of the 11.7 million total visitors. The surveys test satisfaction and intention to return. In addition, focus groups are run in each European country (again in the local language). People for the focus groups are recruited during their stay at the resort.

These focus groups, which are attended by the resort's top operators and local sales management, provide valuable feedback on performance and ideas for further improvements. For example, a group who had travelled to the resort on the Eurostar train experienced some delays. Whilst this was out of the control and no fault of Disneyland Paris, the experience reflected negatively on the levels of satisfaction. Following discussions at the focus group, Disneyland Paris introduced children's entertainers on the dedicated trains. Now the Disney experience starts before people arrive at the resort.

Feedback from customers supplements intensive monitoring of quality standards. Performance measures are also regularly collected and monitored. In addition, staff carry out their own quality checks, visiting different parts of the resort to measure a specific aspect of performance. Staff and their families are also invited to the resort as guests and act as mystery shoppers. They experience the resort as a 'normal' guest but provide extensive reporting of what they experienced.

This constant source of information fed back to the *Small Worlds* teams acts as the basis for continuous improvements. This is part of a crucial process and service improvement process known as 'Keys to Service'. This technique, developed by cast members, looks at the business through the eyes of the customer. It begins with the team developing a mission or purpose statement. The whole experience – a ride or a catering experience – is then broken down into smaller steps and the competencies of the appropriate professions applied. This template of the perfect experience provides a basis for the design and measurement of the process. Weaknesses in the process or experience (as viewed from the customer's perspective) are identified from the performance and customer satisfaction data and improvements initiated.

Managers stay close to the operation of the resort by acting as 'godfathers'. Each staff member not holding a front-line (guest facing) job is trained to carry out duties in a particular *Small World*, a ride for example. When the resort becomes particularly busy, these staff members can be called in by the operating teams. If they receive such a call, staff cancel internal activities and meetings, put on the appropriate costume and enter 'show-time' – they do a front-line job. It is important to note that this work is not a planned event. It is at the behest of the operational teams in the *Small Worlds*; serving the guests takes precedence over all other activities.

Understanding, measuring and improving to meet the needs of customers lies at the heart of the *Small Worlds* organisation model. The dramatic improvements in performance experienced since the introduction is further testament that bringing together the talents of people with an in-depth understanding of customers is a recipe for success.

Disneyland Paris' understanding of customers is best summed up by a short verse derived from listening to the descriptions young children used when describing the resort.

For all children from every country, it's an enchanted world inhabited by marvellous characters.

A sparkling world full of colour both in winter and summer.

A delicious world where you can taste what you want, when you want it.

A world full of friends from whom anything can be asked, who keep us entertained while we are waiting, protect us when we are afraid, who have fun with us.

A fairy tale world where all our dreams come true and makes us want to come back.

13 KLM

THE SERVICE DECATHLON

Understanding the customer is the staple diet of a dynamic organisation. Several years ago people doubted that customer satisfaction could be objectively and effectively measured. Few tried. This case study focuses narrowly on a very effective and thorough approach to understanding and measuring what it is that makes customers want to return to the same organisation.

In many ways service is like sport. It is a human effort. It requires knowledge of the rules and knowledge of one's own talents and weaknesses. It requires a lot of training and resilience. The goal is to make the customer come back. And it is one of the most rewarding things in the world if you win. Success is the smile on the face of the customer.

Service is a string of interactions between individuals. It can only be measured subjectively, by the customer's perception. He or she is the referee, the one who decides who wins or loses. Customer satisfaction data, provided by the International Air Transport Association (an independent industry body), has enabled KLM objectively to compare its position in terms of service performance on all service items. Reliability is a prime asset for an airline. The customer's journey depends on how punctual the airline is. Her or his sense of security depends on the airline's professional behaviour and the state of its equipment. It also depends on how well the customer is kept informed and whether the information can be trusted.

Being reliable is not enough. All major airlines are expected to be reliable: it is a basic. People punish airlines that do not leave and arrive on time, lose their baggage, deny their boarding, make them miss their connection or give them false information. They choose another airline next time, and in most cases they do not inform the airline of their dissatisfaction. Each customer lost this way represents a significant loss of revenue.

The goal for KLM therefore is to develop services that will attract as many customers as possible while retaining all existing customers. Satisfaction data on customer perception of service are a major management tool in this respect, because a close link exists between customers' satisfaction level and their intention to return. Their experiences also influence an airline's image in the market place because they tell other about their good and bad experiences. The service decathlon is an approach developed by KLM to turn qualitative service perception data into concrete product improvements.

Analysis of data shows that excellent ratings have a positive influence on repeat buying behaviour. Figure 13.1 shows that 98 per cent of all passengers that rated an airline 'excellent' indicated that they intended to return to the same airline for their next flight. If the rating was merely 'good', 15 per cent said they would *not* use the same airline next time. This means that excellence must be the goal.

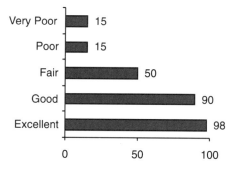

Figure 13.1　Service performance and repurchase intention

Figure 13.1 also shows that there is another side of the coin. A number of passengers rated their flight as fair, poor or very poor. A high percentage of this group said that, because of their experience, they would not return to the same airline. This means that on every Boeing 747 there are at least 10–15 people who will not return. This 'customer at risk' group deserves close attention: it is much more costly to win back a lost customer than to keep a satisfied customer.

According to KLM's onboard questionnaires, only 27 per cent of all passengers consider that none of the factors of service seem insufficient or poor what 25 per cent have encountered a problem with one of the ten service items (Figure 13.2). If people experience a number of service problems simultaneously, their intention not to return increases rapidly. The proportion of customers who experience problems with five service factors on one flight might only be 3 per cent, but 10 per cent of these will never come back. Therefore an airline that has problems with punctuality, catering and baggage on the same flight loses more customers than

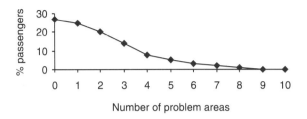

Figure 13.2 Percentage of passengers experiencing problems

if these had occurred separately. From the data KLM can derive the total number of 'customers at risk'.

KLM operates a global network, a consequence of which is dealing with people of all nationalities and cultures. It is not unusual for 40 different nationalities to be on board a Boeing 747 at the same time. It is interesting to see how these different nationalities view service. Figure 13.3 shows how the same KLM product was rated very differently by customers of different nationalities.

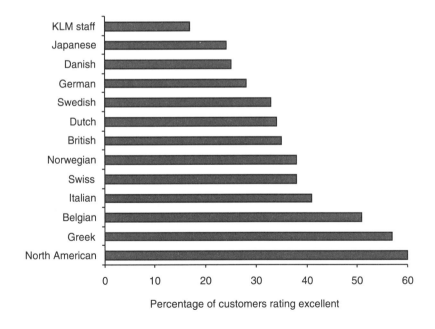

Figure 13.3 Satisfaction ratings by nationality of traveller

This type of data allows KLM to consider each route specifically. In combination with data about the passenger mix, KLM adjusts its product to please specific national characteristics, for example by adjusting meals and in-flight entertainment. KLM calls this 'route dedicated services'. Again, qualitative issues are managed using quantitative data.

THE SERVICE DECATHLON

In the Olympic games the decathlon is the most prestigious sport. Sportsmen pit their strength against each other in 10 different events to win the gold medal. For each event they gain points, which are added together to determine their final position. Not all items are equally weighted. Dan O'Brien, the winner of the last Olympic decathlon, won only three of the ten events. He even scored quite poorly in three other events (see Table 13.1). It is evident that sportsmen concentrate on and train for those events that have the greatest potential for generating points. No athlete, however, can afford to disregard any of his weaker disciplines. O'Brien failed in his last two attempts to break the world record because his 1500 metres time, his weakest event, was not good enough.

Table 13.1   Decathlon scores, 1993

	Gold O'Brien	*Silver* Hamalainen	*Bronze* Meir	Schenk	Blondel	Plaziat	Smith
100 metres	1	3	2	7	6	4	5
Long jump	1	7	4	3	6	5	2
Shot putt	4	2	3	1	7	6	5
High jump	6	3	1	1	7	3	5
400 metres	1	2	3	7	5	4	6
110 metres hurdles	2	1	5	7	4	3	6
Discus	2	1	6	3	5	7	4
Pole vault	3	2	6	5	1	4	6
Javelin	3	5	6	2	4	7	1
1500 metres	6	5	4	2	1	3	7
Overall position	1	2	3	4	5	6	7

In KLM's experience, airline service, like the decathlon, is built up of 10 service items. These 10 items are the focus of the questions included in the on-board questionnaire, of which more than 100 000 are issued annually. The questionnaire provides competitive as well as performance data. Like the decathlon, not all 10 service items influence the overall score to the same degree. And whilst the airline strives to be number one in all items, achieving the gold medal does not mean having to win on every one. Analysis of the service items has revealed the following weightings:

Table 13.2   KLM service decathlon weighting

Group	Service Decathlon Item	Contribution (%)
A	1. Friendly crew	25
A	2. Efficient crew	18
B	3. Ground services	9
B	4. Meal services	9
B	5. Drink service	9
B	6. Seat comfort	9
B	7. Cabin environment	9
C	8. Entertainment	4
C	9. Punctuality	4
C	10. Information	4
Overall score		100

KLM has grouped the 10 items into three categories. 'Crew friendliness' and 'crew efficiency' make up Group A, and are by far the most important contributors to overall satisfaction. They determine the extent to which a customer is made to feel like an important individual. Together these two items contribute 43 per cent of the overall score. This explains why Singapore Airlines, praised for its outstanding cabin crews, scores so well in the perception of the customer. Their Singapore Girl is used image to build and reinforce this in the mind of the customer.

The next five items (Group B), each of which contributes 9 per cent, deal in one way or another with the physical comfort of the customer. This includes the services a customer receives before boarding, and on board the cleanliness, climate and comfort of the cabin, the seating and the meals.

Group C consists of three items, each contributing 4 per cent. Entertainment is the icing on the cake: it kills time and can make flying fun, if done well. KLM sees Virgin as one of the top performers in this area. At 4 per cent it might seem that punctuality is unimportant, but this is not the case. Passengers consider punctuality to be a basic criterion. If it is not upto standard in this area an airline is just not in the game, and therefore punctuality does not influence the excellency rating to a great extent. Information, the last item, has a great 'value for money' rating as it costs relatively little to provide.

The relative contribution of each item does not provide the full picture. Each item can make or break (particularly break) the overall result if performed exceptionally well or badly. If passengers consider that one of the items is extremely good, for example the entertainment provided by Virgin, or Singapore's cabin staff, they will reward this with extra points, thus increasing the overall score. KLM calls this 'the delight bonus'. If one the items is perceived by customers as extremely bad they award a 'disappointment penalty'. This can influence the overall score by up to 8 per cent and make the difference between gold and silver.

DOING THE DECATHLON

The Decathlon is an integral part of KLM's Business Planning Process. Every service delivery department is involved, but can only play their part if targets for improvement and cost are clear. Quality targets are described in KLM's Service Plan and agreed in Quality Cost Contracts between Marketing and the service delivery departments. The objective is to stimulate a continuous improvement of the quality/cost ratio over the years. All the contracts are consistent with each other, and the specific goals are all directed towards the same, shared goal. The planning extends across the organisation and includes key sub-contractors.

The targets set have to meet the following criteria:

- They are relevant to the customer.
- They can be judged, by the customer, through objective and frequent measurement.
- They can be influenced by the departments responsible for delivery.
- They can be (more or less) measured for competitors as well.
- They can be interpreted clearly.

The service decathlon results are the starting point for target setting.

INNOVATE TO SATISFY

Innovation is important in sport and in service. Consider the high jump. Until 1968 everybody used the straddle technique and gradual gains in height came from continually improving technique, fitness and mental attitude. In 1968 Dick Fosbury won the Olympic gold with an entirely new technique – the Fosbury flop – taking the record to a height previously unimagined. Now everyone uses the Fosbury flop.

In service innovation, breakthroughs can be measured by service ratings. The introduction of personal video systems in seat backs or consoles is comparable to the Fosbury flop. The excellence ratings for in-flight entertainment used to hover between 15 per cent and 25 per cent. The old style screens did not offer passengers much control, nor was their quality very good. Everyone had to watch the same film; there was no choice. Since the introduction of personal videos the excellency rating has risen to 45 per cent – a significant increase. However it has also introduced a new problem: passengers expect the personal video system to work as well their own televisions at home and this relatively new technology has not yet fully met their expectations. Quantitative service data can be used to chart progress and point to where innovation is required.

KLM introduced an innovation in the airline industry when it introduced a new class: business class. Passengers responded with high ratings and this forced other airlines to follow. Again, innovation not for innovation's sake, but to satisfy customers.

14 The National and Provincial Building Society

The National and Provincial Building Society (N&P)[1] is one of the UK's ten largest building societies, with a net income of £380.5 million and assets of £14.13 billion. The society employs 4300 staff and operates 324 branches around the UK. This case study, a story of the turnaround at N&P focuses on the implementation of a novel approach to management process.

N&P was one of the first mutual societies to consider becoming a limited company. Work towards this goal started in the late 1980s when the then management team split the society into product-based business units. This resulted in a significant loss of market share in the all-important mortgage market and utter confusion in the customer base. Used to dealing with one society, customers had to determine which part of the organisation they had to deal with. Results took a turn for the worse, aggravated by the collapse of the UK housing market. The move to limited company status was put on hold and a new chief executive appointed.

David O'Brien, a non-executive director of N&P and a member of the senior management team at Rank Xerox, took over at N&P. O'Brien recognised the importance of the customer as the driving force of the organisation and was a great supporter of a process-based approach. The management team set themselves a major challenge: To create an organisation capable of competing in an environment of change where the basis of success is anticipating customer requirements and fulfilling them to their satisfaction.

To meet this challenge, N&P began to redesign the whole organisation as a series of interrelated processes. There are two important under-pinnings to the N&P approach. The first is that there are three key resources to be considered in designing an organisation: people, processes and systems. Elements of these are combined to form a capability. Through the use of its capabilities the organisation anticipates and fulfils customer requirements. The second fundamental element comprises the three questions that form the backbone of all the processes of the organisation: 'what', 'with' and 'how'. 'What' is deciding what the organisation is going to do; 'With' is about defining the resources needed to do the 'what'; and 'how' determines the method to be used to achieve the 'what'. Together with measurement and improvement, 'what, with and how' form the basic process cycle depicted in Figure 14.1.

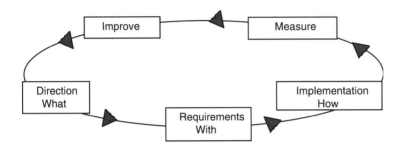

Figure 14.1 The basic process cycle

This cycle is used to design all the process within N&P. It is very much like the simple equation that forms a complex pattern like a fractal. By developing this 'metaprocess' N&P has created a common framework across the organisation that leaves space for people to make their own, individual contributions to the shape of the organisation.

There are two methods of keeping the processes in sync. The first is the overlapping nature of the three questions: what, with and how. This is depicted in Figure 14.2.

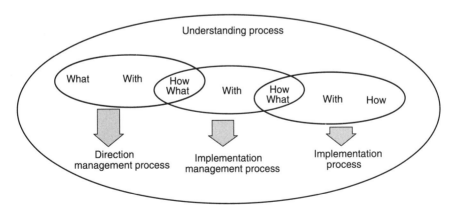

Figure 14.2 Cascading processes

This mechanism ensures consistency between all the processes or, as shown in the figure, between the direction management process, implementation management process and the implementation process. This was also the order in which the processes were instituted. Implementing the direction management process gave management the grip on the organisation they needed to move forward. This was not an academic exercise. Whilst the idea of a process-based organisation was clearly premeditated, along with some of the principles underpinning it, the detail was fleshed out as part of the change itself. The core process was simple, and the basic ideas were worked out by a team of managers in about one week. Making it happen took much longer. The basis of the approach was to replace organisational politics with process and discipline. Key to this was a group of people who could help the rest of the organisation to turn the ideas into reality. As the change progressed, people with the skills to facilitate the change were identified and trained to further embed the new values and processes.

The second mechanism connecting the processes built on the inherent nature of processes. Any process consists of inputs, work and outputs. N&P developed a mechanism called 'events'. These received inputs, processed them and produced outputs. These events are part of the processes, and their associated inputs and outputs are part of a fixed calendar, through which inputs and outputs are synchronised. This of course requires great discipline; missing an event risks a missed output that is relied on by others for their events. This process-based timetable of the organisation provides the rhythm of the business and is timed accordingly. All events consider the performance of that part of the business, and any improvements needed.

VISION AND VALUES

N&P's direction management process produces two key outputs:

- The society's mission, goals, strategy, values and philosophy of management.
- The structure, requirements, roles and responsibilities of the implementation management processes.

The N&P's mission for 1994 was: 'To satisfy our customers' requirements for Homemaking, Security and Protection, managing money and Providing for the Future through quality advice and guidance on our solutions appropriate to their circumstances and consistent with the prosperity of N&P'. This was achieved through the application of eight values:

- *Customer relationship.* 'We develop empathy with our customers through understanding, agreeing, anticipating and fulfilling their requirements throughout their lives.'
- *Quality.* 'We meet requirements first time after understanding and agreeing these requirements.'
- *Teamplay.* 'We play together in a way which enables all the roles necessary to participate in finding and agreeing the best way forward.'
- *Understanding.* 'Seeking to develop your own understanding and that of others in order to move forward with agreed understanding.'
- *Individual contribution.* 'Each individual contributes to the best of their competencies in the context of the team.'
- *Individual development.* 'Each individual seeks to develop to their potential to increase contribution to the team.'
- *Achievement.* 'Determining how to best meet and meeting team achievements.'
- *Recognition and reward.* 'We recognise and reward individual contribution to team achievements.'

These values are applied to the way the society manages itself through its philosophy of management:

> We will succeed in achieving our goals by realising the potential of our people through *Understanding, Teamplay,* and *Individual Contribution* and *Individual Development.*
>
> Through understanding our customers' requirements and fulfilling them in a *Quality* manner, we will build strong *Customer Relationships* which will be sustained through all aspects of our customers' lives.
>
> We will continually challenge ourselves to improve, as we achieve our goals. This will enable individuals and teams to realise a continuous sense of *Achievement* and enjoy *Recognition and Reward* for their contribution.

N&P is probably unique in having explicitly established a clear vision, a set of shared values and a management process, all of which act in unison. Indeed the management process is designed to ensure this happens again and again. Paul Chapman, N&P's director of organisation design and development, believes that making it explicit is an essential part of getting people to understand the process and the rationale behind it.

APPRAISAL AND DEVELOPMENT

The appraisal and development process is based around a single competency framework that applies to the entire organisation. N&P has defined 35 competencies, a mix of interpersonal skills, common organisation/ industry knowledge and behaviours, each of which has eight levels of attainment. Each person plays a role within a process team. This role is defined by the same competency set.

Appraisal is a team-based activity. Each team member is asked to assess each other team member on their contribution to the team according to three criteria: competency, style of play and values. Competency is assessed against the competency profile of the role, evidence is sought of improvement in the 35 competencies. Values are assessed mainly by the intuitive feelings of the people in the organisation, reinforced by some specifically designed psychometric tests. Style of play refers to how individuals have applied these values when carrying out their work. This appraisal forms the basis of agreed roles the individual will play in the team the following year. Again, the team as a whole decides who will play which role when carrying out the elements of process they are responsible for. This will always combine 'business as usual' and some contribution to the on-going development of the team and its associated process. All team members contribute to the assessment, although the final decision about the person's role is made by the individual and the team leader.

Part of the appraisal process is agreement on the development needs of the individual. This is based on the results of their appraisal and focuses on four areas. As N&P is based on a shared vision and values set, it is natural that the first area of development is in the individual's understanding of the society's direction, values and style of play. The main vehicle for this is what N&P calls the 'understanding process', which will be described below. The development of common qualities across N&P's processes is the second area. For example challenge, team-play and creativity are the subject of both specific competency development programmes and coaching within the teams. For the development of the technical skills of the role, for example credit assessment, regulatory requirements or underwriting, N&P uses a combination of formal courses (both in-house and external) and computer-based training. Specific programmes and information bulletins cover recurring items such as interest rate changes and year end customer activities.

REWARD AND RECOGNITION

The appraisal process is directly linked to N&P's reward structure. The system N&P have implemented is simple and again supports their team based culture. There are only four levels in the N&P structure. Using a soccer analogy, these equate to manager, coach, captain and player. These roles relate to the basic process as follows:

Role	Relation	Process
Process leader (What)	Manager	Direction
Manager of implementation and resources (With)	Coach	Requirements
Team Leader (How)	Captain	Implementation
Player (How)	Player	Implementation

Everyone at N&P, irrespective of role, is part of the same opportunity/ risk reward package. Each role has a planned pay based on the individual's competence level and an opportunity/risk element. If the company achieves its targets each individual receives an element of pay over and above that established by his or her competency level. Overperformance results in the payment of a bonus, the size of which is determined by how much the society exceeds its targets. If, however, the targets are not achieved, the risk element comes into play, with staff losing an element of their pay, although it does not fall below the fixed level established by their competency (Figure 14.3).

This reward structure has two effects: it focuses people on developing their competencies and encourages them to take responsibility for their own development. The opportunity/risk element encourages people to perform both individually and collectively.

Unlike other organisations, N&P explicitly chose not to introduce formal recognition programmes. Instead it encouraged people actively to recognise the contribution of their peers within the team. This reinforced the team as a basic building block of the organisation and emphasised that team success, rather than individual heroes, is the all-important goal.

THE UNDERSTANDING PROCESS

A key component of N&P's management process is the 'understanding process'. This is a two-way communication process designed to ensure

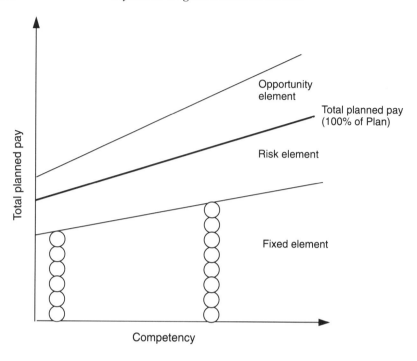

Figure 14.3   N&P's reward system

consistency of understanding of the society's direction, and to identify issues of concern across the organisation. Every two weeks the teams in N&P sit down (not all at the same time) to discuss what they have done in the last two weeks, what has worked or not worked, and the performance of the team, including customer feedback and issues of concern. The issues may be particular to the team, or of concern to the greater organisation. These issues are collected and directed to the appropriate people for resolution. This mechanism allows the organisation to identify issues that are common to the culture of the organisation. People within N&P refer to this as the 'issueometer'. Analysis of the causes of the issues provides data for improvement.

ORGANISATIONAL DESIGN FACILITY

Having the elements of people, processes and systems as building blocks has made it easy for N&P to retune its organisation as customers' needs and circumstances change. Nonetheless this would be a difficult task without a tool to help people identify the elements of capability currently available, and understand the impact changes would happen on the organisation as a whole. To support this N&P has built an organisational modelling and management tool called the Organisation Design Facility (ODF). A fully object-oriented tool, ODF holds all information on the organisation's processes and workflows, the competencies needed to carry out that work, the competencies available among the staff and the computer systems used to support the work. Through an easy-to-use Windows interface, staff can explore these different elements and see how they interrelate. A process leader or team leader considering a change to a process can see which other processes and teams will be affected, which staff will need training and which systems will need further development.

The system is based on an object model of the organisation. The process of thinking through how the different parts of the organisation relate to each other is a powerful exercise in its own right, as it highlights areas of possible conflict, gaps in the organisational design, and possible improvements.

Since the introduction of its new system N&P has gone through three major iterations, each step simplifying the organisation. Throughout all this the core mission and values have remained basically unchanged, as has the basic process cycle. By understanding the issues within the organisation and referring to feedback from customers, people within the organisation are able continually to retune the processes, people and systems. When the new approach to the organisation was implemented the business press had widely differing opinions. Whilst one national newspaper described the approach being taken by N&P as 'a breath of fresh air in an industry not renowned for innovation', another stated that N&P was 'a sect of the Moonies'. Whilst some of the language use by the N&P could be described as jargonistic, executives at N&P point out that their language reflects the new approach and reinforces the break with tradition and the past.

15 RAC Motoring Services Ltd

This case study examines a turnaround that started in the mid 1980s. Elements of understanding the customer, changing processes, people and leadership all exist. A key part of the RAC case is a significant investment in technology. Unlike other major IT investments, however, the RAC shows how success only comes when all the pieces are in place and fit together.

The Royal Automobile Club is the second largest motoring organisation in the UK offering roadside assistance, insurance and other services to motorists. In 1985 the largest of these, the Automobile Association (AA), had six million members compared with the RAC's three million. Although still some way behind, the RAC is catching up fast – the RAC now has almost six million members and the AA 7.5 million.

By the mid 1980s the RAC was handling one million breakdowns a year and wanted to expand its membership base. One of its principal constraints was the bureaucracy involved in handling breakdowns. Every single breakdown was recorded on its own piece of paper: the breakdown slip. Servicing a breakdown required a lot of data, including a location. This in itself frequently required reference to area or street maps, as well as being slow and prone to error. When completed the breakdown slip was passed to a controller, who decided which type of response was required. In the early 1980s, technology was introduced to speed up this process: a conveyor system was installed to carry the breakdown slips from the call handler to the controller. The controller needed great local knowledge to effect the dispatch of a patrolman. Keeping track of the breakdown and the location and work status of the patrols was done by voice radio.

Life for customers was no better. Not only did the poor motorist have the misfortune to break down, but he or she then had to determine where precisely he or she was, as the RAC divided the country into 17 autonomous regions, each with its own control room. Members had a card listing 17 different emergency phone numbers. Only if they called the right number would they get through to the control area that could help.

Callers who picked the wrong number were politely told of their error and instructed to try again.

The system operated adequately, but any further expansion of membership would have been unmanageable. In addition it was impossible to obtain timely and accurate performance information, either to manage the business or to set customer service standards.

The paper-based system, the difficulties customers faced and the complete lack of meaningful management information brought the business to the brink of collapse. The organisation was militaristic, with an institutionalised management structure. Managers were known as superintendents or chief superintendents. Staff saluted their superiors while wearing white gloves and military style uniforms on formal visits.

The catalyst for change was the appointment of Arthur Large as chief executive. Large joined from British Leyland, where he had worked closely with Michael Edwards and the RAC chairman, Jeffrey Rose.

Large began by seeking the views of members. As a motoring organisation the RAC had developed a wide range of products and services. The organisation, however, was failing at its core activity – breakdown services. Large translated his research into a more focused view of the purpose of the RAC. His view was that: 'What the motorist wanted most was for his motoring organisation to answer the phone quickly, to get to him quickly and to re-mobilise him.'

He envisaged the RAC as an efficient and profitable business, unclouded by tradition and rid of its embedded, bureaucratic practices. His objective was to transform the RAC into a customer-focused, business-minded organisation. 'Getting through. Getting there. Getting going' became the rallying call for the changes to follow.

An extensive programme of customer research provided a constant flow of information that stimulated the improvement activities. The research showed that by far the most important aspect of service was responsiveness: getting to the motorist. This is an example of the emotional needs of customers: just having someone there can ease the strain. The problem is half solved even if the car cannot be immediately fixed. To create a sense of urgency and pressure on the organisation, in 1986 the RAC publicly committed itself to reaching eight out of ten stranded motorists within the hour. This standard was far in excess of market performance, although in line with customer expectations. The standard was announced as soon as the processes and systems were fully installed.

An urgent requirement, therefore, was a new process and supporting technology to log and follow up breakdown calls. Rather than start from scratch, the RAC began to search for existing technology to automate the services. This led it to New South Wales in Australia, where a command and control system had been built for an Australian motoring organisation by Yezerski Roper Ltd. Yezerski Roper accepted the challenge of building a similar system for the RAC, but in half the time taken to build the original system – competitors were also investigating similar solutions. In two years CARS (computer assisted rescue services) was developed, tested and implemented.

The CARS system (which absorbed a total investment of £30 million) allows calls to be handled anywhere in the country. It combines a computer-based command and control centre, supported by six regional centres, with direct two-way data communication to the patrols via mobile data terminals. No matter where the breakdown occurs, the motorist now calls a single freephone number. The motorist's information is logged directly into CARS, where upon identification of membership, member's location and an analysis of the fault are processed and the data relayed to the mobile data terminal in the patrolman's car. CARS maintains a comprehensive 'gazetteer' – an electronic map that contains thousands of landmarks to make identification of the member's location easier. This system, together with the mobile data terminals, allows easy identification of a free patrol vehicle closest to the breakdown, which can then be dispatched instantaneously. Since introducing the system the RAC has consistently exceeded its target of reaching 80 per cent of breakdowns within the hour.

The mobile data terminals have revolutionised the organisation. Management information now flows directly from the sharp end of the business to the managers, providing them with timely and accurate information. From its beginnings as an antiquated organisation, the RAC is now probably better organised in its field of operation than any other commercial organisation. The management information available includes detailed data on the performance of each patrol or command and control operator, and provides managers with data that enables them to focus their efforts on improving customer service and controlling costs.

Important though it was, it would be very wrong to believe that the turnaround of the RAC was due to the technology alone. New technology and old management never produce the results hoped for.

During Large's tenure at the RAC unnecessary levels of management were axed, reducing the hierarchy from 13 to six. As part of the cultural change programme, every member of staff was put through a training programme entitled 'People in Mind'. This programme introduced the concept of PACE: Personally Accountable, Caring and Enterprising. PACE summed up the behaviours the new organisation valued. People were encouraged to ignore the extensive rule book and apply the PACE principles in doing what was right for customers.

The impact of technology on the front-line staff was significant. To reduce the bureaucracy, the number of administrative staff was halved. This was matched by an increase in the number of patrolmen from 700 to 1300. Staff were told to ignore the rulebook and follow the new rule: do what is right for the customer. The unions were involved from the start. An open and honest approach, based on consultation and focused on obtaining the full involvement of staff in designing the new processes and systems, was crucial to the success of the change. Not all was sweetness and light, but the common understanding that change was essential for survival and a long-term future bound the company and the union to a single cause.

If technology had its greatest impact on work at the front line, it was the change in culture that most impacted on the RAC management. The RAC's militaristic and autocratic style had pervaded the organisation, and managers were accustomed to giving and receiving commands. But worse than this was the creeping bureaucracy that had stifled all initiative and caused the inevitable decay. The change was not gentle. Within three years 90 per cent of the directors and senior executives had moved on and in their wake came a new breed of managers, bringing a fresh, commercial approach and a more open and participative style.

Great effort was put into communicating the change The personnel department was charged with sorting out internal communication. One of the major problems in communication was dealing with remote staff, that is, the patrolmen, who spend all their time on the road. The RAC introduced 'Call Sign', a monthly audio tape sent to all 1300 patrolmen. Team briefings a two-way, face-to-face programme of managers meeting the staff – was introduced to further improve dialogue across the organisation.

An unusual but fundamental part of the strategy concerned property. Call centres were concentrated into five supercentres, each housing between 250 and 500 staff at locations throughout the UK. These new centres were designed as expressions of the company's new culture: high tech, high profile and focused on its motoring members. The first of these centres was built at the end of the M1 in London, quickly followed by the opening of the RAC's flagship control centre beside the M6 near Walsall. More recently (November 1994) a super centre was built beside the M5 near Bristol, where on one floor 200 RAC staff provide a 24-hour telephone-based service to members. All the buildings are open plan and single status, reinforcing the culture in which communication and team-work are paramount.

The change at RAC, began with an understanding of customers, and it is from there that it has continued. One of the more important events to impact on the service was the realisation that the RAC could no longer be a service that simply fixed vehicles. Improvements in vehicle reliability, along with changing customer needs, require staff to be incident managers first and good mechanics second.

Recognition of this culminated in the launch of a comprehensive service in 1990 called Reflex. Reflex is simply a promise to get the motorist moving whatever it takes. A new role was created, of personal incident manager, who is mandated to meet the customer's requirements irrespective of what that involves. New services were introduced, including replacement vehicles and overnight accommodation for members stranded away from home. This endeavour to bring complete peace of mind to the motorist has been a huge commercial success. Moreover, the creation of personal incident managers sent a powerful message through the company, reinforcing the idea of commitment to customers whatever it takes.

Reflex is an example of how continuous dialogue between an organisation and its customers creates new revenue opportunities, as well as maximising the returns from existing products. The RAC makes a great effort to build this dialogue.

Another key development was the introduction of motor manufacturer accounts. The marketing and sales departments set up teams to sell bulk memberships to car manufacturers, securing deals that would form the basis of phenomenal growth. In the period 1986 to 1994 the RAC won 70 per cent of such contracts, under which RAC membership is part of the new car purchase.

The RAC's service managers now have the ability to manage. This in turn has enabled budgetary control to be devolved to the area service managers, who now have control over service costs, vans and patrolmen and how well these, and agent resources, are used.

In tandem with its investment in IT, the RAC launched a programme to provide motoring services to company fleet operators and, through agreements with manufacturers, to the purchasers of new cars. This programme has been pivotal in developing the business of the RAC. The CARS system, discussed above, has proved key to securing many of the new motor manufacturer contracts and adding two million new members. Two factors were responsible for this success. The first was the RAC's ability to demonstrate its lead in service quality. The second was the comprehensive fault and diagnostic information generated by CARS. This information is extremely valuable to manufacturers seeking to improve the quality and reliability of their vehicles.

The increase in the quality, quantity and availability of management information, has not only improved operational efficiency, but also enabled the organisation to be streamlined.

At the heart of the RAC's organisation is the quality management system (Figure 15.1), a management process that addresses direction, strategy, objectives, process improvement and measurement.

Figure 15.1 RAC's quality management system

Leadership is, as always, at the heart of the RAC. Leadership in the RAC is about commitment to a common vision, described as shared enthusiasm. The RAC has two types of manager; those that have this commitment, and new managers. Without this shared commitment the organisation will not reproduce the progress it has achieved in the past, and that it continues to want. Building this commitment has taken time and a great deal of communication. However, commitment alone has not been sufficient: the RAC introduced a programme to develop executive capability, designed and run by its own managers, with support from an external consultancy.

The RAC's investment in change has paid off in increased membership, market share and profits. After an initial period of four years, when the bulk of the investment was made, it was generating profits in double figures by 1991 whilst market share increased by 3–4 per cent. The improved service has led to a vast increase in customer satisfaction, which now exceeds 95 per cent. The RAC is determined not to rest on its laurels, and continues to invest in its people and the latest technology to achieve still higher standards. Strong leadership, focused on releasing the creativity of people to meet customers' needs, and the application of technology are what changed the RAC. They are also the factors that will keep it at the forefront of its market.

Appendix I The Voice of the Customer Handbook

The following pages provide a guide to a technique to help build a customer-focused organisation.

NEW PURPOSE, NEW DIRECTIONS

An increasing number of companies are finding themselves between a rock and a hard place. As markets mature and product life cycles shrink, relying on the differentiation of core products or services is becoming increasingly difficult. Organisations are also faced with customers who are more demanding, more vocal and know they have a choice. Many organisations will be crushed. Those that survive will be those that are best at tapping the experience and wisdom of their people to understand and meet the needs of their customers.

Today, success depends upon customer satisfaction. Achieving a high level of customer satisfaction requires more than simply offering good products or services at reasonable prices. Customers' buying decisions are increasingly based on non-price issues, such as quality, relationships and problem solving. This provides all companies with a challenge. A truly customer-oriented approach is vital to the achievement of long-term success. Voice of the Customer is a key programme in providing excellent service to customers and enabling continuous improvement.

Voice of the Customer provides a way of improving through a process of listening, mutual learning, and action (Figure A1.1). During the process we learn to listen to what customers have to say. By working with invited customers the process seeks to understand their needs, to share mutual knowledge and expertise and to make improvements based on that input. The clear link between feedback and action is a powerful tool for securing greater commitment and loyalty from customers.

QUALITY FUNCTION DEPLOYMENT

Voice of the Customer (VoC) is based on a Japanese quality tool called Quality Function Deployment. This was brought to the attention of the West in a *Harvard Business Review* article entitled 'The House of Quality' by D. Clausing and J. R. Hauser (1988). The title takes it name from the shape of the matrix used (Figure A1.2).

At its most simple, Quality Function Deployment is a matrix for relating a customer needs to the features of a product or service and using this to generate

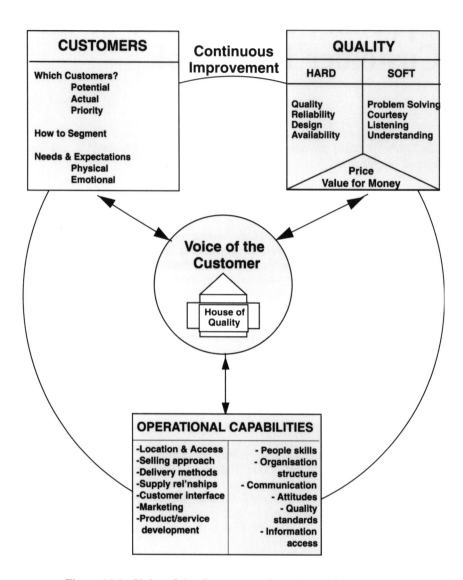

Figure A1.1   Voice of the Customer and continuous improvement

improvement actions. With VoC I have extended this use to cater for the overall relationship between a supplier and its customers. In this way VoC provides a vehicle for accessing information that otherwise might not surface. The power of the approach is limited only by the willingness of the organisation to act on the data, and the ability of its people to develop answers to the problems and aspirations customer express.

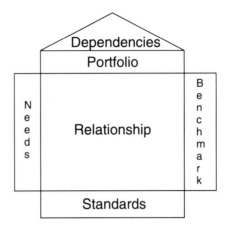

Figure A1.2 The House of Quality

USING VOICE OF THE CUSTOMER

This section outlines the stages of running a VoC project. It is advisable to use a knowledgeable facilitator for the first project. The goal must be to embed the approach in the organisation. Listening to customers is not a project, it must be a way of life.

The Steps

There are three major stages in the VoC project:

- Establish the project.
- Data gathering.
- Analysis and action.

Each of these steps is described briefly below. This sequence of activities has been shown to work and it is recommended for initial VoC projects. After that, adapt the process to suit your own needs. Remember, the goal is to make listening to customers a way of life; adaptation is a natural part of embedding the approach in your organisation.

1. Establish the Project

First, set the scope of the project. The narrower the focus, the more specific the actions that are generated. A broad, organisation-wide approach will produce broad organisation actions. You must find where the problems are and what scope (and authority) there is for initiating meaningful action. Remember, like charity, quality begins at home.

Second, establish the team. The following roles are needed:

- Sponsor: an initial project will need a sponsor. This person should be a senior in the business adopting VoC.
- Project Manager: someone to manage the day-to-day activities of the project. Needs to be a good organiser.
- Consultant: someone independent of the business and experienced in facilitating customer events to run the workshops, design the materials and act as 'honest broker' between the organisation and its customers.

Third, the customers. To be effective a VoC project needs between four and ten customers. Fewer means views are often too specific; more than ten are difficult to manage. Choose customers who are demanding; those that complain most have most to offer – they know what your weaknesses are.

You will have to sell their involvement in the project to them – what's in it for them. The selling points I have used are:

- Improvements in the service/product the customer receives.
- Better relationships with key suppliers.
- Influence in the direction and processes of the supplier's business.
- Knowledge of the VoC approach and tools.

Remember not to promise too much. Be clear and honest about which changes are within your remit and which are not.

Fourth, kick off the meeting. An initial half-day meeting of all participants is used to familiarise them with the objectives of the project, the timetable and the approach being used. It is important to establish a sense of openness, which is essential if meaningful data is to be obtained. The goal of the event is to build commitment to and understanding of the project and its results. The agenda should include:

- The objectives of the project
  - for the supplier
  - for the customers.
- The players and their roles.
- The methodology (QFD).
- Timetable.

Remember, this is a customer-focused activity – start as you mean to go on.

2. Data Gathering

VoC is all about obtaining from the customer meaningful data upon which action can be based. Like any data-related activity, 'Garbage in; garbage out' applies.

First, for each customer, run an individual *data gathering workshop*. This allows customers to be open without constraint. Remember, most people don't like to complain, so this 'privacy' is important to them.

Use the time – again about half a day is required – to identify the customers' needs. Use open questions such as 'What would you like to see improved?' to solicit their views. Encourage openness and candour. Capture these points on cards or a flipchart – they are the raw data upon which the House of Quality is built. Find the logical groupings, using the customers to help with this.

Once the data gathering is complete, explain the next steps and thank people for their involvement.

Second, run an *integration workshop*. This workshop, with all customers present, will need three quarters of a day. The objective here is to identify common problems as the basis for priority actions.

Present the raw data from the initial workshops and ask the customers to identify common threads – supergroups of data. From these supergroups, ask customers to identify and weight the issues.

Many people try to eliminate this step by doing the grouping in-house. This is dangerous. The temptation for people to prioritise the work based on what they can do easily, or what *they* think the problem is, is too great. Remember, you cannot second-guess a customer.

Third, the issues identified in the integration workshop are used as the basis for a *questionnaire* for further data collection. Questionnaires are useful for proving the validity of the priorities and increasing the size of the data sample. Do not use questionnaires as a substitute for the workshops. Service is a personal thing. Workshops represent an opportunity to build relationships, questionnaires don't.

Take the issues statements and translate them into positive benefit-oriented statements. For example the problem 'I can't find the right person to contact' can become 'I know who to contact.' These statements become the expectation statements in the VoC matrix. Compile a questionnaire around these statements, asking four questions:

- How important is this aspect?
- How important will this aspect be in the future?
- How do you rate our performance?
- How do you rate the performance of our competitors?

Ask people to rank these statements on a 0–5 scale. The importance figure is added to the expectation statements to form the basis of a weighting. The performance data forms the input for the benchmark.

Allow space at the end of each question or section for comments. These can often be a source of information and ideas when it comes to action planning.

Fourth, run a *portfolio workshop*. The objective of this workshop is to identify the supplier's view of the world. A cross-sample of the organisation is needed to describe the range of offerings. A suggested agenda for this workshop is as follows:

- Explanation of the VoC project and update on status.
- Collect and group data on service offerings.
- Compare with customer expectations – assess the match using a 0–5 scale.
- Identify any dependencies between the offerings (the roof of the matrix).
- Brainstorm initial improvement ideas.

Update the matrix with the data generated by the workshop.

3. Analysis and Action

The data collected is no use without action. Indeed, having asked customers their needs automatically raises their expectation that something will be done to address them. Failure to show that their inputs have been acted on is fatal.

First, build the *House of Quality*. The QFD matrix is a vehicle for structuring the data. Build up the matrix as follows:

- Insert the customers' expectations statements in the left-hand column with the priority scores (this data comes from the questionnaires).
- Insert the portfolio statements (offerings) from the portfolio workshop.
- Calculate and insert the relationship. This is calculated by multiplying the importance (from the questionnaire) with the match (from the portfolio workshop).
- Insert the benchmark. This figure is the difference between our performance and our competitors' performance collected in the questionnaire.
- Calculate the influence factor. This is the sum of each column.

Second, set up *action planning workshops*. This is the key part of the exercise. The first part is attended by the suppliers' staff, the second part by both supplier and customer representatives. With the help of the data the supplier workshops identify the areas for action and propose specific improvement suggestions. The combined workshop receives these suggestions and accepts or amends them. This second group can also add suggestions. At the end of this, the project has generated a set of customer-approved improvements.

Remember to thank the customers for their help. Check to make sure you have met their expectations and take corrective action where necessary.

Third, provide the customers with periodic *feedback* on the progress of the actions. The data will have made sure the right issues are addressed; seeing them addressed is the biggest compliment you can pay your customers.

Remember, a most important aspect of business is the relationship you have with customers. Ignore it at your peril.

SUMMARY

When it comes to listening to customers, deafness is a life-threatening disease. VoC is a proven approach to starting this important dialogue in a way that focuses on issues that are important to customers and provides measurable benefits for them and for you.

Remember that constant listening and action is what separates the winners from the also-rans. Teach this technique widely in your organisation. Strive for the time when listening to the voice of the customer is not a project, but a way of life.

Good listening and good luck!

Appendix II Dynamic Organisation Audit

This simple self-diagnostic is based on my research of the characteristics of a dynamic organisation. This version is a subset of the complete instrument, which includes techniques for the more rigorous benchmarking of some of the factors. It is designed to generate a discussion of, and proposals to address, the steps needed to improve organisational performance.

Please feel free to use the audit, adapting it as you feel appropriate. The key is to gather views from across the organisation, and if appropriate from customers and other stakeholders. The objective is to generate conversations from which a large number of improvements can stem. Remember the importance of participation in effecting change.

Beware of building a picture based on your perceptions alone. You should continuously challenge your opinions, looking for evidence to support your view from customers, staff and competitors. In this way you will build a more accurate picture of your organisation's capabilities.

Does your organisation focus on the customer?

Issue	Importance					Improvement					Proposals for action
	1	2	3	4	5	1	2	3	4	5	
We have sharply defined the customer groups we serve.											
Customers are clear about what products and services we offer.											
We use regular and systematic methods for measuring customers' perceptions of us.											
We use systematic and imaginative methods to monitor customers' changing needs.											
We actively encourage, monitor and act on complaints.											
We measure customer's repurchase intentions and retention.											
We seek and develop long-term relationships with chosen customers.											
We can rapidly identify all aspects of our relationship with a given customer.											
We capture and use information from the front-line in our decision making.											
There is total commitment to satisfying customers throughout the organisation.											

Does your organisation exite, empower and develop people?

Issue	Importance					Improvement					Proposals for action
	1	2	3	4	5	1	2	3	4	5	
People have the right skills, knowledge and behaviours to carry out their roles.											
People believe they make a valued contribution to the organisation.											
People have a real say in what they do.											
We actively monitor employee satisfaction.											
People believe they are fairly rewarded for the contribution they make.											
Training and development is freely available to all our people.											
People have the authority to make decisions.											
We recognise efforts to satisfy customers and 'go the extra mile.'											
Success is actively and publicly celebrated.											
Middle managers play an effective role in coaching and developing people's performance.											
This is an organisation where people are encouraged to try new things.											
Our organisational structure focuses effort and resources on the things customers value.											
We make effective use of teams within and across organisational boundaries.											

Do you have integrated and effective management processes?

Issue	Importance					Improvement					Proposals for action
	1	2	3	4	5	1	2	3	4	5	
We understand our core competencies.											
We have a clear statement of direction, which is understood by and guides our people.											
We have a clear set of values, which are understood by and guide our people.											
We have effective processes to convert direction into hard and soft operating results.											
Our values guide our actions and decisions throughout the organisation.											
Our management style encourages active participation and debate.											
Ideas, experience and knowledge are freely shared throughout the organisation.											
We are good at communicating.											
We track key operational (non-financial) performance indicators.											
Performance measures are openly shared and discussed.											
Managers have the skills, knowledge and behaviours to do their jobs effectively.											
The best people get promoted.											

Does your organisation have effective business processes?

Issue	Importance					Improvement					Proposals for action
	1	2	3	4	5	1	2	3	4	5	
Our products and services are rated highly by customers and competitors.											
We rapidly identify and correct failing in our products and services.											
Customers regard us as easy to do business with.											
Customers find it easy to contact the right person.											
We set targets for improvements based on customer feedback.											
We involve customers in the design of processes that affect them.											
We continually increase the productivity of our business processes.											
Our processes are non-bureaucratic. Meetings, manuals and paperwork are minimal.											
Functional boundaries do not get in the way of our processes.											
People have the information to do their work well.											
We have working partnerships with key suppliers.											
We outsource non-core activities that can be done more effectively by specialists.											

Is your organisation externally focused?

Issue	Importance					Improvement					Proposals for action
	1	2	3	4	5	1	2	3	4	5	
We actively monitor the activities of our major competitors.											
We use benchmarking to compare performance with and learn from the best in class.											
We monitor key socioeconomic trends.											
We share and discuss the changing environment with our people.											
We experiment with new approaches to management.											
We monitor technology developments that might lead to new opportunities.											

Notes

1. Since these events, Management Centre Europe has changed considerably. It continues to be a provider of excellent executive development programmes and conferences.
2. Based on conversations primarily with Nissan's Andy Green, but also with Ian Gibson and Brian Carolin. Nissan's former Personnel Director, Peter Wickens, gives a full insider's account of the establishment of Nissan's UK plant in his book *The Road to Nissan. Flexibility, Quality, Teamwork* (Basingstoke, Macmillan, 1987).

1 A NEW SCHEME OF THINGS

1. This quotation is from Buckminster Fuller's book, *Synergetics* (1975). I thought it worth quoting more of this as it explains the impact of decomposition and specialisation (a common trait of organisations) particularly well: 'We are in an age that assumes the narrowing trends of specialisation to be logical, natural and desirable. Consequently, society expects all earnestly responsible communication to be crisply brief. Advancing science has now discovered that all the known causes of biological extinction have been caused by overspecialisation, whose concentration of selected genes sacrifices general adaptability. Thus, the specialist brief for pinpoint brevity is dubious. In the meantime, humanity has been deprived of comprehensive understanding. Specialisation has bred feelings of isolation, futility and confusion in individuals. It has resulted in the individual's leaving responsibility for thinking and social action to others.'
2. Service Excellence: A Survey of Executive Opinion' research by John Humble and Management Centre Europe. The study examined the opinions of 4000 executives in North America, Europe and Japan, trading blocs representing over 60 per cent of world trade.
3. Ibid.
4. I picked this term up from Colin Adamson, who was then managing director of TARP Europe.
5. Bob Galvin, former chairman of Motorola, described the level of service Motorola was seeking to develop as that which the customer receiving would say 'wow!'
6. 'Corporate Values: The Bottom Line Contribution' studied the opinions of 450 senior managers in the UK. The research report, developed by John

Humble and sponsored by Digital Equipment Company, generated huge interest. It again showed how many organisations pay only scant regard to important issues like values.

7. Referenced in *The Machine That Changed the World* by James P. Womack, Daniel T. Jones and Daniel Roos (Rawson Associates, 1990).
8. This term was introduced by Professor Dorothy Leonard-Barton in her book *Wellsprings of Knowledge* (1995). Whilst the book focuses on product development, the term is equally applicable across the organisation.
9. The butterfly effect was described by James Gleick in his book Chaos (1987). The book opens by quoting Edward Lorenz's remarks about chaos theory. Pondering whether a butterfly flapping its wings in Tokyo had an effect on a tornado in Texas, Lorenz answered yes. There is much interest about what we, in management circles, can learn from chaos theory, and the other new ideas in science. Recent articles have been included in the *Harvard Business Review* and *Management Today* exploring this fascinating subject. I believe there is much to be gained from drawing these parallels.

2 GETTING CLOSE TO CUSTOMERS

1. From his book *Thriving on Chaos. Handbook for a Management Revolution* (London, Macmillan, 1988).
2. Quoted in *Managing on the edge* by Richard Tanner Pascale (1990).
3. Paul Fifield developed the concept of context marketing into a customer-led approach to developing organisations. The approach will be discuased in greater detail in Paul's book, *Customer Strategy*, to be published by Butterworth Heinemann in 1997.
4. The study, reported in the *Financial Times* on 23 October 1995, was carried out by Mintel and Coley Bell Porter. More than 1000 adults were questioned about the characteristics of 25 of the largest companies in the UK.
5. I am grateful to my friend Charles Savage, who has worked as a consultant to ABB, for bringing this to my attention and to Dr Arun Gairola of ABB Germany for permission to reproduce it here.
6. Technical Assistance Research Programmes (TARP) have carried out extensive research on complaints and their impact and the measurement of customer satisfaction. TARP research shows that in the travel and leisure industry, 59 per cent of people experience some type of problem compared with 36 per cent in financial services, 41 per cent in telecommunications, 50 per cent in petrochemical, 37 per cent in small packaged goods and 28 per cent in utilities. I have not researched this, but to me the figures suggest that problems and complaints are roughly in proportion to the contact between staff and customers. The less frequent the personal contact, the fewer the problems. This ties into the opinions some people express that we have been good at getting products and processes right, but not so good at getting the people aspects right.
7. This approach was developed by me and a group of consultants at Digital. It was applied very successfully to improve relationships with key customers of

the software maintenance business. QFD is extensively used by many organisations for product development.

8. Peter Senge, *The Fifth Discipline: The Art and Practice of The Learning Organization* (1990). This book is packed with examples of the quick fix and the problems they can lead to. Early in the book he recounts the Beer game, a simple business simulation in which the seemingly right answer leads the players into chaos. Chapter 4, 'The Laws of the Fifth Discipline', includes:
   - Today's problems come from yesterday's solutions.
   - The easy way out usually leads back in.
   - The cure can be worse than the disease.
   - Faster is slower.
   - Small changes can produce big results – but the areas of highest leverage are often the least obvious.

   These are all illustrations of the danger of not thinking systemically before acting.
9. Ibid.
10. Christopher Lloyd, 'Junk mail will do nicely' *Sunday Times*, 14 April 1996.
11. Ibid.
12. 'What Keeps Customers?', a special report on customer retention strategies, November 1995. The study asked 150 executives – chosen from among the 250 largest US banking companies – for their opinions on the importance and practice of customer retention.

3 A NEW APPROACH TO CHANGE

1. This phrase relates to the approach to change, adopted by many organisations, suggested by Kurt Lewin. They recommended that the current organisations be unfrozen, changed and refrozen. This of course fits perfectly with a paradigm of organisations where the bosses (or the consultants) decide when the changes are needed and what they will be, and then go back to business as usual until the next change.
2. *The Fifth Discipline: The Art and Practice of the Learning Organisation* (1990). Peter Senge's work is of great importance. His explanation of the personal and organisational mechanisms that are needed for on-going learning should be studied and practiced by all managers.
3. Robert M. Pirsig details the problems of the reductionist school of thinking in his novel *Zen and the Art of Motorcycle Maintenance*, (London: Bodley Head, 1974).
4. Henry Minzberg, 'Crafting Strategy', *Harvard Business Review*, July/August 1987.
5. For a fuller description see *The State We're In* by Will Hutton (London: Jonathan Cape, 1995).
6. Collins and Porras, 'Organisational Visions and Visionary Organisations', Research Paper 1159, Stanford University Graduate Business School, 1991.
7. Ibid.
8. I am indebted to the work of Anne and Paul Thorne from DOCSA who have shaped my thinking on values and culture. Their toolkit (described

briefly in this section) for measuring organisational culture (based on the original work of Professor Geert Hofstede) is a valuable addition to the armoury of the manager in a dynamic organisation.

9. This excellent piece of research is described in *Corporate Culture and Performance* by John P. Kotter and James L. Heskett published by The Free Press 1992. Much of the book is taken up by the quantitative results of the research, but the commentary and case studies are particularly enlightening for any student of the dynamic organisation.
10. This model of organisations was originally developed by Professor Geert Hofstede and is detailed in his book *Culture and Organizations* (New York: McGraw Hill, 1991).
11. The toolkit has been developed by DOCSA and is the copyright of DOCSA Ltd.
12. O'Brien shared this when speaking at a seminar with Peter Senge in London.
13. 'The Information Executives Truly Need', *Harvard Business Review*, Jan.–Feb. 1995.
14. Kaplan and Norton introduced the concept of the balanced scorecard in their article 'The Balanced Scorecard: Measures That Drive Performance', *Harvard Business Review*, Jan.–Feb. 1992.

4 LEADERSHIP IN THE POST-INDUSTRIAL ERA

1. 'What Leaders Really Do', *Harvard Business Review*, May–June 1990.
2. Gore's complete set of values are:
    Fairness: a dedication to maintaining it.
    Commitment: if you make one, you keep it.
    Freedom: the company allows individuals the freedom to grow beyond what they are doing, and they are expected to use it.
    Waterline: a hole above a ship's waterline won't cause it to sink, but one below it will. Certain decisions, say building a new plant, demand consultation and agreement. Others, such as launching a new product, don't. This value substitutes for budgets.
    Quoted in *Fortune*, 21 February 1994.
3. Peter Wickens, *The Road to Nissan: Flexibility, Quality and Teamwork* (London: Macmillan, 1987). Wickens described the role of the supervisor in Nissan's manufacturing plant near Sunderland. In the book he also says that much of what Nissan implemented in team working could have been learned by studying the practices of Careras Rothman based a few miles down the road. It is clear that the UK is not short of excellent practices; the best UK companies are up with the best in the world. Unfortunately our average level of performance is below that of other countries.
4. The survey, carried out by International Survey Research of California, examined the thoughts of managers in corporations that conducted major restructuring between 1991 and 1995.
5. Ibid.
6. Prahalad's comments were part of a presentation urging corporate executives to give young, able managers a say in the future of their

companies. He added 'Pay is important, but a 5 per cent pay rise is not going to keep these young people excited. What they need is to have a shared voice in the company'. Report in *Financial Times* on 26 October 1995: 'Bosses urged to give young managers a say' by Richard Donkin.

7. I am indebted to Geoff Elliott for his help and ideas. It is based on our ideas and research with a number of organisations who share an interest in the future competencies of leaders. I would be pleased to hear from anyone interested in joining in the development of this.

8. System archetypes are a technique developed by Peter Senge and reported in his excellent book, *The Fifth Discipline: The Art and Practice of Learning Organisations* (1990), which should be required reading for any practising and aspiring leaders. Systems archetype seeks to identify the structural elements of a problem or situation, thereby avoiding the simple cause and effect solution that so often exacerbates things.

5 PEOPLE DO IT ALL

1. Maslow's hierarchy of needs postulates that people's needs differ according to their circumstances. He developed his hierarchy as a classification of these needs, as shown in the diagram below.

Maslow explained how higher needs only motivate when the lower needs have been met. Equally, when they are met, lower needs are no longer a source of motivation. As Western economies have developed, most people do not have to struggle with the physiological needs.

2. Quoted in *A book about the classic Avis advertising campaign of the 60s* (1995) by Henri Holmgren and Peer Eriksson.

3. DOCSA, Diagnosing Organisation Culture for Strategic Advantage, is a powerful tool with which to measure organisation culture from multiple perspectives. I have used it in a number of organisations, where it has provided valuable data and generated useful insights into the nature of the organisation's culture. See Chapter 3 for a discussion of organisational values and culture, including the role of DOCSA. DOCSA is the copyright of DOCSA Ltd.

4. Skills Passport was a scheme launched by the Confederation of British Industry to establish a mechanism for individuals to record their skills in a way that other employees would recognise.

6   BUILDING A WELL-OILED MACHINE

1. This information was quoted by Dr Albert Thienel at a conference in Dusseldorf organised by EuroForum. The research was carried out by the Kienbaum und Partnership GmbH.
2. *Harvard Business Review*, vol. 68, no. 2 (July–August 1990).
3. Quoted in 'Quality: What motivates American workers?', *Business Week*, 12 April 1993.
4. Many figures have been quoted for the success and failure of BPR projects. The figure I quote is based on a report from industry analysts and researchers, New Science Associates. In their report on BPR (February 94), they quoted the following figures:

Organisation success in meeting BPR goals (per cent)	
Very successful	6.7
Successful	25.4
Somewhat	44.7
Not very	20.7
Unsuccessful	2.5

They went on to add that the biggest challenges of BPR projects were change management and communication. This is typical of the BPR advocates who believe that changing processes is all it takes. They all too often completely ignore, or relegate to afterthought, the management of change which is essentially a people thing.
5. *Financial Times*, October 1994.
6. *Financial Times*, October 1994. Lorenz ends the article by saying 'That is why easily misunderstood metaphors such as re-engineering are so attractive yet so dangerous. It is not surprising that wary companies avoid them like the plague'.
7. Drucker quoted this in an article published in the *Wall Street Journal*. Unfortunately I have been unable to trace the date of publication.
8. Laurence Megson and John Horsley, who were at the time part of Digital's internal organisation consulting group, led the team through the change.
9. The group that developed the Organisation Design Facility have left N&P and formed Adaptive Solutions for Business Ltd to provide this capability, now called 'The Adaptive Frmework', to other organisations.
10. *Newsweek*, 27 February 1995.
11. This data was produced by Paul A Strassmann and discussed in his article 'The Value of Computers, Information and Knowledge'. The article, and

further information on Strassmann's interesting views and research can be found on the World Wide Web at URL http:\\www.strassmann.com.

12. Quoted in his speech to Management Centre Europe's first global conference on service excellence.

13. Ken Olsen, founder of Digital Equipment Corporation developed the minicomputer because he had a cultural problem with the concept of mainframes and glass-house data centres. He built up Digital from nothing to a turnover of $13 billion in 30 years, collecting along the way the description 'The Ultimate Entrepreneur' from *Fortune* magazine.

14. Quoted in Louise Kehoe, 'OK, let's reengineer the planet', *Financial Times*, 17 July 1995.

15. This system was described in Pawson, Bravard and Cameron, 'The Case for Expressive Systems', *Sloan Management Review*, Winter 1995.

16. 'A hand across the great divide', *Financial Times*, 6 March 1996.

7 DYNAMIC ORGANISATIONS: THE GREATER CONTEXT

1. Extracted from a speech given by Parker Follett to the London Business School. Quoted in Gordon Wills, 'Mary Parker Follett and the Integration of Business Administration', in Anthony D. Tillet, Thomas Kempner and Gorden Wells (eds), *Management Thinkers* (Middlesex: Pelican Books, 1970).

2. In *The New Paradigm of Business* (by Michael Ray and Alan Rinzler, published by G. P. Putnam's Sons, 1993) a series of articles explores some of the fundamental shifts of business. Many see a whole new role for business as the centrepiece of society. They argue that to meet this changing role, the purpose of an organisation will change, placing greater importance on the spiriual needs of people to balance the economic needs. We see the emergence of this in the dynamic organisation, where much greater emphasis is placed on people.

3. Taken from CBI News, September 1995.

4. This figure is taken from the World Economic Forum's 1995 report, quoted in CBI News, March 1996.

5. 'Prepared for the Future? The British and Technology', a research report conducted by MORI on behalf of Motorola.

8 CHANGE: SEVEN SINS, SEVEN VIRTUES

1. Peter Wickens, *The Ascendant Organisation* (London: MacMillan, 1995).

9 AVIS EUROPE

1. This model was developed in association with John Seddon. Further details can be found in his book *I want you to cheat* (Vanguard Press, 1992).

10 BIRMINGHAM MIDSHIRES BUILDING SOCIETY

1. A mutual society is an organisation owned by its customers: savings and mortgage account holders. This ownership structure removes the need to pay dividends to shareholders but imposes some constraints on what the society can do and how it can raise cash.
2. It is an all too common characteristic, and perhaps the most salutary lesson in corporate management, that existing management teams seem unable either to perceive the need to change or to effect the necessary change. This is not a universal trait. The dynamic organisation focuses effort on regularly assessing the fit between culture, strategy and the external environment; with the environment acting as the source of energy.

14 THE NATIONAL AND PROVINCIAL BUILDING SOCIETY

1. At the time of writing the National and Provincial Building Society was in the process of merging with the Abbey National plc.

References

Argyris, Chris (1994) *Good Communication That Blocks Learning* Harvard Business Review, July–Aug.

Beer, Michael; R. A. Eisenstat and Bert Spector (1990) 'Why change programs don't produce change' *Harvard Business Review,* Nov.–Dec.

Beer, Stafford (1972) *The Brain of the Firm* Penguin, London

Bennis, Warren (1989) *On Becoming A Leader* Hutchinson Business, London

Brandt, John R. (1994) 'Middle Management: Where the action will be' *Industry Week*, 2 May

Buckminster Fuller, Richard (1975) *Synergetics: Explorations in the Geometry of Thinking.* Macmillan, New York.

Clausing, Don and J. R. Hauser (1988) 'The House of Quality' *Harvard Business Review,* May–Jun.

Davis, Stanley M. and William H. Davidson (1991) *2020 Vision* Simon & Schuster, New York

de Geuss, Arie (1988) 'Planning as Learning' *Harvard Business Review,* Mar–Apr

Digital Equipment Company (1990) *Service Excellence: A Study of Executive Opinions* Digital Equipment Company

Digital Equipment Company (1992) *Corporate Values: The Bottom Line Contribution* Digital Equipment Company

Drucker. Peter F. (1955) *The Practice of Management* Heinemann, London

Drucker, Peter F. (1964) *Managing for Results* Heinemann, London

Drucker, Peter F. (1994) 'The Theory of the Business' *Harvard Business Review,* Sep.–Oct.

Drucker, Peter F. (1995) 'The Information Executives Truly Need' *Harvard Business Review,* Jan.–Feb.

Freedman, David H. (1992) 'Is Management Still a Science?' *Harvard Business Review,* Nov.–Dec.

Galbraith, John K. (1994) *The World Economy Since the War* Sinclair-Stevenson, London

258 *References*

Hammer, Michael (1990)   'Reengineering Work: *Harvard Business Review,*
                         Don't Automate,   July–Aug.
                         Obliterate'
Handy, Charles (1989)   *The Age of Unreason*   Random House, London
Handy, Charles (1991)   'What is a company for?' *RSA Journal,* March
                         Michael Shanks
                         Memorial Lecture
Hoff, Benjamin (1982)   *The Tao of Pooh & The* Methuen, London
                         Te of Piglet
Holmgren, Henri and   *A book about the classic* HHAAB, Järfälla
Peer Eriksson (1995)   *Avis advertising*
                         campaign of the 60s
Howard, Robert (1990)   'Values make the   *Harvard Business Review,*
                         company. An interview   Sep.–Oct.
                         with Robert Haas'
Howard, Robert (ed)   *The Learning Imperative* HBS Press, Boston
(1993)
Hout, Thomas M. and   'Getting it done: New   *Harvard Business Review,*
John C. Carter (1995)   roles for senior   Nov.–Dec.
                         executives'
Hsieh, Tsun-Yan (1992)   'The Road to Renewal'   *McKinsey Quarterly,* no.
                                                   3
Hutton, Will (1995)   *The State We're In*   Jonathan Cape, London
IT Management   'Managing the Move to   *IT Management*
Programme (1995)   Client-Server'   *Programme,*
                                                   January
Jackson, David and John 'Middle Managers. New   *Journal of Management*
Humble (1994)   purpose; new direction'   *Development,* vol. 13,
                                                   no. 3
Jackson, D. and Roland   *The Management of*   IFS Publications,
P. Toone (eds) (1987)   *Manufacturing*   Bedford
Jay, Anthony (1967)   *Management and*   Hutchinson Business,
                         Machiavelli   London
Johnston, William B.   'Global Workforce 2000:   *Harvard Business Review,*
(1991)   The New Labor   Mar.–Apr.
                         Market'
Kaplan, Robert S. and   'The Balanced Scorecard   *Harvard Business Review,*
David P. Norton   – Measures That Drive   Jan.–Feb.
(1992)   Performance'
Kirk, David (1992)   'World-class teams'   *McKinsey Quarterly,*
                                                   no. 4
Korn/Ferry International *Reinventing the CEO*   Korn Ferry International
and Columbia   and Columbia
University (1989)   University Graduate
                                                   Business School
Kotter, John P. (1990)   'What Leaders Really   *Harvard Business Review,*
                         Do'   May–June

Kotter, John P. and James L. Heskett (1992) — *Corporate Culture and Performance* — The Free Press, New York

Lash, Linda (1989) — *The Complete Guide to Customer Service* — John Wiley & Sons, New York

Leonard-Barton, Dorothy (1995) — *Wellsprings of Knowledge* — HBS Press, London

London Business School (1994) — *Building Global Excellence* — London Business School/ BOC Group

Lynch, Dudley and Paul M. Kordis (1988) — *Strategy of a Dolphin* — Arrow Books, London

Minzberg, Henry (1987) — 'Crafting Strategy' — *Harvard Business Review*, July–Aug.

Minzberg, Henry (1989) — *Minzberg on Management* — The Free Press, New York

Minzberg, Henry (1994) — 'The Fall and Rise of Strategic Planning' — *Harvard Business Review*, Jan.–Feb.

Mos-Kanter, Rosabeth (1989) — *When Giants Learn to Dance* — Simon & Schuster, New York

Musashi, Miyamoto; translated by Victor Harris (1974) — *A Book of Five Rings* — Alison & Busby Ltd, London

Naisbett, John and Patricia Aburdene, (1985) — *Re-inventing the Corporation* — Megatrends, New York

Pascale, Richard Tanner (1990) — *Managing on the edge* — Simon & Schuster, New York

Pawson, Richard, Jean–Louis Bravard and Lorette Cameron (1995) — 'The Case for Expressive Systems' — *Sloane Management Review*, vol. 36, no. 2 (Winter)

Peppers, Don and Marsha Rodgers (1993) — *The One to One Future* — Currency Doubleday, New York

Peters, Tom (1987) — *Thriving on Chaos* — MacMillan, London

Pirsig, Robert M. (1974) — *Zen and the Art of Motorcycle Maintenance* — Vintage, London

Pirsig, Robert M. (1991) — *Lila. An Inquiry Into Morals* — Bantam, London

Ray, Michael and Alan Rinzler (1993) — *The New Paradigm in Business* — G. P. Putnams, New York

Savage, Charles M. (1990) — *5th Generation Management* — Digital Press, Newton

Schapiro, Eileen C. (1995) — *Fad Surfing in the Boardroom* — Addison-Wesley, Reading, Mass.

Seely Brown, John (1991) — 'Research That Reinvents the Corporation' — *Harvard Business Review*, Jan.–Feb.

Senge, Peter M. (1990)	*The Fifth Discipline. The Art and Practice of The Learning Organisation*	Currency Doubleday, New York
Senge, Peter M., Art Kleiner, Charlotte Roberts, Richard B. Ross and Bryan J. Smith (1994)	*The Fifth Discipline Fieldbook*	Nicholas Brearley, London
Sieff, Marcus (1987)	*Don't Ask The Price*	Weidenfeld & Nicolson, London
Slater, R. (1993)	*The New GE*	Business One Irwin, New York
TARP (1995)	'TARP's approach to customer driven quality'	TARP Europe, London
Tichy, Noel M. and Ram Charan (1989)	'Speed, simplicity, self-confidence: An interview with Jack Welch	*Harvard Business Review*, Sep.–Oct.
Tichy, Noel M. and Stratford Sherman, (1993)	*Control Your Destiny Or Someone Else Will*	Currency Doubleday, New York
Tillet, A., T. Kempner and G. Wills (eds) (1970)	*Management Thinkers*	Penguin, London
Walton, Sam and John Huey	*Sam Walton – Made in America: My Story*	Doubleday, New York
Wheatley, Margaret J. (1992)	*Leadership and the New Science*	Berrett-Koehler, San Francisco
Wickens, Peter D. (1987)	*The Road to Nissan*	Macmillan, London
Wickens, Peter D. (1995)	*The Ascendant Organisation*	Macmillan, London
Yokoyama, Yoshinori (1992)	'An architect looks at organisation design'	*McKinsey Quarterly*, no. 4

Index

ABB 33, 34
Ackoff, Russell 92
appraisal 192, 203, 212, 226
Argyris, Chris 92
arrogance 24, 40, 58
Audit, Dynamic Organisation 243–8
Avis 36, 65, 79, 92, 118, 120, 126, 130, 171, 173–84

Babbage, Charles 88
balanced business scorecard 81–4, 180
Barnevick, Percy 20
Beer, Stafford 5
behaviour 13, 64, 122–3
benchmarking 17
Birmingham Midshires Building Society (BMBS) 35, 114, 171, 185–6
Body Shop 152
Branson, Richard 7
bureaucracy 11, 42
business process reengineering (BPR) 13, 54, 128
Buzan, Tony 104

career paths 103–4
Cathcart, Alun 20, 62, 120, 171
Champy, James 129
change 3, 4, 54–86, 95, 99–100, 158–68, 203–4
  approaches to 162
  delivering 73–5
Chapman, Paul 225
Churchill, Lawrence 141
CIA (complacency, arrogance, ignorance) 23, 31, 158
Cigna UK 92, 114, 171, 197–206
clarity 164–5
Clausing, Don 38
Colyer, Lesley 62, 171
commitment 95
communication 90–1, 191, 200, 233–5
compassion 166
competencies, leadership 92, 107–11
competency 76–8, 120, 123, 226, 228
competition 7, 16–17, 25

competitive advantage 34
complacency 23
complaints 37, 51
complexity 4
control, management 90
conversations 70–1, 100
Cowieson, Douglas 114, 171, 204
creativity 104
culture 13, 64–72, 174, 186, 202–3, 207, 217
  change 67–72, 232–5
  dimensions of 67–70
customer
  satisfaction 113, 120, 178, 215
  satisfaction measurement 35, 193–4, 212–13, 216–19
customer, contact management 48–52, 182
  focus 9, 81
  retention 31,50, 177
  understanding 11, 22–53, 181–2, 212–13

De Bono, Edward 104
de Soet, Jan 62, 71
decathlon 215
Deming xiii
Digital Equipment Corporation 24, 62–3, 132, 161
discipline 96, 118
Disney 113, 126, 207
Disneyland Paris 171, 207–12
DOCSA 65–70, 122
Drucker, Peter 79, 129

EDS 21
employment 154
empowerment 14, 43, 50, 116–19, 205
environment 16, 18, 57, 59, 63, 74, 110
expoliting ideas 92

facilitator skills 200–1
Falotti, Pier-Carlo 62–3
Fayol, Henri 88, 91
Fifield, Paul 30

focus   164–5, 167
Forrester, Jay   92, 133

Galvin, Bob   12, 62, 85
Gartner Group   5
Gerstner, Lou   107
Gore, Bill   94
Green, Andy   19

Haas, Robert   15
Hammer, Michael   128
Handy, Charles   28, 123, 137, 155
Hannover Insurance   92, 114, 171
Herzberg, Frederick   xv
Heskett, James   65, 126
Hewitt, Ron   171
Heywood, John   4
Hofstede, Geert   67
Hughes, John   171
Humble, John   xi, 25, 106
ignorance   24
industrial
   era   8
   revolution   xiv
information   5, 41–8, 50, 74, 80, 156,
      179, 208, 231–2
information, technology   20, 102–3,
      133–49, 231
infrastructure   140, 142–4,   156–7
innovation   27, 81, 175, 220
involvement   165

Jackson, Mike   114, 186
Jacobs, Klaus   55
Johnson & Johnson   95

Kaplan, Robert   81
Kirk, David   165
Klecha, Denis   171
KLM   171, 215–21
knowledge   9, 13, 33, 91, 101, 121–2
Kotler, Philip   29
Kotter, John   65, 91, 92

Langler, Gerald   87
Large, Arthur   23, 114, 165, 231
Lash, Linda   126
leadership   14–16, 62, 87–111, 125, 154,
      165, 174–5, 190, 235
learning   xiv, 41, 56, 57, 81, 107, 155–6
Leonard-Barton, Dorothy   19
Levitt, Ted   16
listening   35, 39, 237

logic   159
Lorenz, Christopher   21, 129
Lund-Jensen, Ib   62

Machiavelli   10, 118
Management Centre Europe   xiii
management processes   15, 54, 59,
      72–86, 175–80, 187, 220, 222–4,
      227–8, 235
managers   87
   middle   100–10, 117
market research   46
marketing   29–30, 41
Matsushita, Konosuke   93
Mayo, Elton   xv
McGarahan, Tony   171
McNealy, Scott   137
measurement   79–86, 141, 193–4
Minzberg, Henry   58
Mitsubishsi Heavy Industries   82–3
Morgan, J.P.   12, 145
Morita, Akio   7
Moss-Kanter, Rosabeth   102
Moyes, Peter   162

National & Provincial Building Society
      (N&P)   75, 77, 79, 92, 113, 114,
      149–50, 171, 222–9
Nissan   xix, 19, 79
Nolan, Lord   153
Norton, David   81
object technology   138, 146

O'Brien, Bill   20, 63, 75, 100, 114
O'Brien, Dan   218
O'Brien, David   114, 222
Olsen, Ken   24, 136
operational excellence   12
opportunities   93
Organisation Design Facility
      (ODF)   78, 133, 145, 228
organisation model   142
organisation, integration   47
outsourcing   149

Parker-Follet, Mary   98, 151
partnership   13, 36, 149–50
Patrick, John   171
pay   114, 203, 228
people   9,13, 21, 34, 49, 51, 56, 105,
      112–26, 131, 162, 183–4, 192
perceptions   36
plans   160

power xv
Prahalad, CK 109
Prentice, Derek 43
processes
    management 15, 54, 59, 72–86,
        175–80, 187, 220, 222–4, 227–8,
        235
    business 34, 127, 199
purpose 55, 98, 131, 139, 140–1

quality 33, 65
Quality Function Deployment
    (QFD) 38, 237

RAC 23, 114, 165, 171, 230–6
Rapaille, G. Clotaire 128
recognition 78, 114–16, 192, 227
recruitment 178, 192
Reich, Robert 149
relationships 53, 112
Reseigh, Tom 68
reward 78, 114–16, 178–9, 227
Richardson, Frank 171
Rodgers, John 171
roles and responsibilities 140, 144–6
Rothmeir, Steve 167

S-curve 6
Schaper, Frank 171
scorecard, balanced business 81–4, 180
segmentation 29, 49
Semler, Riccardo 20
Senge, Peter 40, 92, 171
Shell 26
Simpson, George 114
skills 13, 120–1
Smith, Fred 4
soft factors 34
specialisation xv
Strassmann, Paul 135

strategic planning xvi, 55, 63
strategy 82
strategy, IT 137–40
structure, organisation 15, 209
surveys 35
systems
    development 147
    thinking 57, 111

TARP 37
Taylor, F.W. xiv, 88
teams 97–8, 119–20, 226
    management of 14, 190
    maturity 205
    self-managed 198
Total Quality Management (TQM) 33,
    54
training and development 124, 155–6,
    184, 200
trends, socio-economic 26
Turner, Adair 114

uncertainty 6

values 14–16, 64–72, 97,105, 153–4,
    163–4, 174–5, 189, 224–5
Venkatraman, Ven 144
vision 14–16, 60–4, 111, 163–4, 174–5,
    187, 189, 209–10, 224–5
Voice of the Customer (VOC) 38,
    237–42

Walton, Sam 107
Welch, Jack 15, 20, 58, 64, 70, 94, 97,
    104, 171
Wickens, Peter xix, 98, 165
Wolffson, Brian 109
work 152, 154
workforce, flexible 124
World Business Academy 152